Praise for *Refactoring HTML*

"Wow, what a compendium of great information and how-to's! I am *so* impressed! Elliotte's written a book whose title comes nowhere near to doing it justice. Covering much more than just refactoring, this book explains how to do it right the first time around, in a clear and lucid voice. Harold obviously knows his stuff. A must-read!"

—Howard Katz,
Proprietor,
Fatdog Software

"After working with people who require the skills and tools necessary to continually improve the quality and security of their applications, I have discovered a missing link. The ability to rebuild and recode applications is a key area of weakness for web designers and web application developers alike. By building refactoring into the development process, incremental changes to the layout or internals efficiently averts a total rewrite or complete make-over. This is a fantastic book for anyone who needs to rebuild, recode, or refactor the web."

—Andre Gironda,
tssci-security.com

"Elliotte's book provides a rare collection of hints and tricks that will vastly improve the quality of web pages. Virtually any serious HTML developer, new or tenured, in any size organization will reap tremendous benefit from implementing even a handful of his suggestions."

—Matt Lavallee,
Development Manager,
MLS Property Information Network, Inc.

Refactoring HTML

The Addison-Wesley Signature Series

The **Addison-Wesley Signature Series** provides readers with practical and authoritative information on the latest trends in modern technology for computer professionals. The series is based on one simple premise: great books come from great authors. Books in the series are personally chosen by expert advisors, world-class authors in their own right. These experts are proud to put their signatures on the covers, and their signatures ensure that these thought leaders have worked closely with authors to define topic coverage, book scope, critical content, and overall uniqueness. The expert signatures also symbolize a promise to our readers: you are reading a future classic.

THE ADDISON–WESLEY SIGNATURE SERIES
SIGNERS: KENT BECK AND MARTIN FOWLER

Kent Beck has pioneered people-oriented technologies like JUnit, Extreme Programming, and patterns for software development. Kent is interested in helping teams do well by doing good — finding a style of software development that simultaneously satisfies economic, aesthetic, emotional, and practical constraints. His books focus on touching the lives of the creators and users of software.

Martin Fowler has been a pioneer of object technology in enterprise applications. His central concern is how to design software well. He focuses on getting to the heart of how to build enterprise software that will last well into the future. He is interested in looking behind the specifics of technologies to the patterns, practices, and principles that last for many years; these books should be usable a decade from now. Martin's criterion is that these are books he wished he could write.

TITLES IN THE SERIES

Implementation Patterns
Kent Beck, ISBN 0321413091

Test-Driven Development: By Example
Kent Beck, ISBN 0321146530

User Stories Applied: For Agile Software Development
Mike Cohn, ISBN 0321205685

Implementing Lean Software Development: From Concept to Cash
Mary and Tom Poppendieck, ISBN 0321437381

Refactoring Databases: Evolutionary Database Design
Scott W. Ambler and Pramodkumar J. Sadalage, ISBN 0321293533

Continuous Integration: Improving Software Quality and Reducing Risk
Paul M. Duvall, with Steve Matyas and Andrew Glover, 0321336380

Patterns of Enterprise Application Architecture
Martin Fowler, ISBN 0321127420

Refactoring HTML: Improving the Design of Existing Web Applications
Elliotte Rusty Harold, ISBN 0321503635

Beyond Software Architecture: Creating and Sustaining Winning Solutions
Luke Hohmann, ISBN 0201775948

Enterprise Integration Patterns: Designing, Building, and Deploying Messaging Solutions
Gregor Hohpe and Bobby Woolf, ISBN 0321200683

Refactoring to Patterns
Joshua Kerievsky, ISBN 0321213351

xUnit Test Patterns: Refactoring Test Code
Gerard Meszaros, 0131495054

For more information, check out the series web site at www.awprofessional.com

Refactoring HTML

Improving the Design
of Existing Web Applications

Elliotte Rusty Harold

✦✦ Addison-Wesley

Upper Saddle River, NJ • Boston • Indianapolis • San Francisco
New York • Toronto • Montreal • London • Munich • Paris • Madrid
Capetown • Sydney • Tokyo • Singapore • Mexico City

Many of the designations used by manufacturers and sellers to distinguish their products are claimed as trademarks. Where those designations appear in this book, and the publisher was aware of a trademark claim, the designations have been printed with initial capital letters or in all capitals.

The author and publisher have taken care in the preparation of this book, but make no expressed or implied warranty of any kind and assume no responsibility for errors or omissions. No liability is assumed for incidental or consequential damages in connection with or arising out of the use of the information or programs contained herein.

The publisher offers excellent discounts on this book when ordered in quantity for bulk purchases or special sales, which may include electronic versions and/or custom covers and content particular to your business, training goals, marketing focus, and branding interests. For more information, please contact:

U.S. Corporate and Government Sales
(800) 382-3419
corpsales@pearsontechgroup.com

For sales outside the United States, please contact:

International Sales
international@pearson.com

Visit us on the Web: www.informit.com/aw

This Book Is Safari Enabled

The Safari® Enabled icon on the cover of your favorite technology book means the book is available through Safari Bookshelf. When you buy this book, you get free access to the online edition for 45 days.

Safari Bookshelf is an electronic reference library that lets you easily search thousands of technical books, find code samples, download chapters, and access technical information whenever and wherever you need it.

To gain 45-day Safari Enabled access to this book:

- Go to informit.com/onlineedition
- Complete the brief registration form
- Enter the coupon code YFLX-3BEM-1IBF-VSMV-M9IY

If you have difficulty registering on Safari Bookshelf or accessing the online edition, please e-mail customer-service@safaribooksonline.com.

Library of Congress Cataloging-in-Publication Data

Harold, Elliotte Rusty.
    Refactoring HTML : improving the design of existing Web applications / Elliotte Rusty Harold.
        p. cm.
    Includes index.
    ISBN-13: 978-0-321-50363-3 (pbk. : alk. paper)
    ISBN-10: 0-321-50363-5 (pbk. : alk. paper)
    1. Web sites—Design. 2. Software refactoring. 3.Web servers—Computer programs. 4. Application software—Development. 5. HTML editors (Computer programs) I. Title.

TK5105.888.H372 2008
006.7'4—dc22   2008008645

Text printed in the United States on recycled paper at Courier in Westford, Massachusetts.
First printing, April 2008

Contents

Foreword by Martin Fowler

In just over a decade the Web has gone from a technology with promise to major part of the world's infrastructure. It's been a fascinating time, and many useful resources have been built in the process. But, as with any technology, we've learned as we go how best to use it and the technology itself has matured to help us use it better.

However complex a web application, it finally hits the glass in the form of HTML—the universal web page description language. HTML is a computer language, albeit a very limited and specialized one. As such, if you want a system that you can evolve easily over time, you need to pay attention to writing HTML that is clear and understandable. But just like any computer language, or indeed any writing at all, it's hard to get it right first time. Clear code comes from writing and rewriting with a determination to create something that is easy to follow.

Rewriting code carries a risk of introducing bugs. Several years ago, I wrote about a technique called refactoring, which is a disciplined way of rewriting code that can greatly reduce the chances of introducing bugs while reworking software. Refactoring has made a big impact on regular software languages. Many programmers use it as part of their daily work to help them keep code clear and enhance their future productivity. Tools have sprung up to automate refactoring tasks, to further improve the workflow.

Just as refactoring can make a big improvement to regular programming, the same basic idea can work with HTML. The refactoring steps are different, but the underlying philosophy is the same. By learning how to refactor your HTML, you can keep your HTML clean and easy to change into the future, allowing you to make the inevitable changes more quickly. These techniques can also allow you to bring web sites into line with the improvements in web technologies, specifically allowing you to move toward supporting XHTML and CSS.

Elliotte Rusty Harold has long had a permanent place on my bookshelf for his work on XML technologies and open source software for XML processing. I've always respected him as a fine programmer and writer. With this book he brings the benefits of refactoring into the HTML world.

—Martin Fowler

Foreword by Bob DuCharme

A key to the success of the World Wide Web has always been the ease with which just about anyone can create a web page and put it where everyone can see it. As people create sets of interlinked pages, their web sites become more useful to a wider audience, and stories of web millionaires inspire these web developers to plan greater things.

Many find, though, that as their web sites get larger, they have growing pains. Revised links lead to nowhere, pages look different in different browsers, and it becomes more difficult to keep track of what's where, especially when trying to apply changes consistently throughout the site. This is when many who built their own web site call in professional help, but now with *Refactoring HTML,* you can become that professional. And, if you're already a web pro, you can become a better one.

There are many beginner-level introductions to web technologies, but this book is the first to tie together intermediate-level discussions of all the key technologies for creating professional, maintainable, accessible web sites. You may already be an expert in one or two of the topics covered by this book, but few people know all of them as well as Elliotte, and he's very good at explaining them. (I know XML pretty well, but this book has shown me that some simple changes to my CSS habits will benefit all of the web pages I've created.)

For each recommendation in the book, Elliotte lays out the motivation for why it's a good idea, the potential trade-offs for following the recommendation, and the mechanics of implementing it, giving you a full perspective on the how and why of each tip. For detecting problems, I'll stop short of comparing his use of smell imagery with Proust's, but it's pretty evocative nevertheless.

I've read several of Elliotte's books, but not all of them. When I heard that *Refactoring HTML* was on the way, I knew right away that I'd want to read it, and I was glad to get an advanced look. I learned a lot, and I know that you will, too.

—Bob DuCharme
Solutions Architect, Innodata Isogen

About the Author

Elliotte Rusty Harold is an internationally respected writer, programmer, and educator. His Cafe con Leche web site (www.cafeconleche.org) has become one of the most popular sites for information on XML. In addition, he is the author and coauthor of numerous books, the most recent of which are *Java I/O* (O'Reilly, 2006), *Java Network Programming* (O'Reilly, 2004), *Effective XML* (Addison-Wesley, 2003), and *XML in a Nutshell* (O'Reilly, 2002).

Chapter 1

Refactoring

Refactoring. What is it? Why do it?

In brief, **refactoring** is the gradual improvement of a code base by making small changes that don't modify a program's behavior, usually with the help of some kind of automated tool. The goal of refactoring is to remove the accumulated cruft of years of legacy code and produce cleaner code that is easier to maintain, easier to debug, and easier to add new features to.

Technically, refactoring never actually fixes a bug or adds a feature. However, in practice, when refactoring I almost always uncover bugs that need to be fixed and spot opportunities for new features. Often, refactoring changes difficult problems into tractable and even easy ones. Reorganizing code is the first step in improving it.

If you have the sort of personality that makes you begin a new semester, project, or job by thoroughly cleaning up your workspace, desk, or office, you'll get this immediately. Refactoring helps you keep the old from getting in the way of the new. It doesn't let you start from a blank page. Instead, it leaves you with a clean, organized workspace where you can find everything you need, and from which you can move forward.

The concept of refactoring originally came from the object-oriented programming community and dates back at least as far as 1990 (William F. Opdyke and Ralph E. Johnson, "Refactoring: An Aid in Designing Application Frameworks and Evolving Object-Oriented Systems," Proceedings of the Symposium on Object-Oriented Programming Emphasizing Practical Applications [SOOPPA], September 1990, ACM), though likely it was in at least limited use before then. However, the term was popularized by Martin Fowler in 1999 in his book *Refactoring* (Addison-Wesley, 1999). Since then, numerous IDEs and other tools such as Eclipse, IntelliJ IDEA, and C# Refactory have implemented many of his catalogs of refactorings for languages such as Java and C#, as well as inventing many new ones.

However, it's not just object-oriented code and object-oriented languages that develop cruft and need to be refactored. In fact, it's not just programming languages at all. Almost any sufficiently complex system that is developed and maintained over time can benefit from refactoring. The reason is twofold.

1. Increased knowledge of both the system and the problem domain often reveals details that weren't apparent to the initial designers. No one ever gets everything right in the first release. You have to see a system in production for a while before some of the problems become apparent.

2. Over time, functionality increases and new code is written to support this functionality. Even if the original system solved its problem perfectly, the new code written to support new features doesn't mesh perfectly with the old code. Eventually, you reach a point where the old code base simply cannot support the weight of all the new features you want to add.

When you find yourself with a system that is no longer able to support further developments, you have two choices: You can throw it out and build a new system from scratch, or you can shore up the foundations. In practice, we rarely have the time or budget to create a completely new system just to replace something that already works. It is much more cost-effective to add the struts and supports that the existing system needs before further work. If we can slip these supports in gradually, one at a time, rather than as a big-bang integration, so much the better.

Many sufficiently complex systems with large chunks of code are not object-oriented languages and perhaps are not even programming languages at all. For instance, Scott Ambler and Pramod Sadalage demonstrated how to refactor the SQL databases that support many large applications in *Refactoring Databases* (Addison-Wesley, 2006).

However, while the back end of a large networked application is often a relational database, the front end is a web site. Thin client GUIs delivered in Firefox or Internet Explorer everywhere are replacing thick client GUIs for all sorts of business applications, such as payroll and lead tracking. Adventurous users at companies such as Sun and Google are going even further and replacing classic desktop applications like word processors and spreadsheets with web apps built out of HTML, CSS, and JavaScript. Finally, the Web and the ubiquity of the web browser have enabled completely new kinds of applications that never existed before, such as eBay, Netflix, PayPal, Google Reader, and Google Maps.

HTML made these applications possible, and it made them faster to develop, but it didn't make them easy. It didn't make them simple. It certainly didn't make them less fundamentally complex. Some of these systems are now on their second, third, or fourth generation—and wouldn't you know it? Just like any other sufficiently complex, sufficiently long-lived application, these web apps are developing cruft. The new pieces aren't merging perfectly with the old pieces. Systems are slowing down because the whole structure is just too ungainly. Security is being breached when hackers slip in through the cracks where the new parts meet the old parts. Once again, the choice comes down to throwing out the original application and starting over, or fixing the foundations, but really, there's no choice. In today's fast-moving world, nobody can afford to wait for a completely new replacement. The only realistic option is to refactor.

Why Refactor

How do you know when it's time to refactor? What are the smells of bad code that should set your nose to twitching? There are quite a few symptoms, but these are some of the smelliest.

Smell: Illegible Code

The most obvious symptom is that you do a View Source on the page, and it might as well be written in Greek (unless, of course, you're working in Greece). Most coders know ugly code when we see it. Ugly code *looks* ugly. Which would you rather see, Listing 1.1 or Listing 1.2? I don't think I have to tell you which is uglier, and which is going to be easier to maintain and update.

LISTING 1.1 Dirtier Code

```
<TABLE BORDER="0" CELLPADDING="0" CELLSPACING="0" WIDTH="100%">
<TR><TD WIDTH="70">    <A HREF="http://www.example.com/" TARGET=
"_blank"
>
           <IMG SRC="/images/logo-footer.gif"
HSPACE = 5 VSPACE="0" BORDER="0"></A></TD>
    <td class="footer" VALIGN="top"> &#169;2007 <A HREF="http://
www.example.com/" TARGET="_blank">Example Inc.</A>.
All rights reserved.<br>
       <A HREF="http://www.example.com/legal/index.html"
TARGET="_blank">Legal Notice</A> -
       <A HREF="http://www.example.com/legal/privacy.htm"
TARGET="_blank">Privacy Policy</A> - <A HREF="http://www.example.com/
legal/permissions.html"
TARGET="_blank">

       Permissions</A>
</td>
  </TR></TABLE>
```

LISTING 1.2 Cleaner Code

```
<div id='footer'>
  <a href="http://www.example.com/">
    <img src="/images/logo-footer.gif" alt="Example Inc."
       width='70' height='41' />
  </a>
  <ul>
  <li>© 2007 <a href="http://www.example.com/">Example Inc.</a>.
  All rights reserved.</li>
  <li><a href="http://www.example.com/legal/index.html">
     Legal Notice
  </a></li>
  <li><a href="http://www.example.com/legal/privacy.htm">
    Privacy Policy
  </a></li>
  <li><a href="http://www.example.com/legal/permissions.html">
    Permissions
  </a></li>
  </ul>
</div>
```

Now, you may object that in Listing 1.2 I haven't merely reformatted the code. I've also changed it. For instance, a table has turned into a `div` and a list, and some hyphens have been removed. However, Listing 1.2 is actually much closer to the meaning of the content than Listing 1.1. Listing 1.2 may here be assumed to use an external CSS stylesheet to supply all the formatting details I removed from Listing 1.1. As you'll see, that's going to be one of the major techniques you use to refactor pages and clean up documents.

I've also thrown away the `TARGET="_blank"` attributes that open links in new windows or tabs. This is usually not what the user wants, and it's rarely a good idea. Let the user use the back button and history list if necessary, but otherwise open most links in the same window. If users want to open a link in a new window, they can easily do so from the context menu, but the choice is now theirs. Sometimes half the cleanup process consists of no more than removing pieces that shouldn't have been there in the first place.

Line Length

Listing 1.2 is still a little less than ideal. I'm a bit constrained by the need to fit code within the margins of this printed page. In real source code, I could fit a little more onto one line. However, don't take this to extremes. More than 80 or so characters per line becomes hard to read and is itself a minor code smell.

A small exception can be made here for code generated out of a content management system (CMS) of some kind. In this case, the code you see with View Source is not really the source code. It's more of a compiled machine format. In this case, it's the input to the CMS that should look good and appear legible.

Nonetheless, it's still better if tools such as CMSs and web editors generate clean, well-formed code. Surprisingly often, you'll find that the code the tool generates is a start, not an end. You may want to add stylesheets, scripts, and other things to the code after the tool is through with it. In this case, you'll have to deal with the raw markup, and it's a lot easier to do that when it's clean.

Smell: The CEO Can't Fill Out His Travel Expense Vouchers

Usability on the Web has improved in the past few years, but not nearly as much as it can or should. All but the best sites can benefit by refocusing more on the readers and less on the writers and the designers. A few simple changes aimed at improving usability—such as increasing the font size (or not specifying it at all) or combining form fields—can have disproportionately great returns in productivity. This is especially important for intranet sites, and any site that is attempting to sell to consumers.

Smell: Slow Page-Rendering Times

If any major browser takes more than half a second to display a page, you have a problem. This one can be a little hard to judge, because many slow pages are caused by network latency or overloaded databases and HTTP servers. These are problems, too, though they are ones you usually cannot fix by changing the HTML. However, if a page saved on a local file system takes more than half a second to render in the web browser, you need to refactor it to improve that time.

Smell: Pages Appear Different in Different Browsers

Pages do not need to look identical in different browsers. However, all content and functionality should be accessible to everyone using any reasonably current browser. If the page is illegible or nonfunctional in Safari, Opera, Internet Explorer, or Firefox, you have a problem. For instance, you may see the page starting with a full-screen-width sidebar, followed by the content pane. Alternatively, the sidebar may show up below the content rather than above it. This usually means the page looks perfectly fine in the author's browser. However, she did not bother to check it in the one you're using. Be sure to check your pages in all the major browsers.

Anytime you see something like "Best Viewed with Internet Explorer," you have a code smell, and refactoring is called for. Anytime you see something like Figure 1.1, you have a huge code smell—

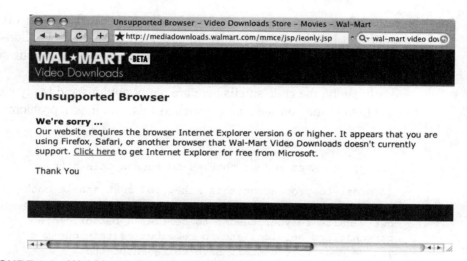

FIGURE 1.1   Wal-Mart locks out non-IE users.

and one that all your readers can smell, too. Internet Explorer has less than 80% market share, and that's dropping fast. In fact, even that is probably vastly overestimated because most spiders and bots falsely identify themselves as IE, and they account for a disproportionate number of hits. Mac OS X and Linux users don't even have an option to choose Internet Explorer. The days when you could design your site for just one browser are over.

A common variant of this is requiring a particular screen size—for instance, "This page is best viewed with a screen resolution of 1024 × 768. To change your monitor/display resolution, go to. . . ." Well-designed web pages do not require any particular screen size or browser.

Smell: Pages Require Dangerous or Nonstandard Technologies

Many sites require cookies, JavaScript, Flash, PDF, Java, or other non-HTML technologies. Although all of these have their place, they are vastly overused on the Web. They are not nearly as interoperable or reliable in the wild as most web designers think. They are all the subject of frequent security notices telling users to turn them off in one browser or another to avoid the crack of the week. They are often unsupported by Google and most other search engine robots. Consequently, you should strive to make sure that most pages on your site function properly even if these technologies are unavailable.

Fortunately, the code smells here are really obvious and really easy to detect. Anytime you see a notice such as this, you have a problem:

```
Cookies Required

Sorry, you must accept cookies to access this site.

In order to proceed on this site, you must enable cook-
ies on your Internet browser. We use cookies to tailor
our website to your needs, to deliver a better, more
personalized service, and to remember certain choices
you've made so you don't have to re-enter them.
```

Not only is this annoying to users, but these sites are routinely locked out of Google and get hideous search engine placement.

Embarrassingly, this next example actually comes from a page that's talking about cleaning up HTML:

```
Notice: There is a Table of Contents, but it is dynami-
cally generated. Please enable JavaScript to see it.
```

The right way to do dynamic content is to use server-side templating, but still sending static HTML to the client.

One site I found managed to hit almost all of these:

```
This site uses JavaScript, Cookies, Flash, Pop-up win-
dows, and is designed for use with the latest versions
of Internet Explorer, Netscape Navigator (NOT Netscape
6), and Opera.
```

If only they had asked for a specific screen size, they would have hit the superfecta.

This site also added a new one. I had forgotten about pop-ups. Given the rampant abuse of pop-ups and the consequent wide deployment of pop-up blockers, no legitimate site should rely on them.

Of course, some things you can only do with JavaScript or other non-HTML technologies. I don't intend to tell you not to design the next

Google Maps or YouTube, if that is indeed what you're trying to do. Just try to keep the fancy tricks to a minimum, and make sure everything you can do without Java/JavaScript/Flash/and so on is done without those technologies. This Flickr message is a lot less troublesome:

```
To take full advantage of Flickr, you should use a Java-
Script-enabled browser and install the latest version of
the Macromedia Flash Player.
```

The key difference is that I saw this on a page that still managed to show me the content I'd come to see, despite disabling JavaScript and Flash. I may not see everything, or have full functionality, but I'm not locked out. This is much friendlier to the reader and to search engines such as Google.

As a site developer, I'd still take a second look at this page to see if I might be able to remove some of the requirements on clients. However, it wouldn't be my first priority.

Smell: Your Company's Home Page Suddenly Says, "Pwned by Elite Doodz"

Web-site defacements are a major wake-up call, and one that gets everybody's attention really quick. This can happen for a number of reasons, but by far the most common is a code injection attack directed at a poorly designed form processing script.

Frankly, if all that happens is that your web site is defaced, you're lucky and you should thank the hackers who pointed this out to you. More serious attacks can steal confidential data or erase critical information.

Smell: Your First Appearance on Google Is on Page 17

Search engine optimization is a major driver for web-site refactoring. Search engines value text over images and early text over later text. They don't understand table layouts, and they don't much care for cookies or JavaScript. However, they do love unique titles and maybe even meta tags.

Smell: Readers Send E-mail Saying Your Site Is Broken

This is one of the absolute best ways to find out you have a problem. For example, I recently received this e-mail from one of my readers:

> The links in the "Further Reading" section of Cafe au Lait to "The Next Big Language?" and "Testing HopStop" are broken.
>
> Best regards,
>
> Kent

That was a bit of a surprise because the section Kent was complaining about was automatically generated using XSLT that transformed an Atom feed from another site. I checked the feed and it was correct. However, Kent was right and the link was broken. I eventually tracked it down to a bug in the XSLT stylesheet. It was reading an element that was usually but not always the same as the link, rather than the element that was indeed the link. Five minutes later, the site was fixed.

Ninety-nine percent of your readers will just grumble and never tell you that your site is broken. The 1% who do complain are gold. You need to treat them well and listen to what they say. Do not make it hard for them to find you. Every site and almost every page should have an obvious person to contact for any problems that arise. These responses need to be carefully considered and acted on quickly.

Readers may also send you e-mail about many things not directly related to the site: canceled orders, shipping dates, link requests, political disagreements, and a thousand other things. You need to be able to separate the technical problems from the nontechnical ones so that the correspondence can be routed appropriately. Some sites use an online form and ask readers to self-classify the problem. However, this is unreliable because readers don't usually think of the site in the same way the developers do. For example, if a customer can't enter a nine-digit ZIP Code with a hyphen into your shipping address form, you may think of that as a technical mistake (and you'd be right), but the customer is likely to classify it as a shipping problem and direct it to a department that won't even understand the question, much less know what to do about it. You may need a triage person or team that identifies each piece of e-mail and decides who in your organization is the right person to respond to it. This is a critical function that should not be outsourced to the lowest bidder.

Whatever you do, do not let problem reports drop into the black hole of customer service. Make sure that the people who have the power to fix the problems receive feedback directly from the users of the site, and that they pay attention to it. Too many sites use e-mail and contact forms to *prevent* users from reaching them and firewall developers off from actual users. Do not fall into this trap. Web sites pay a lot of money to hire QA teams. If people volunteer to do this for you, love them for it and take advantage of them.

When to Refactor

When should you refactor? When do you say the time has come to put new features on hold while you clean up and get a handle on your legacy code? There are several possible answers to this question, and they are not mutually exclusive.

The first time to refactor is before any redesign. If your site is undergoing a major redevelopment, the first thing you need to do is get its content under control. The first benefit to refactoring at this point is simply that you will create a much more stable base on which to implement the new design. A well-formed, well-organized page is much easier to reformat.

The second reason to refactor before redesigning is that the process of refactoring will help to familiarize developers with the site. You'll see where the pages are, how they fit together in the site hierarchy, which elements are common across pages, and so forth. You'll also likely discover new ideas for the redesign that you haven't had before. Don't implement them yet, but do write them down (better yet, add them to the issue tracker) so that you can implement them later, after the refactoring is done. Refactoring is a very important tool for bringing developers up to speed on a site. If it's a site they've never previously worked on, refactoring will help teach them about it. If it's a site they've been working on for the past ten years, refactoring will remind them of things they have forgotten. In either case, refactoring helps to make developers comfortable with the site.

Perhaps the new functions are on completely new pages, maybe even a completely new site. If there's still some connection to the old site, you'll want to look at it to see what you can borrow or reuse. Styles, graphics, scripts, and templates may be candidates for reuse. Indeed, doing so may help you keep a consistent look and feel between the old parts and the new parts of the site. However, if the old parts that you want to reuse have any problems, you'll need to clean them up first. For similar reasons, you should consider refactoring before any major new project that builds on top of the old one. For example, if you're going to implement one-click shopping, make sure the old shopping cart makes sense first. If the legal department is making you add small print at the bottom of every page, find out whether each page has a consistent footer into which you can easily insert it. You don't have to refactor everything, but do make those changes that will help you more easily integrate the new content into your site.

Finally, you may wish to consider semicontinuous refactoring. If you find a problem that's bothering you, don't wait for an uninterrupted two-week block during which you can refactor everything. Figure out what you can do to fix that problem right away, even if you don't fix everything else. To the extent possible, try to use agile development practices. Code a little, test a little, refactor a little. Repeat. Although many projects will be starting from a large base of crufty legacy code, if you do have a green-field project try not to let it turn into a large base of crufty code in the first place. When you see yourself repeating the same code, extract it into external templates or stylesheets. When you notice that one of your hired HTML guns has been inserting deprecated elements, replace them with CSS (and take the opportunity to educate the hired gun about why you're doing that). A stream of many small but significant changes can have great effect over time.

Whatever you do, don't let the perfect be the enemy of the good. If you only have time to do a little necessary refactoring right now, do a little. You can always do more later. Huge redesigns are splashy and impressive, but they aren't nearly as important as the small and gradual improvements that build up over time. Make it your goal to leave the code in better shape at the end of the day than at the beginning. Do this over a period of months, and sooner than you know it, you'll have a clean code base that you'll be proud to show off.

What to Refactor To

There is one critical difference between refactoring in a programming language such as Java and refactoring in a markup language such as HTML. Compared to HTML, Java really hasn't changed all that much. C++ has changed even less, and C hardly at all. A program written in Java 1.0 still runs pretty much the same as a program written in Java 6. A lot of features have been added to the language, but it has remained more or less the same.

By contrast, HTML and associated technologies have evolved much faster over the same time frame. Today's HTML is really not the same language as the HTML of 1995. Keywords have been removed. New ones have been added. Syntax and parsing algorithms have changed. Although a modern browser such as Firefox or Internet Explorer 7 can usually make some sense out of an old-fashioned page, you may discover that a lot of things don't work quite right. Furthermore, entirely new components such as CSS and ECMAScript have been added to the stew that a browser must consume.

Most of the refactorings in this book are going to focus on upgrading sites to web standards, specifically:

- XHTML
- CSS
- REST

They are going to help you move away from

- Tag soup
- Presentation-based markup
- Stateful applications

These are not binary choices or all-or-nothing decisions. You can often improve the characteristics of your sites along these three axes without going all the way to one extreme. An important characteristic of refactoring is that it's linear. Small changes generate small improvements. You do not need to do everything at once. You can implement well-formed XHTML before you implement valid XHTML. You can implement valid XHTML before you move to CSS. You can have a fully valid CSS-laid-out site before you consider what's required to eliminate sessions and session cookies.

Nor do you have to implement these changes in this order. You can pick and choose the refactorings from the catalog that bring the most benefit to your applications. You may not require XHTML, but you may desperately need CSS. You may want to move your application architecture to REST for increased performance but not care much about converting the documents to XHTML. Ultimately, the decision rests with you. This book presents the choices and options so that you can weigh the costs and benefits for yourself.

It is certainly possible to build web applications using tag-soup table-based layout, image maps, and cookies. However, it's not possible to scale those applications, at least not without a disproportionate investment in time and resources that most of us can't afford. Growth both horizontally (more users) and vertically (more features) requires a stronger foundation. This is what XHTML, CSS, and REST provide.

Why XHTML

XHTML is simply an XML-ized version of HTML. Whereas HTML is at least theoretically built on top of SGML, XHTML is built on top of XML. XML is a much simpler, clearer spec than SGML. Therefore, XHTML is a simpler, clearer version of HTML. However, like a gun, a lot depends on whether you're facing its front or rear end.

XHTML makes life harder for document authors in exchange for making life easier for document consumers. Whereas HTML is forgiving, XHTML is not. In HTML, nothing too serious happens if you omit an end-tag or leave off a quote here or there. Some extra text may be marked in boldface or be improperly indented. At worst, a few words here or there may vanish. However, most of the page will still display. This forgiving nature gives HTML a very shallow learning curve.

Although you can make mistakes when writing HTML, nothing horrible happens to you if you do.

By contrast, XHTML is much stricter. A trivial mistake such as a missing quote or an omitted end-tag that a browser would silently recover from in HTML becomes a four-alarm, drop-everything, sirens-blaring emergency in XHTML. One little, tiny error in an XHTML document, and the browser will throw up its hands and refuse to display the page, as shown in Figure 1.2. This makes writing XHTML pages harder, especially if you're using a plain text editor. Like writing a computer program, one syntax error breaks everything. There is no leeway and no margin for error.

Why, then, would anybody choose XHTML? Because the same characteristics that make authoring XHTML a challenge (draconian error handling) make consuming XHTML a walk in the park. Work has been shifted from the browser to the author. A web browser (or anything else that reads the page) doesn't have to try to make sense out of a confusing mess of tag soup and guess what the page really meant to say. If the page is unclear in any way, the browser is allowed, in fact required, to throw up its hands and refuse to process it. This makes the browser's job much simpler. A large portion of today's browsers devote a large chunk of their HTML parsing code simply to correcting errors in pages. With XHTML they don't have to do that.

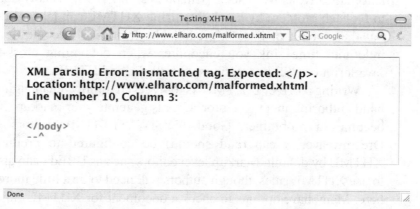

FIGURE 1.2   Firefox responding to an error in an XHTML page

Of course, most of us are not browser vendors and are never going to write a browser. What do we gain from XHTML and its draconian error handling? There are several benefits. First of all, though most of us will never write a browser, many of us do write programs that consume web pages. These can be mashups, web spiders, blog aggregators, search engines, authoring tools, and a dozen other things that all need to read web pages. These programs are much easier to write when the data you're processing is XHTML rather than HTML.

Of course, many people working on the Web and most people authoring for the Web are not classic programmers and are not going to write a web spider or a blog aggregator. However, there are two things they are very likely to write: JavaScript and stylesheets. By number, these are by far the most common kinds of programs that read web pages. Every JavaScript program embedded in a web page itself reads the web page. Every CSS stylesheet (though perhaps not a program in the traditional sense of the word) also reads the web page. JavaScript and CSS are much easier to write and debug when the pages they operate on are XHTML rather than HTML. In fact, the extra cost of making a page valid XHTML is more than paid back by the time you save debugging your JavaScript and CSS.

While fixing XHTML errors is annoying and takes some time, it's a fairly straightforward process and not all that hard to do. A validator will list the errors. Then you go through the list and fix each one. In fact, errors at this level are fairly predictable and can often be fixed automatically, as we'll see in Chapters 3 and 4. You usually don't need to fix each problem by hand. Repairing XHTML can take a little time, but the amount of time is predictable. It doesn't become the sort of indefinite time sink you encounter when debugging cross-browser JavaScript or CSS interactions with ill-formed HTML.

Writing correct XHTML is only even mildly challenging when hand authoring in a text editor. If tools generate your markup, XHTML becomes a no-brainer. Good WYSIWYG HTML editors such as Dreamweaver 8 can (and should) be configured to produce valid XHTML by default. Markup level editors such as BBEdit can also be set to use XHTML rules, though authors will need to be a little more careful here. Many have options to check a document for XHTML validity and can even automatically correct any errors with the click of a button.

Make sure you have turned on the necessary preference in your editor of choice. Similarly good CMSs, Wikis, and blog engines can all be told to generate XHTML. If your authoring tool does not support XHTML, by all means get a better tool. In the 21st century, there's no excuse for an HTML editor or web publishing system not to support XHTML.

If your site is using a hand-grown templating system, you may have a little more work to do; and you'll see exactly what you need to do in Chapters 3 and 4. Although the process here is a little more manual, once you've made the changes, valid XHTML falls out automatically. Authors entering content through databases or web forms may not need to change their workflow at all, especially if they're already entering data in a non-HTML format such as markdown or wikitext. The system can make the transition to XHTML transparent and painless.

The second reason to prefer XHTML over HTML is cross-browser compatibility. In practice, XHTML is much more consistent in today's browsers than HTML. This is especially true for complex pages that make heavy use of CSS for styling or JavaScript for behavior. Although browsers can fix markup mistakes in classic HTML, they don't always fix them the same way. Two browsers can read the same page and produce very different internal models of it. This makes writing one stylesheet or script that works across browsers a challenge. By contrast, XHTML doesn't leave nearly so much to browser interpretation. There's less room for browser flakiness. Although it's certainly true that browsers differ in their level of support for all of CSS, and that their JavaScript dialects and internal DOMs are not fully compatible, moving to XHTML does remove at least one major cause of cross-browser issues. It's not a complete solution, but it does fix a lot.

The third reason to prefer XHTML over HTML is to enable you to incorporate new technologies in your pages in the future. For reasons already elaborated upon, XHTML is a much stronger platform to build on. HTML is great for displaying text and pictures, and it's not bad for simple forms. However, beyond that the browser becomes primarily a host for other technologies such as Flash, Java, and AJAX. There are many things the browser cannot easily do, such as math and music notation. There are other things that are much harder to do than they should be, such as alerting the user when he types an incorrect value in a form field.

Technologies exist to improve this, and more are under development. These include MathML for equations, MusicXML for scores, Scalable Vector Graphics (SVG) for animated pictures, XForms for very powerful client-side applications, and more. All of these start from the foundation of XHTML. None of them operates properly with classic HTML. Refactoring your pages into XHTML will enable you to take advantage of these and other exciting new technologies going forward. In some cases, they'll let you do things you can't already do. In other cases, they'll let you do things you are doing now, but much more quickly and cheaply. Either way, they're well worth the cost of refactoring to XHTML.

Why CSS

The separation of presentation from content is one of the fundamental design principles of HTML. Separating presentation from content allows you to serve the same text to different clients and let them decide how to format it in the way that best suits their needs. A cell phone browser doesn't have the same capabilities as a desktop browser such as Firefox. Indeed, a browser may not display content visually at all. For instance, it may read the document to the user.

Consequently, the HTML should focus on what the document means rather than on what it looks like. Most important, this style of authoring respects users' preferences. A reader can choose the fonts and colors that suit her rather than relying on the page's default. One size does not fit all. What is easily readable by a 30-year-old airline pilot with 20/20 vision may be illegible to an 85-year-old grandmother. A beautiful red and green design may be incomprehensible to a color-blind user. And a carefully arranged table layout may be a confusing mishmash of random words to a driver listening to a page on his cell phone while speeding down the Garden State Parkway.

Thus, in HTML, you don't say that "Why CSS" a few paragraphs up should be formatted in 11-point Arial bold, left-aligned. Instead, you say that it is an H2 header. At least you did, until Netscape came along and invented the font tag and a dozen other new presentational elements that people immediately began to use. The W3C responded with CSS, but the damage had been done. Web pages everywhere were created with a confusing mix of font, frame, marquee, and other presentational elements. Semantic elements such as `blockquote`, `table`, `img`, and `ul` were subverted to support layout goals. To be honest, this never really worked all that well, but for a long time it was the best we had.

That is no longer true. Today's CSS enables not just the same, but better layouts and presentations than one can achieve using hacks such as frames, spacer GIFs, and text wrapped up inside images. The CSS layouts are not only prettier, but they are leaner, more efficient, and more accessible. They cause pages to load faster and display better. With some effort, they can produce pages that work better in a wide variety of browsers on multiple platforms.

Shifting the markup out of the page and into a separate stylesheet allows us to start with a simple page that is at least legible to all readers, even those with ten-year-old browsers. We can then apply beautiful effects to these pages that improve the experience for users who are ready to handle them. However, no one is left out completely. Pages degrade gracefully.

Shifting the markup out of the page also has benefits for the developers. First of all, it allows different people with different skills to work on what they're best at. Writers can write words in a row without worrying about how everything will be formatted. Designers can organize and reorganize a page without touching the writers' words. Programmers can write scripts that add activity to the page without interfering with the appearance. CSS allows everyone to do what they are best at without stepping on each other's toes.

Whereas CSS is a boon to writers and designers, it's a godsend to developers. From a programmer's perspective, a page is much, much simpler when all the layout and style information is pulled out and extracted into a separate CSS stylesheet. The document tree has fewer elements in it and isn't nested as deeply. This makes it much easier to write scripts that interact with the page.

Finally, the biggest winners are the overworked webmasters who manage the entire site. Moving the markup out of the pages and into separate stylesheets allows them to combine common styles and maintain a consistent look and feel across the entire site. Changing the default font from Arial to Helvetica no longer requires editing thousands of HTML documents. It can now be a one-line fix in a single stylesheet file.

CSS enables web developers, webmasters, and web designers to follow the DRY principle: Don't Repeat Yourself. By combining common rules into single, reusable files, they make maintenance, updates, and editing far simpler. Even the end-users benefit because they load the style rules for a site only once rather than with every page. The smaller pages load faster and display quicker. Everyone wins.

Finally, let's not neglect the importance of CSS for our network managers and accountants. There may be only a kilobyte or two of purely presentational information in each page. However, summed over thousands of pages and millions of users, those kilobytes add up. You get real bandwidth savings by loading the styles only once instead of with every page. When ESPN switched to CSS markup it saved about *two terabytes of data a day.* At that level, this translates into real cost savings that you can measure on the bottom line. Now, admittedly, most of us are not ESPN and can only dream of having two terabytes of daily traffic in the first place, much less two terabytes of daily traffic that we can save. Nonetheless, if you are experiencing overloaded pipes or are unexpectedly promoted to the front page of Digg, moving your style into external CSS stylesheets can help you handle that.

Why REST

Representational State Transfer (REST) is the oldest and yet least familiar of the three refactoring goals I present here. Although I'll mostly focus on HTML in this book, one can't ignore the protocol by which HTML travels. That protocol is HTTP, and REST is the architecture of HTTP.

Understanding HTTP and REST has important consequences for how you design web applications. Anytime you place a form in a page, or use AJAX to send data back and forth to a JavaScript program, you're using HTTP. Use HTTP correctly and you'll develop robust, secure, scalable applications. Use it incorrectly and the best you can hope for is a marginally functional system. The worst that can happen, however, is pretty bad: a web spider that deletes your entire site, a shopping center that melts down under heavy traffic during the Christmas shopping season, or a site that search engines can't index and users can't find.

Although basic static HTML pages are inherently RESTful, most web applications that are more complex are not. In particular, you must consider REST anytime your application involves the following common things:

- Forms
- User authentication
- Cookies
- Sessions
- State

These are very easy to get wrong, and more applications to this day get them wrong than right. The Web is not a LAN. The techniques that worked for limited client/server systems of a few dozen to a few hundred users do not scale to web systems that must accommodate thousands to millions of users. Client/server architectures based on sessions and persistent connections are simply not possible on the Web. Attempts to recreate them fail at scale, often with disastrous consequences.

REST, as implemented in HTTP, has several key ideas, which are discussed in the following sections.

All Resources Are Identified by URLs

Tagging distinct resources with distinct URLs enables bookmarking, linking, search engine storage, and painting on billboards. It is much easier to find a resource when you can say, "Go to http://www.example .com/foo/bar" than when you have to say, "Go to http://www.example .com/. Type 'bar' into the form field. Then press the foo button."

Do not be afraid of URLs. Most resources should be identified only by URLs. For example, a customer record should have a URL such as http://example.com/patroninfo/username rather than http:// example.com/patroninfo. That is, each customer should have a separate URL that links directly to her record (protected by a password, of course), rather than all your customers sharing a single URL whose content changes depending on the value of some login cookie.

Safe, Side-Effect-Free Operations Such as Querying or Browsing Operate via GET

Google can only index pages that are accessed via GET. Users can only bookmark pages that are accessed via GET. Other sites can only link to pages with GET. If you care about raising your site traffic at all, you need to make as much of it as possible accessible via GET.

Nonsafe Operations Such as Purchasing an Item or Adding a Comment to a Page Operate via POST

Web spiders routinely follow links on a page that are accessible via GET, sometimes even when they are told not to. Users type URLs into browser location bars and then edit them to see what happens. Browsers prefetch linked pages. If an operation such as deleting content, agreeing to a contract, or placing an order is performed via GET, some program somewhere is going to do it without asking or consulting an actual user, sometimes with disastrous consequences. Entire sites have disappeared when Google discovered them and began to follow "delete this page" links, all because GET was used instead of POST.

Each Request Is Independent of All Others

The client and server may each have state, but neither relies on the other side remembering what its state is. All necessary information is transferred in each communication. Statelessness enables scalability through caching and proxy servers. It also enables a server to be easily replaced by a server farm as necessary. There's no requirement that the same server respond to the same client two times in a row.

Robust, scalable web applications work with HTTP rather than against it. RESTful applications can do everything that more familiar client/server applications do, and they can do it at scale. However, implementing this may require some of the largest changes to your systems. Nonetheless, if you're experiencing scalability problems, these can be among the most critical refactorings to make.

Objections to Refactoring

It is not uncommon for people ranging from the CEO to managers to HTML grunts to object to the concept of refactoring. The concern is expressed in many ways, but it usually amounts to this:

We don't have the time to waste on cleaning up the code. We have to get this feature implemented now!

There are two possible responses to this comment. The first is that refactoring saves time in the long run. The second is that you have more time than you think you do. Both are true.

Refactoring saves time in the long run, and often in the short run, because clean code is easier to fix and easier to maintain. It is easier to build on bedrock than quicksand. It is much easier to find bugs in clean code than in opaque code. In fact, when the source of a bug doesn't jump out at me, I usually begin to refactor until it does. The process of refactoring changes both the code itself and my view of the code. Refactoring can move my eyes into new places and allow me to see old code in ways I didn't see it before.

Of course, for maximum time savings, it's important to automate as much of the refactoring as possible. This is why I'm going to emphasize tools such as Tidy and TagSoup, as well as simple, regular-expression-based solutions. Although some refactorings require significant human effort—converting a site from tables to CSS layouts, for example—many others can be done with the click of a button—converting a static page to well-formed XHTML, for example. Many refactorings lay somewhere in between.

Less well recognized is that a lot more time is actually available for refactoring than most managers count on their timesheets. Writing new code is difficult, and it requires large blocks of uninterrupted time. A typical workday filled with e-mail, phone calls, meetings, smoking breaks, and so on sadly doesn't offer many long, uninterrupted blocks in which developers can work.

By contrast, refactoring is not hard. It does not require large blocks of uninterrupted time. Sixty minutes of refactoring done in six-minute increments at various times during the day has close to the same impact as one 60-minute block of refactoring. Sixty minutes of uninterrupted time is barely enough to even start to code, though, and six-minute blocks are almost worthless for development.

It's also worth taking developers' moods into account. The simple truth is that you're more productive at some times than at other times. Sometimes you can bang out hundreds of lines of code almost as fast as you can type, and other times it's an effort to force your fingers to the keyboard. Sometimes you're in the zone, completely focused on the task at hand. Other times you're distracted by an aching tooth, an upcoming client meeting, and your weekend plans. Coding, design, and other complex tasks don't work well when you're distracted, but refactoring isn't a complex task. It's an easy task. Refactoring enables you to get something done and move forward, even when you're operating at significantly reduced efficiency.

Perhaps most important, I find that when I am operating at less than peak efficiency, refactoring enables me to pick up speed and reach the zone. It's a way to dip a toe into the shallow end of the pool and acclimatize to the temperature before plunging all the way in. Taking on a simple task such as refactoring allows me to mentally move into the zone to work on more challenging, larger problems.

Getting Things Done

Refactoring is not unique in this, by the way. There are a lot of productive tasks you can use to nudge yourself into the zone. Writing tests, measuring and improving code coverage, fixing known bugs, using static code analyzers, and even spellchecking can help you to be productive and get things done when you just aren't in the mood to perform major tasks. The key is to not become blocked on any one task. Always have something else (ideally several something elses) ready to go at any time. Sometimes you just need to find the task that fits the time rather than finding the time to fit the task.

Refactoring is really a classic case of working smarter, not harder. Although that maxim can be a cliché ripe for a Dilbert parody, it really does apply here.

Chapter 2
Tools

Automatic tools are a critical component of refactoring. Although you can perform most refactoring manually with a text editor, and although I will sometimes demonstrate refactoring that way for purposes of illustration, in practice we almost always use software to help us. To my knowledge no major refactoring browsers are available for HTML at the time of this writing. However, a lot of tools can assist in many of the processes. In this section, I'll explain some of them.

Backups, Staging Servers, and Source Code Control

Throughout this book, I'm going to show you some very powerful tools and techniques. As the great educator Stan Lee taught us, "With great power comes great responsibility." Your responsibility is to not irretrievably break anything while using these techniques. Some of the tools I'll show can misbehave. Some of them have corner cases where they get confused. A huge amount of bad HTML is out there, not all of which the tools discussed here have accounted for. Consequently, refactoring HTML requires at least a five-step process.

1. Identify the problem.
2. Fix the problem.
3. Verify that the problem has been fixed.
4. Check that no new problems have been introduced.
5. Deploy the solution.

Because things can go wrong, you should not use any of these techniques on a live site. Instead, make a local copy of the site before making any changes. After making changes to your local copy, carefully verify all pages once again before you deploy.

Most large sites today already use staging or development servers where content can be deployed and checked before the public sees it. If you're just working on a small personal static site, you can make a local copy on your hard drive instead; but by all means work on a copy and check the changes before deploying them. How to check the changes is the subject of the next section.

Of course, even with the most careful checks, sometimes things slip by and are first noticed by end-users. Sometimes a site works perfectly well on a staging server and has weird problems on the production server due to unrecognized configuration differences. Thus, it's a very good idea to have a full and complete backup of the production site that you can restore to in case the newly deployed site doesn't behave as expected. Regular, reliable, tested backups are a must.

Finally, you should very seriously consider storing all your code, including all your HTML, CSS, and images, in a source code control system. Programmers have been using source code control for decades, but it's a relatively uncommon tool for web developers and designers. It's time for that to change. The more complex a site is, the more likely it is that subtle problems will slip in unnoticed at first. When refactoring, it is critical to be able to go back to previous versions, maybe even from months or years ago, to find out which change introduced a bug. Source code control also provides timestamped backups so that it's possible to revert your site to its state at any given point in time.

I strongly recommend Subversion for web development, mostly because of its strong support for moving files from one directory to another, though its excellent Unicode support and decent support for binary files are also helpful. Most source code control systems are set up for programmers who rarely bother to move files from one directory to another. By contrast, web developers frequently reorganize site structures (more frequently than they should, in fact). Consequently, a system really needs to be able to track histories across file moves. If your organization has already set up some other source code control system such as CVS, Visual SourceSafe, ClearCase, or Perforce, you can use that system instead; but Subversion is likely to work better and cause you fewer problems in the long run.

The topic of managing Subversion could easily fill a book on its own; and indeed, several such books are available. (My favorite is *Pragmatic Version Control Using Subversion* by Mike Mason [The Pragmatic Bookshelf, 2006].) Many large sites hire people whose sole responsibility is to manage the source code control repository. However, don't be scared off. Ultimately, setting up Subversion or another source code control repository is no harder than setting up Apache or another web server. You'll need to read a little documentation. You'll need to tweak some config files, and you may need to ask for help from a newsgroup or conduct a Google search to get around a rough spot. However, it's eminently doable, and it's well worth the time invested.

You can check files into or out of Subversion from the command line if necessary. However, life is usually simpler if you use an editor such as BBEdit that has built-in support for Subversion. Plug-ins are available that add Subversion support to editors such as Dreamweaver that don't natively support it. Furthermore, products such as Tortoise-SVN and SCPlugin are available that integrate Subversion support directly into Windows Explorer or the Mac Finder.

Some content management systems (CMSs) have built-in version control. If yours does, you may not need to use an external repository. For instance, MediaWiki stores a record of all changes that have been made to all pages. It is possible at any point to see what any given page looked like at any moment in time and to revert to that appearance. This is critical for MediaWiki's model installation at Wikipedia, where vandalism is a real problem. However, even private sites that are not publicly editable can benefit greatly from a complete history of the site over time. Although Wikis are the most common use of version control on the Web, some other CMSs such as Siteline also bundle this functionality.

Validators

There really are standards for HTML, even if nobody follows them. One way to find out whether a site follows HTML standards is to run a page through a validation service. The results can be enlightening.

They will provide you with specific details to fix, as well as a good idea of how much work you have ahead of you.

The W3C Markup Validation Service

For public pages, the validator of choice is the W3C's Markup Validation Service, at http://validator.w3.org/. Simply enter the URL of the page you wish to check, and see what it tells you. For example, Figure 2.1 shows the result of validating my blog against this service.

It seems I had misremembered the syntax of the `blockquote` element. I had mistyped the `cite` attribute as the `source` attribute. This was actually better than I expected. I fixed that and rechecked, as shown in Figure 2.2. Now the page is valid.

It is usually not necessary to check each and every page on your site for these sorts of errors. Most errors repeat themselves. Generally, once you identify a class of errors, it becomes possible to find and automatically fix the problems. For example, here I could simply search for `<blockquote source=` to find other places where I had made the same mistake.

This page was actually cleaner than normal to begin with. I next tried one of the oldest and least-maintained pages I could find on my sites. This generated 144 different errors.

Private Validation

The W3C is reasonably trustworthy. Still, you may not want to submit private pages from your intranet to the site. Indeed, for people dealing with medical, financial, and other personal data, it may be illegal to do so. You can download a copy of the HTML validator scripts from http://validator.w3.org/docs/install and install them locally. Then your pages don't need to travel outside your firewall when validating.

This style of validation is good when authoring. It is also extremely useful for spot-checking a site to see how much work you're likely to do, or for working on a single page. However, at some point, you'll want to verify all of the pages on a site, not just a few of them. For this, an automatic batch validator is a necessity.

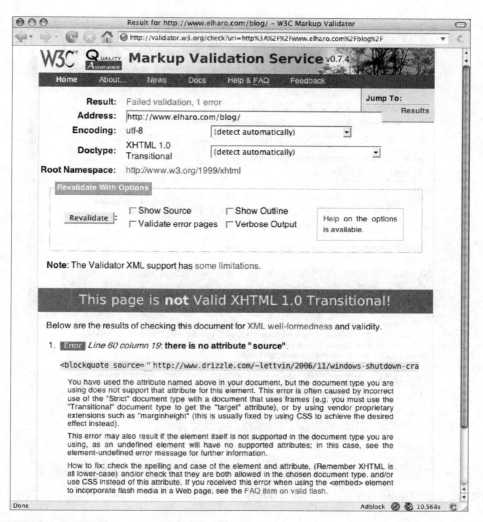

FIGURE 2.1   The W3C Markup Validation Service

The Log Validator

The W3C Markup Validation Service has given birth to the Log Validator (www.w3.org/QA/Tools/LogValidator/), a command-line tool written in Perl that can check an entire site. It can also use a web server's log files to determine which pages are the most popular and start its

FIGURE 2.2   Desired results: a valid page

analysis there. Obviously, you care a lot more about fixing the page that gets 100 hits a minute than the one that gets 100 hits a year. The Log Validator will provide you with a convenient list of problems to fix, prioritized by seriousness and popularity of page. Listing 2.1 shows the beginning of one such list.

LISTING 2.1   Log Validator Output

```
Results for module HTMLValidator
********************************************************************
Here are the 10 most popular invalid document(s) that I could
find in the logs for www.elharo.com.

Rank    Hits    #Error(s)                                    Address
------  ------  -----------    ------------------------------------
1       2738    21             http://www.elharo.com/blog/feed/atom/
2       1355    21             http://www.elharo.com/blog/feed/
3       1231    3              http://www.elharo.com/blog/
4       1127    6              http://www.elharo.com/
6       738     3              http://www.elharo.com/blog/networks
/2006/03/18/looking-for-a-router/feed/
11      530     3              http://www.elharo.com/journal
/fruitopia.html
20      340     1              http://www.elharo.com/blog
/wp-comments-post.php
23      305     3              http://www.elharo.com/blog/birding
/2006/03/15/birding-at-sd/
25      290     4              http://www.elharo.com/journal
/fasttimes.html
26      274     1              http://www.elharo.com/journal/
```

The first two pages in this list are Atom feed documents, not HTML files at all. Thus, it's no surprise that they show up as invalid. The third and fourth ones are embarrassing, though, since they're my blog's main page and my home page, respectively. They're definitely worth fixing. The fifth most visited page on my site is valid, however, so it doesn't show up in the list. Numbers 11, 25, and 26 are very old pages that pre-date XML, much less XHTML. It's no surprise that they're invalid, but because they're still getting hits, it's worth fixing them.

Number 20 is also a false positive. That's just the comments script used to post comments. When the validator tries to GET it rather than POST to it, it receives a blank page. That's not a real problem, though I might want to fix it one of these days to show a complete list of the comments. Or perhaps I should simply set up the script to return "HTTP error 405 Method Not Allowed" rather than replying with "200 OK" and a blank document.

After these, various other pages that aren't as popular are listed. Just start at the top and work your way down.

xmllint

You can also use a generic XML validator such as xmllint, which is bundled on many UNIX machines and is also available for Windows. It is part of libxml2, which you can download from http://xmlsoft.org/.

There are advantages and disadvantages to using a generic XML validator to check HTML. One advantage is that you can separate well-formedness checking from validity checking. It is usually easier to fix well-formedness problems first and then fix validity problems. Indeed, that is the order in which this book is organized. Well-formedness is also more important than validity.

The first disadvantage of using a generic XML validator is that it won't catch HTML-specific problems that are not specifically spelled out in the DTD. For instance, it won't notice an a element nested inside another a element (though that problem doesn't come up a lot in practice). The second disadvantage is that it will have to actually read the DTD. It doesn't assume anything about the document it's checking.

Using xmllint to check for well-formedness is straightforward. Just point it at the local file or remote URL you wish to check from the command line. Use the --noout option to say that the document itself shouldn't be printed and --loaddtd to allow entity references to be resolved. For example:

```
$ xmllint --noout --loaddtd http://www.aw.com
http://www.aw-bc.com/:118: parser error : Specification mandate
value for attribute nowrap
<TD class="headerBg" bgcolor="#004F99" nowrap align="left">
                                              ^
http://www.aw-bc.com/:118: parser error :
attributes construct error
<TD class="headerBg" bgcolor="#004F99" nowrap align="left">
                                              ^
http://www.aw-bc.com/:118: parser error : Couldn't find end of
Start Tag TD line 118
<TD class="headerBg" bgcolor="#004F99" nowrap align="left">
                                              ^
http://www.aw-bc.com/:120: parser error : Opening and ending
tag mismatch: IMG line 120 and A
 Benjamin Cummings" WIDTH="84" HEIGHT="64" HSPACE="0"
VSPACE="0" BORDER="0"></A>
...
```

When you first run a report such as this, the number of error messages can be daunting. Don't despair—start at the top and fix the problems one by one. Most errors fall into certain common categories that we will discuss later in the book, and you can fix them en masse. For instance, in this example, the first error is a valueless nowrap attribute. You can fix this simply by searching for nowrap and replacing it with nowrap="nowrap". Indeed, with a multifile search and replace, you can fix this problem on an entire site in less than five minutes. (I'll get to the details of that a little later in this chapter.)

After each change, you run the validator again. You should see fewer problems with each pass, though occasionally a new one will crop up. Simply iterate and repeat the process until there are no more well-formedness errors.The next problem is an IMG element that uses a start-tag rather than an empty-element tag. This one isn't quite as easy, but you can fix most occurrences by searching for BORDER="0"> and replacing it with border="0" />. That won't catch all of the problems with IMG elements, but it will fix a lot of them.

It is important to start with the first error in the list, though, and not pick an error randomly. Often, one early mistake can cause multiple well-formedness problems. This is especially true for omitted start-tags and end-tags. Fixing an early problem often removes the need to fix many later ones.

Once you have achieved well-formedness, the next step is to check validity. You simply add the --valid switch on the command line, like so:

```
$ xmllint --noout --loaddtd --valid  valid_aw.html
```

This will likely produce many more errors to inspect and fix, though these are usually not as critical or problematic. The basic approach is the same, though: Start at the beginning and work your way through until all the problems are solved.

Editors

Many HTML editors have built-in support for validating pages. For example, in BBEdit you can just go to the Markup menu and select Check/Document Syntax to validate the page you're editing. In Dreamweaver, you can use the context menu that offers a Validate Current Document item. (Just make sure the validator settings indicate XHTML rather than HTML.) In essence, these tools just run the document through a parser such as xmllint to see whether it's error-free.

If you're using Firefox, you should install Chris Pederick's Web Developer plug-in (https://addons.mozilla.org/firefox/60/). Once you've done that, you can validate any page by going to Tools/Web Developer/ Tools/Validate HTML. This loads the current page in the W3C validator. The plug-in also provides a lot of other useful options in Firefox.

Whatever tool or technique you use to find the markup mistakes, validating is the first step to refactoring into XHTML. Once you see what the problems are, you're halfway to fixing them.

Testing

In theory, refactoring should not break anything that isn't already broken. In practice, it isn't always so reliable. To some extent, the catalog later in this book shows you what changes you can safely make. However, both people and tools do make mistakes, and it's always possible that refactoring will introduce new bugs. Thus, the refactoring process really needs a good automated test suite. After every refactoring, you'd like to be able to press a button and see at a glance whether anything broke.

Although test-driven development has been a massive success among traditional programmers, it is not yet so common among web developers, especially those working on the front end. In fact, any automated testing of web sites is probably the exception rather than the rule, especially when it comes to HTML. It is time for that to change. It is time for web developers to start to write and run test suites and to use test-driven development.

The basic test-driven development approach is as follows.

1. Write a test for a feature.

2. Code the simplest thing that can possibly work.

3. Run all tests.

4. If tests passed, goto 1.

5. Else, goto 2.

For refactoring purposes, it is very important that this process be as automatic as possible. In particular:

- The test suite should not require any complicated setup. Ideally, you should be able to run it with the click of a button. You don't want developers to skip running tests because they're too hard to run.

- The tests should be fast enough that they can be run frequently; ideally, they should take 90 seconds or less to run. You don't want developers to skip running tests because they take too long.

- The result must be pass or fail, and it should be blindingly obvious which it is. If the result is fail, the failed tests should generate more output explaining what failed. However, passing tests should generate no output at all, except perhaps for a message such as "All tests passed." In particular, you want to avoid the common problem in which one or two failing tests get lost in a sea of output from passing tests.

Writing tests for web applications is harder than writing tests for classic applications. Part of this is because the tools for web application testing aren't as mature as the tools for traditional application testing. Part of this is because any test that involves *looking* at something and figuring out whether it looks right is hard for a computer. (It's easy for a person, but the goal is to remove people from the loop.) Thus, you may not achieve the perfect coverage you can in a Java or .NET application. Nonetheless, some testing is better than none, and you can in fact test quite a lot.

One thing you will discover is that refactoring your code to web standards such as XHTML is going to make testing a lot easier. Going forward, it is much easier to write tests for well-formed and valid XHTML pages than for malformed ones. This is because it is much easier to write code that consumes well-formed pages than malformed ones. It is much easier to see what the browser sees, because all browsers see the same thing in well-formed pages and different things in malformed ones. Thus, one benefit of refactoring is improving test-ability and making test-driven development possible in the first place. Indeed, with a lot of web sites that don't already have tests, you may need to refactor them enough to make testing possible before moving forward.

You can use many tools to test web pages, ranging from decent to horrible and free to very expensive. Some of these are designed for programmers, some for web developers, and some for business domain experts. They include

- HtmlUnit
- JsUnit
- HttpUnit
- JWebUnit
- FitNesse
- Selenium

In practice, the rough edges on these tools make it very helpful to have an experienced agile programmer develop the first few tests and the test framework. Once you have an automated test suite in place, it is usually easier to add more tests yourself.

JUnit

JUnit (www.junit.org/) is the standard Java framework for unit testing and the one on which a lot of the more specific frameworks such as HtmlUnit and HttpUnit are built. There's no reason you can't use it to test web applications, provided you can write Java code that pretends to be a browser. That's actually not as hard as it sounds.

For example, one of the most basic tests you'll want to run is one that tests whether each page on your site is well-formed. You can test this simply by parsing the page with an XML parser and seeing whether it throws any exceptions. Write one method to test each page on the site, and you have a very nice automated test suite for what we checked by hand in the previous section.

Listing 2.2 demonstrates a simple JUnit test that checks the well-formedness of my blog. All this code does is throw a URL at an XML parser and see whether it chokes. If it doesn't, the test passes. This version requires Sun's JDK 1.5 or later, and JUnit 3.8 or later somewhere in the classpath. You may need to make some modifications to run this in other environments.

LISTING 2.2 A JUnit Test for Web Site Well-Formedness

```
import java.io.IOException;
import junit.framework.TestCase;
import org.xml.sax.*;
import org.xml.sax.helpers.XMLReaderFactory;

public class WellformednessTests extends TestCase {

    private XMLReader reader;

    public void setUp() throws SAXException {
        reader = XMLReaderFactory.createXMLReader(
        "com.sun.org.apache.xerces.internal.parsers.SAXParser");
    }

    public void testBlogIndex()
      throws SAXException, IOException {
        reader.parse("http://www.elharo.com/blog/");
    }

}
```

You can run this test from inside an IDE such as Eclipse or NetBeans, or you can run it from the command line like so:

```
$ java -cp .:junit.jar
  junit.swingui.TestRunner WellformednessTests
```

If all tests pass, you'll see a green bar as shown in Figure 2.3.

To test additional pages for well-formedness, you simply add more methods, each of which looks exactly like `testBlogIndex`, just with a different URL. Of course, you can also write more complicated tests. You can test for validity by setting the http://xml.org/sax/features/validation feature on the parser and attaching an error handler that throws an exception if a validity error is detected.

You can use DOM, XOM, SAX, or some other API to load the page and inspect its contents. For instance, you could write a test that checks whether all links on a page are reachable. If you use TagSoup as the parser, you can even write these sorts of tests for non-well-formed HTML pages.

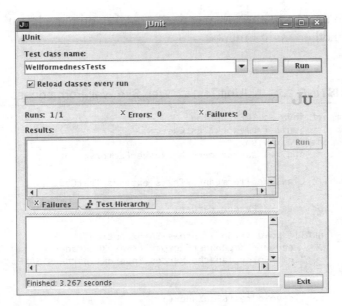

FIGURE 2.3   All tests pass.

You can submit forms using the `HttpURLConnection` class or run JavaScript using the Rhino engine built into Java 6. This is all pretty low-level stuff, and it's not trivial to do, but it's absolutely possible to do it. You just have to roll up your sleeves and start coding.

If nondevelopers are making regular changes to your site, you can set up the test suite to run periodically with cron and to e-mail you if anything unexpectedly breaks. (It's probably not reasonable to expect each author or designer to run the entire test suite before every check-in.) You can even run the suite continuously using a product such as Hudson or Cruise Control. However, that may fill your logs with a lot of uncountable test traffic, so you may wish to run this against the development server instead.

Many similar test frameworks are available for other languages and platforms: PyUnit for Python, CppUnit for C++, NUnit for .NET, and so forth. Collectively these go under the rubric *xUnit*. Whichever one you and your team are comfortable working with is fine for writing web test suites. The web server doesn't care what language your tests are written in. As long as you have a one-button test harness and enough HTTP client support to write tests, you can do what needs to be done.

HtmlUnit

HtmlUnit (http://htmlunit.sourceforge.net/) is an open source JUnit extension designed to test HTML pages. It will be most familiar and comfortable to Java programmers already using JUnit for test-driven development. HtmlUnit provides two main advantages over pure JUnit.

- The WebClient class makes it much easier to pretend to be a web browser.
- The HTMLPage class has methods for inspecting common parts of an HTML document.

For example, HtmlUnit will run JavaScript that's specified by an onLoad handler before it returns the page to the client, just like a browser would. Simply loading the page with an XML parser as Listing 2.2 did would not run the JavaScript.

Listing 2.3 demonstrates the use of HtmlUnit to check that all the links on a page are not broken. I could have written this using a raw parser and DOM, but it would have been somewhat more complex. In particular, methods such as getAnchors to find all the a elements in a page are very helpful.

LISTING 2.3   An HtmlUnit Test for a Page's Links

```
import java.io.IOException;
import java.net.*;
import java.util.*;
import com.gargoylesoftware.htmlunit.*;
import com.gargoylesoftware.htmlunit.html.*;

import junit.framework.TestCase;

public class LinkCheckTest extends TestCase {

    public void testBlogIndex()
      throws FailingHttpStatusCodeException, IOException {
        WebClient webClient = new WebClient();
        URL url = new URL("http://www.elharo.com/blog/");
        HtmlPage page = (HtmlPage) webClient.getPage(url);
        List links = page.getAnchors();
        Iterator iterator = links.iterator();
        while (iterator.hasNext()) {
            HtmlAnchor link = (HtmlAnchor) iterator.next();
            URL u = new URL(link.getHrefAttribute());
            // Check that we can download this page.
```

```
            // If we can't, getPage throws an exception and
            // the test fails.
            webClient.getPage(u);
        }
    }
}
```

This test is more than a unit test. It checks all the links on a page, whereas a real unit test would check only one. Furthermore, it makes connections to external servers. That's very unusual for a unit test. Still, this is a good test to have, and it will let us know that we need to fix our pages if an external site breaks links by reorganizing its pages.

HttpUnit

HttpUnit (http://httpunit.sourceforge.net/) is another open source JUnit extension designed to test HTML pages. It is also best suited for Java programmers already using JUnit for test-driven development and is in many ways quite similar to HtmlUnit. Some programmers prefer HttpUnit, and others prefer HtmlUnit. If there's a difference between the two, it's that HttpUnit is somewhat lower-level. It tends to focus more on the raw HTTP connection, whereas HtmlUnit more closely imitates a browser. HtmlUnit has somewhat better support for Java-Script, if that's a concern. However, there's certainly a lot of overlap between the two projects.

Listing 2.4 demonstrates an HttpUnit test that verifies that a page has exactly one H1 header, and that its text matches the web page's title. That may not be a requirement for all pages, but it is a requirement for some. For instance, it would be a very apt requirement for a newspaper site.

LISTING 2.4 An HttpUnit Test That Matches the Title to a Unique H1 Heading

```
import java.io.IOException;
import org.xml.sax.SAXException;
import com.meterware.httpunit.*;
import junit.framework.TestCase;
```

```
public class TitleChecker extends TestCase {

    public void testFormSubmission()
      throws IOException, SAXException {

        WebConversation wc = new WebConversation();
        WebResponse     wr = wc.getResponse(
          "http://www.elharo.com/blog/");
        HTMLElement[]   h1 = wr.getElementsWithName("h1");
        assertEquals(1, h1.length);
        String title = wr.getTitle();
        assertEquals(title, h1[0].getText());

    }

}
```

I could have written this test in HtmlUnit, too, and I could have written Listing 2.3 with HttpUnit. Which one you use is mostly a matter of personal preference. Of course, these are hardly the only such frameworks. There are several more, including ones not written in Java. Use whichever one you like, but by all means use something.

JWebUnit

JWebUnit is a higher-level API that sits on top of HtmlUnit and JUnit. Generally, JWebUnit tests involve more assertions and less straight Java code. These tests are somewhat easier to write without a large amount of Java expertise, and they may be more accessible to a typical web developer. Furthermore, tests can very easily extend over multiple pages as you click links, submit forms, and in general follow an entire path through a web application.

Listing 2.5 demonstrates a JWebUnit test for the search engine on my web site. It fills in the search form on the main page and submits it. Then it checks that one of the expected results is present.

LISTING 2.5   A JWebUnit Test for Submitting a Form

```
import junit.framework.TestCase;
import net.sourceforge.jwebunit.junit.*;

public class LinkChecker extends TestCase {

    private WebTester tester;
```

```
public LinkChecker(String name) {
    super(name);
    tester = new WebTester();
    tester.getTestContext().setBaseUrl(
      "http://www.elharo.com/");
}

public void testFormSubmission() {

    // start at this page
    tester.beginAt("/blog/");

    // check that the form we want is on the page
    tester.assertFormPresent("searchform");

    /// check that the input element we expect is present
    tester.assertFormElementPresent("s");

    // type something into the input element
    tester.setTextField("s", "Linux");

    // send the form
    tester.submit();

    // we're now on a different page; check that the
    // text on that page is as expected.
    tester.assertTextPresent("Windows Vista");
}

}
```

FitNesse

FitNesse (http://fitnesse.org/) is a Wiki designed to enable business users to write tests in table format. Business users like spreadsheets. The basic idea of FitNesse is that tests can be written as tables, much like a spreadsheet. Thus, FitNesse tests are not written in Java. Instead, they are written as a table in a Wiki.

You do need a programmer to install and configure FitNesse for your site. However, once it's running and a few sample fixtures have been written, it is possible for savvy business users to write more tests. FitNesse works best in a pair environment, though, where one programmer and one business user can work together to define the business rules and write tests for them.

For web app acceptance testing, you install Joseph Bergin's Html-Fixture (http://fitnesse.org/FitNesse.HtmlFixture). It too is based on HtmlUnit. It supplies instructions that are useful for testing web applications such as typing into forms, submitting forms, checking the text on a page, and so forth.

Listing 2.6 demonstrates a simple FitNesse test that checks the `http-equiv` meta tag in the head to make sure it's properly specifying UTF-8. The first three lines set the classpath. Then, after a blank line, the next line identifies the type of fixture as an HtmlFixture. (There are several other kinds, but HtmlFixture is the common one for testing web applications.)

The external page at http://www.elharo.com/blog/ is then loaded. In this page, we focus on the element named `meta` that has an `id` attribute with the value `charset`. This will be the subject for our tests.

The test then looks at two attributes of this element. First it inspects the `content` attribute and asserts that its value is `text/html; charset=utf-8`. Next it checks the `http-equiv` attribute of the same element and asserts that its value is `content-type`.

LISTING 2.6   A FitNesse Test for <meta name="charset" http-equiv= "Content-Type" content="text/html; charset=UTF-8" />

```
!path fitnesse.jar
!path htmlunit-1.5/lib/*.jar
!path htmlfixture20050422.jar

!|com.jbergin.HtmlFixture|
|http://www.elharo.com/blog/|
|Element Focus|charset   |meta|
|Attribute    |content   |text/html; charset=utf-8|
|Attribute    |http-equiv|content-type|
```

This test would be embedded in a Wiki page. You can run it from a web browser just by clicking the Test button, as shown in Figure 2.4. If all of the assertions pass, and if nothing else goes wrong, the test will appear green after it is run. Otherwise, it will appear pink. You can use other Wiki markup elsewhere in the page to describe the test.

Selenium

Selenium is an open source browser-based test tool designed more for functional and acceptance testing than for unit testing. Unlike with HttpUnit and HtmlUnit, Selenium tests run directly inside the web

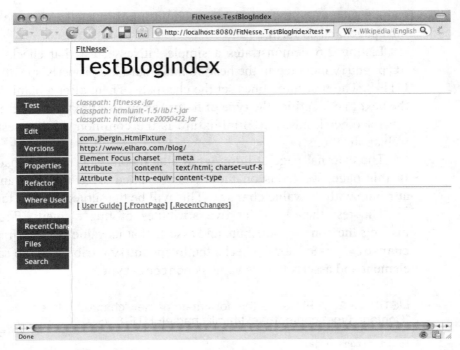

FIGURE 2.4   A FitNesse page

browser. The page being tested is embedded in an `iframe` and the Selenium test code is written in JavaScript. It is mostly browser and platform independent, though the IDE for writing tests, shown in Figure 2.5, is limited to Firefox.

Although you can write tests manually in Selenium using remote control, it is really designed more as a traditional GUI record and playback tool. This makes it more suitable for testing an application that has already been written and less suitable for doing test-driven development.

Selenium is likely to be more comfortable to front-end developers who are accustomed to working with JavaScript and HTML. It is also likely to be more palatable to professional testers because it's similar to some of the client GUI testing tools they're already familiar with.

Listing 2.7 demonstrates a Selenium test that verifies that www .elharo.com shows up in the first page of results from a Google search

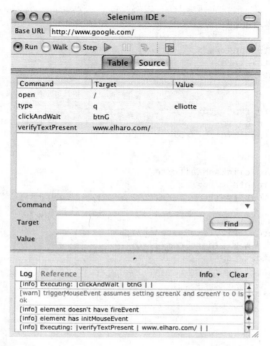

FIGURE 2.5 The Selenium IDE

for "Elliotte." This script was recorded in the Selenium IDE and then edited a little by hand. You can load it into and then run it from a web browser. Unlike the other examples given here, this is not Java code, and it does not require major programming skills to maintain. Selenium is more of a macro language than a programming language.

LISTING 2.7 Test That elharo.com Is in the Top Search Results for Elliotte

```
<html>
<head>
<meta http-equiv="Content-Type"
      content="text/html; charset=UTF-8">
<title>elharo.com is a top search results for Elliotte</title>
</head>
<body>
<table cellpadding="1" cellspacing="1" border="1">
<thead>
```

```
<tr><td rowspan="1" colspan="3">New Test</td></tr>
</thead><tbody>
<tr>
        <td>open</td>
        <td>/</td>
        <td></td>
</tr>
<tr>
        <td>type</td>
        <td>q</td>
        <td>elliotte</td>
</tr>
<tr>
        <td>clickAndWait</td>
        <td>btnG</td>
        <td></td>
</tr>
<tr>
        <td>verifyTextPresent</td>
        <td>www.elharo.com/</td>
        <td></td>
</tr>

</tbody></table>
</body>
</html>
```

Obviously, Listing 2.6 is a real HTML document. You can open this with the Selenium IDE in Firefox and then run the tests. Because the tests run directly inside the web browser, Selenium helps you find bugs that occur in only one browser or another. Given the wide variation in browser CSS, HTML, and JavaScript support, this capability is very useful. HtmlUnit, HttpUnit, JWebUnit, and the like use their own JavaScript engines that do not always have the same behavior as the browsers' engines. Selenium uses the browsers themselves, not imitations of them.

The IDE can also export the tests as C#, Java, Perl, Python, or Ruby code so that you can integrate Selenium tests into other environments. This is especially important for test automation. Listing 2.8 shows the same test as in Listing 2.7, but this time in Ruby. However, this will not necessarily catch all the cross-browser bugs you'll find by running the tests directly in the browser.

LISTING 2.8 Automated Test That elharo.com Is in the Top Search
Results for Elliotte

```
require "selenium"
require "test/unit"

class GoogleSearch < Test::Unit::TestCase
  def setup
    @verification_errors = []
    if $selenium
      @selenium = $selenium
    else
      @selenium = Selenium::SeleneseInterpreter.new("localhost",
        4444, *firefox", "http://localhost:4444", 10000);
      @selenium.start
    end
    @selenium.set_context("test_google_search", "info")
  end

  def teardown
    @selenium.stop unless $selenium
    assert_equal [], @verification_errors
  end

  def test_google_search
    @selenium.open "/"
    @selenium.type "q", "elliotte"
    @selenium.click "btnG"
    @selenium.wait_for_page_to_load "30000"
    begin
        assert @selenium.is_text_present("www.elharo.com/")
    rescue Test::Unit::AssertionFailedError
        @verification_errors << $!
    end
  end
end
```

Getting Started with Tests

Because you're refactoring, you already have a web site or application;
and if it's like most I've seen, it has limited, if any, front-end tests.
Don't let that discourage you. Pick the tool you like and start to write a
few tests for some basic functionality. Any tests at all are better than
none. At the early stages, testing is linear. Every test you write makes a
noticeable improvement in your code coverage and quality. Don't get
bogged down thinking you have to test everything. That's great if you
can do it, but if you can't, you can still do something.

Before refactoring a particular page, subdirectory, or path through a site, take an hour and write at least two or three tests for that section. If nothing else, these are smoke tests that will let you know if you totally muck up everything. You can expand on these later when you have time.

If you find a bug, by all means write a test for the bug before fixing it. That will help you know when you've fixed the bug, and it will prevent the bug from accidentally reoccurring in the future after other changes. Because front-end tests aren't very unitary, it's likely that this test will indirectly test other things besides the specific bit of buggy code.

Finally, for new features and new developments beyond refactoring, by all means write your tests first. This will guarantee that the new parts of the site are tested, and tests will often leak over into the older pages and scripts as well.

Automatic testing is critical to developing a robust, scalable application. Developing a test suite can seem daunting at first, but it's worth doing. The first test is the hardest. Once you've set up your test framework and written your first test, subsequent tests will flow much more easily. Just as you can improve a site linearly through small, automatic refactorings that add up over time, so too can you improve your test suite by adding just a few tests a week. Sooner than you know, you'll have a solid test suite that helps to ensure reliability by telling you when things are broken and showing you what to fix.

Regular Expressions

Manually inspecting and changing each file on even a small site is tedious and often cost-prohibitive. It is much more effective to let the computer do the work by searching for mistakes and, when possible, automatically fixing them. A number of tools support this, including command-line tools such as grep, egrep, and sed; text editors such as jEdit, BBEdit, TextPad, and PSPad; and programming languages such as Java, Perl, and PHP. All these tools provide a specialized search syntax known as *regular expressions*. Although there are small differences from one tool to the next, the basic regular expression syntax is much the same.

For purposes of illustration, I'm going to use the jEdit text editor as my search and replace tool in this section. I chose it because it provides pretty much all the features you need, it has a reasonable GUI, it's open source, and it's written in Java, so it runs on essentially any platform you're likely to want. You can download a copy from http://jedit.org/.

However, the techniques I'm showing here are by no means limited to that one editor. In my work, I normally use BBEdit instead because it has a slightly nicer interface. However, it's payware and only runs on the Mac. There are numerous other choices. If you prefer a different program, by all means use it. What you'll need are

- Full regular expression search and replace
- The ability to recursively search a directory
- The ability to filter the files you search
- A tool that shows you what it has changed, but does not require you to manually approve each change
- Automatic recognition of different character encodings and line-ending conventions

Any tool that meets these criteria should be sufficient.

Searching

The first goal of a regular expression is to find things that may be wrong. For example, I recently noticed that I had mistyped some dates as 20066 instead of 2006 in one of my files. That's an error that's likely to have happened more than once, so I checked for it by searching for that string.

In jEdit, you perform a multifile search using the Search/Search in Directory menu item. Selecting this menu item brings up the dialog shown in Figure 2.6. This is normally configured more or less as shown here.

- The string you're searching for (the target string) goes in the first text field.
- The string that will replace the target string goes in the second text field. Here I'm just going to find, not replace, so I haven't entered a replacement string.

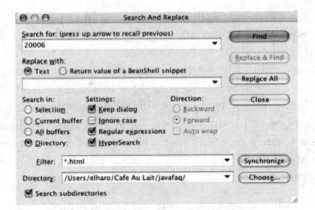

FIGURE 2.6   jEdit multifile search

- The Directory radio button is checked to indicate that you're going to search multiple files. You can also search just in the current file, or even the current selection.

- The filter is set to *.html to search only those files that end in .html. You can modify this to search different kinds of or subsets of files. For instance, I often want to search only my old news files, which are named news2000.html, news2001.html, news2002.html, and so on. In that case, I would set the filter to news2.*html. I could search even older files including news1999.html by rewriting the filter regular expression in a form such as news\d\d\d\d.html.

- I specify the directory where I've stored my local copy of the files I'm searching. In my case, this is /Users/elharo/Cafe au Lait/javafaq.

- "Search subdirectories" is checked. If it weren't, jEdit would search only the javafaq directory, but not any directories that directory contains.

- "Keep dialog" is checked. This keeps the dialog box open after the search is completed.

- "Ignore case" is checked. This will allow the regular expression to match regardless of case. This isn't always what you want, but more often than not, it is.

- "Regular expressions" is checked. You don't need to check this when you're only searching for a constant string, as here. However, most searches are more complex than that.

- HyperSearch is checked. This will bring up a window showing all matches, rather than just finding the next match.

Fortunately, that particular problem seems to have been isolated. However, I also recently noticed another, more serious problem. For some unknown reason, I somehow had managed to write links with double equals signs, as shown here, throughout one of my sites:

```
<a href=="../../index.html">Cafe au Lait</a>
```

Consequently, links were breaking all over the place. The first step was to find out how broad the problem was. In this case, the mistaken string was constant and was unlikely to appear in correct text, so it was easy to search for. This problem turned up 4,475 times in 476 files, as shown in the HyperSearch results in Figure 2.7.

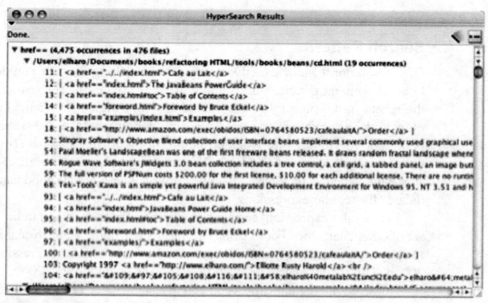

FIGURE 2.7 jEdit search results

When there aren't a lot of mistakes, you can click on each one to open the document and fix it manually. Sometimes this is needed. Sometimes this is even the easiest solution. However, when there are thousands of mistakes, you have to fix them with a tool. In this case, the solution is straightforward. Put `href=` in the "Replace with" field, and then click the "Replace all" button.

Do be careful when performing this sort of operation, though. A small mistake can cause bigger problems. A bad search and replace likely caused this problem in the first place. You should test your regular expression search and replace on a few files first before trying it on an entire site.

Most important, always work on a backup copy of the site, always run your test suite after each change, and always spot-check at least some of the files that have been changed to make sure nothing went wrong. If something does go wrong, an editor with undo capability can be very useful. Not all editors support multifile undo with a buffer that's large enough to handle thousands of changes. If yours doesn't, be ready to delete your working copy and replace it with the original in case the search goes wrong. Like any other complex bit of code, sometimes you have to try several times to fully debug a regular expression.

Search Patterns

Often, you don't know exactly what you're searching for, but you do know its general pattern. For example, if you're searching for years in the recent past, you might want to find any four-digit number beginning with 200. You may want to search for attribute name=value pairs, but you're not sure whether they're in the format `name=value`, `name='value'`, or `name="value"`. You may want to search for all `<p>` start-tags, whether they have attributes or not. These are all good candidates for regular expressions.

In a regular expression, certain characters and patterns stand in for a set of other characters. For example, \d means any digit. Thus, to search for any year from 2000 to 2009, one could use the regular expression 200\d. This would match 2000, 2001, 2002, and so on through 2009.

However, the regular expression 200\d also matches 12000, 200032, 12320056, and other strings that are probably not years at all. (To be precise, it matches the substrings in the form 200\d, not the entire string.) Thus, you might want to indicate that the string you're matching must be preceded and trailed by whitespace of some kind. The metacharacter \s matches whitespace, so we can now rewrite the expression as \s200\d\s to match only those strings that look like years in this decade.

Of course, there's still no guarantee that every string you match in this form is a year. It could be a price, a population, a score, a movie title, or something else. You'll want to scan the list of matches to verify that it is what you expect. False positives are a real concern, especially for simple cases such as this. However, it's normally possible to either further refine the regular expression to avoid any false positives or manually remove the accidental matches.

There usually are other ways to do many things. For instance, we could write this search as \b200\d\b. The metacharacter \b matches the beginning or end of a word, without actually selecting any characters. This would avoid the whitespace at the beginning and end of words. This would also allow us to recognize a year that came at the end of a sentence right before a period, as in "This is 2008." However, it can't distinguish periods from decimal points and would also match the 2005 in 2005.3124.

You could even simply list the years separated by the OR operator, |, like so:

2000|2001|2002|2003|2004|2005|2006|2007|2008|2009

However, this still has the word boundary problems of the previous matches.

Sometimes you stop with a search. In particular, if the content is generated automatically from a CMS, template page, or other program, the search is used merely to find bugs: places where the program is generating incorrect markup. You then must change the program to generate correct markup. If this is the case, false positives don't worry you nearly so much because all changes will be performed manually anyway. The search only identifies the bug. It doesn't fix it.

If you don't stop with a search, and you go on to a replacement, you need to be cautious. Regular expressions can be tricky, and ones involving HTML are often much trickier than the textbook examples. Nonetheless, they are invaluable tools in cleaning up HTML.

Note

If you don't have a lot of experience with regular expressions, please refer to Appendix 1 for many more examples. I also recommend *Mastering Regular Expressions,* 3rd Edition, by Jeffrey E. F. Friedl (O'Reilly, 2006).

Tidy

Regular expressions are well and good for individual, custom changes, but they can be tedious and difficult to use for large quantities of changes. In particular, they are designed more to work with plain text than with semistructured HTML text. For batch changes and automated corrections of common mistakes, it helps to have tools that take advantage of the markup in HTML. The first such tool is Dave Raggett's Tidy (www.w3.org/People/Raggett/tidy/), the original HTML fixer-upper. It's a simple, multiplatform command-line program that can correct most HTML mistakes.

-asxhtml

For purposes of this book, you want to use Tidy with the -asxhtml command-line option. For example, this command converts the file index.html to well-formed XHTML and stores the result back into the same file (-m):

```
$ tidy -asxhtml -m index.html
```

Frankly, you could do worse than just running Tidy across all your HTML files and calling it a day, but please don't stop reading just yet. Tidy has a few more options that can improve your code further, and there are some problems it can't handle or handles incorrectly. For example, when I used this command on one of my older pages that I

hadn't looked at in at least five years, Tidy generated the following
error messages:

```
line 1 column 1 - Warning: missing <!DOCTYPE> declaration
line 7 column 1 - Warning: <body> attribute "bgcolor" has
invalid value "#ffffff"
line 16 column 2 - Warning: <table> lacks "summary" attribute
line 230 column 1 - Warning: <table> lacks "summary" attribute
line 14 column 91 - Warning: trimming empty <p>
Info: Document content looks like XHTML 1.0 Transitional
5 warnings, 0 errors were found!
```

These are problems that Tidy mostly didn't know how to fix. It
actually was able to supply a DOCTYPE because I specified XHTML
mode, which has a known DOCTYPE. However, it doesn't know what
to do with `bgcolor="#ffffff"`. The problem here is an extra *f* which
should be removed, or perhaps the entire `bgcolor` attribute should be
removed and replaced with CSS.

Tip

Once you've identified a problem such as this, it's entirely possible that the same problem crops up in multiple documents. Having noticed this in one file, it's worth doing a search and replace
across the entire directory tree to catch any other occurrences.
Given the prevalence of copy and paste coding, few mistakes
occur only once.

The second two problems are tables that lack a `summary` attribute.
This is an accessibility problem, and you should correct it. Tidy actually prints some further details about this:

```
The table summary attribute should be used to describe
the table structure. It is very helpful for people using
non-visual browsers. The scope and headers attributes for
table cells are useful for specifying which headers apply
to each table cell, enabling non-visual browsers to provide
a meaningful context for each cell.

For further advice on how to make your pages accessible
see http://www.w3.org/WAI/GL. You may also want to try
"http://www.cast.org/bobby/" which is a free Web-based
service for checking URLs for accessibility.
```

Table summaries are certainly a good thing, and you should definitely add one. However, Tidy can't summarize your table itself. You'll have to do that.

The final message warns you that Tidy found an empty paragraph element and threw it away. This common message is probably misleading and definitely worth a second look. What it meant in this case (and in almost every other one you'll see) is that the <P> tag was being used as an end-tag rather than a start-tag. That is, the markup looked like this:

```
Blah blah blah<P>
Blah blah blah<P>
Blah blah blah<P>
```

Tidy reads it as this:

```
Blah blah blah
<P>Blah blah blah</P>
<P>Blah blah blah</P>
<P></P>
```

Thus, it throws away that last empty paragraph. However, what you almost certainly wanted was this:

```
<P>Blah blah blah</P>
<P>Blah blah blah</P>
<P>Blah blah blah</P>
```

There's no easy search and replace for this flaw, though XHTML strict validation will at least alert you to the files in which the problem lies. You can use XSLT (discussed shortly) to fix some of these problems; but if there aren't too many of them, it's safer and not hugely onerous to manually edit these files.

If you specify the --enclose-text yes option, Tidy will wrap any such unparented text in a p element. For example:

```
$ tidy -asxhtml --enclose-text yes  example.html
```

Tidy may alert you to a few other serious problems that you'll still have to fix manually. These include

- A missing end quote for an attribute value, for example, `<p id="c1>`

- A missing `>` to close a tag, for example, `<p` or `</p`

- Misspelled element and attribute names, for example, `<tabel>` instead of `<table>`

-clean

The next important option is `-clean`. This replaces deprecated presentational elements such as `i` and `font` with CSS markup. For example, when I used `-clean` on the same document, Tidy added these CSS rules to the head of my document:

```
<style type="text/css">
/*<![CDATA[*/
 body {
  background-color: #ffffffff;
  color: #000000;
 }
 p.c2 {text-align: center}
 h1.c1 {text-align: center}
/*]]>*/
</style>
```

It also added the necessary `class` attributes to the elements that had previously used a `center` element. For example:

```
<h1 class="c1">Java Virtual Machines</h1>
```

That's as far as Tidy goes with CSS, but you might want to consider revisiting all these files to see if you can extract a common external stylesheet that can be shared among the documents on your site, rather than including the rules in each separate page. Furthermore, you should probably consider more semantic class names rather than Tidy's somewhat prosaic default.

For example, I've sometimes used the `i` element to indicate that I'm *talking about* a word rather than *using* the word. For example:

```
<p><i>May</i> can be very ambiguous in English, meaning might,
can, or allowed, depending on context.</p>
```

Here the italics are not used for emphasis, and replacing them with em is not appropriate. Instead, they should be indicated with a span and a class, like so:

```
<p><span class='wordasword'>May</span> can be very ambiguous
in English, meaning might, can, or allowed, depending on
context.</p>
```

Then, add a CSS rule to the stylesheet to format this as italic:

```
span.wordasword { font-style: italic; }
```

Tidy, however, is not smart enough to figure this out and will need your help. Still, Tidy is a good first step.

Encodings

Tidy is surprisingly bad at detecting the character encoding of HTML documents, despite the relatively rich metadata in most HTML documents for specifying exactly this. If your content is anything other than ASCII or ISO-8859-1 (Latin-1), you'd best tell Tidy that with the --input-encoding option. For example, if you've saved your documents in UTF-8, invoke Tidy thusly:

```
$ tidy -asxhtml --input-encoding utf8 index.html
```

Tidy generates ASCII text as output unless you tell it otherwise. It will escape non-ASCII characters using named entities when available, and numeric character references when not. However, Tidy supports several other common encodings. The only other one I recommend is UTF-8. To get it use the --output-encoding option:

```
$ tidy -asxhtml --output-encoding utf8 index.html
```

The input encoding does not have to be the same as the output encoding. However, if it is you can just specify -utf8 instead:

```
$ tidy -asxhtml -utf8 index.html
```

For various reasons, I strongly recommend that you stick to either ASCII or UTF-8. Other encodings do not transfer as reliably when documents are exchanged across different operating systems and locales.

Pretty Printing

Tidy also has a couple of options that don't have a lot to do with the HTML itself, but do make documents prettier to look at and thus easier to work with when you open them in a text editor.

The -i option indents the text so that it's easier to see how the elements nest. Tidy is smart enough not to indent whitespace-significant elements such as pre.

The -wrap option wraps text at a specified column. Usually about 80 columns are nice.

```
$ tidy -asxhtml -utf8 -i -wrap 80 index.html
```

Generated Code

Tidy has limited support for working on PHP, JSP, and ASP pages. Basically, it will ignore the content inside the PHP, ASP, or JSP sections and try to work on the rest of the HTML markup. However, that is very tricky to do. In particular, most templating languages do not respect element boundaries. If code is generating half of an element or a start-tag for an element that is later closed by a literal end-tag, it is very easy for Tidy to get confused. I do not recommend using Tidy directly on these sorts of pages.

Instead, download some fully rendered pages from your web site after processing by the template engine. Run Tidy on a representative sample of these pages, and then compare the results to the original pages. By looking at the differences, you can usually figure out what needs to be changed in your templates; then make the changes manually.

Although this does require more manual work and human intelligence, if each template is generating multiple static pages, this process can finish sooner than semiautomated processing of large numbers of static HTML pages.

Use As a Library

TidyLib is a C library version of Tidy that you can integrate into your own programs. This might be useful for writing scripts that tidy an entire site, for example. Personally, though, I do not find C to be the most conducive language for simple scripting. I usually prefer to write a shell or Perl script that invokes the Tidy command line directly.

TagSoup

John Cowan's TagSoup (http://home.ccil.org/~cowan/XML/tagsoup/) is an open source HTML parser written in Java that implements the Simple API for XML, or SAX. Cowan describes TagSoup as "a SAX-compliant parser written in Java that, instead of parsing well-formed or valid XML, parses HTML as it is found in the wild: poor, nasty, and brutish, though quite often far from short. TagSoup is designed for people who have to process this stuff using some semblance of a rational application design. By providing a SAX interface, it allows standard XML tools to be applied to even the worst HTML."

TagSoup is not intended as an end-user tool, but it does have a basic command-line interface. It's also straightforward to hook it up to any number of XML tools that accept input from SAX. Once you've done that, feed in HTML, and out will come well-formed XHTML. For example:

```
$ java -jar tagsoup.jar index.html
<?xml version="1.0" standalone="yes"?>
<html lang="en-US" xmlns="http://www.w3.org/1999/
xhtml"><head><title>Java Virtual Machines</title><meta
name="description" content="A Growing
list of Java virtual machines and their capabilities">
</meta></head><body bgcolor="#ffffff" text="#000000">

<h1 align="center">Java Virtual Machines</h1>
…
```

You can improve its output a little bit by adding the `--omit-xml-declaration` and `-nodefaults` command-line options:

```
$ java -jar tagsoup.jar --omit-xml-declaration
        -nodefaults index.html
<html lang="en-US" xmlns="http://www.w3.org/1999/
xhtml"><head><title>Java Virtual Machines</title><meta
name="description" content="A Growing
list of Java virtual machines and their capabilities"></meta>
</head><body bgcolor="#ffffff" text="#000000">
```

```
<h1 align="center">Java Virtual Machines</h1>
...
```

This will remove a few pieces that are likely to confuse one browser or another.

You can use the `--encoding` option to specify the character encoding of the input document. For example, if you know the document is written in Latin-1, ISO 8859-1, you could run it like so:

```
$ java -jar tagsoup.jar --encoding=ISO-8859-1 index.html
```

TagSoup's output is always UTF-8.

Finally, you can use the `--files` option to write new copies of the input files with the extension .xhtml. Otherwise, TagSoup prints the output on stdout, from where you can redirect it to any convenient location. TagSoup cannot change a file in place like Tidy can.

However, TagSoup is primarily designed for use as a library. Its output from command-line mode leaves something to be desired compared to Tidy. In particular:

- It does not convert presentational markup to CSS.

- It does not include a DOCTYPE declaration, which is needed before some browsers will recognize XHTML.

- It does include an XML declaration, which needlessly confuses older browsers.

- It uses start-tag and end-tag pairs for empty elements such as `br` and `hr`, which may confuse some older browsers.

TagSoup does not guarantee absolutely valid XHTML (though it does guarantee well-formedness). There are a few things it cannot handle. Most important, XHTML requires all `img` elements to have an `alt` attribute. If the `alt` attribute is empty, the image is purely presentational and should be ignored by screen readers. If the attribute is not empty, it is used in place of the image by screen readers. TagSoup has no way of knowing whether any given `img` with an omitted `alt` attribute is presentational or not, so it does not insert any such attributes. Similarly, TagSoup does not add summaries to tables. You'll have to do that by hand, and you'll want to validate after using TagSoup to make sure you catch all these instances.

However, despite these limits, TagSoup does do a huge amount of work for you at very little cost.

TagSoup versus Tidy

For an end-user, the primary difference between TagSoup and Tidy is one of philosophy. Tidy will sometimes give up and ask for help. There are some things it does not know how to fix and will not try to fix. Tag-Soup will never give up. It will always produce well-formed XHTML as output. It does not always produce perfectly valid XHTML, but it will give you something. For the same reasons, TagSoup does not warn you about what it could not handle so that you can fix it manually. Its assumption is that you really don't care that much. If that's not true, you might prefer to use Tidy instead. Tidy is more careful. If it isn't pretty sure it knows what the document means, it won't give you any-thing. TagSoup will always give you something.

For a programmer, the differences are a little more striking. First, TagSoup is written in Java and Tidy is written in C. That alone may be enough to help you decide which one to use (though there is a Java port of Tidy, called JTidy). Another important difference is that TagSoup operates in streaming mode. Rather than working on the entire docu-ment at once, it works on just a little piece of it at a time, moving from start to finish. That makes it very fast and allows it to process very large documents. However, it can't do things such as add a style rule to the head that applies to the last paragraph of the document. Because HTML documents are rarely very large (usually a few hundred kilo-bytes at most), I think a whole-document approach such as Tidy's is more powerful.

XSLT

XSLT (Extensible Stylesheet Language Transformations) is one of many XML tools that work well on HTML documents once they have first been converted into well-formed XHTML. In fact, it is one of my favorite such tools, and the first thing I turn to for many tasks. For instance, I use it to automatically generate a lot of content, such as RSS and Atom feeds, by screen-scraping my HTML pages. Indeed, the possibility of using XSLT on my documents is one of my main reasons for refactoring documents into well-formed XHTML. XSLT can query documents for things you need to fix and automate some of the fixes.

When refactoring XHTML with XSLT, you usually leave more alone than you change. Thus, most refactoring stylesheets start with the identity transformation shown in Listing 2.9.

LISTING 2.9 The Identity Transformation in XSLT

```
<xsl:stylesheet xmlns:xsl='http://www.w3.org/1999/XSL/Transform'
  version='1.0'>
  xmlns:html='http://www.w3.org/1999/xhtml'
  xmlns='http://www.w3.org/1999/xhtml'
  exclude-result-prefixes='html'>

  <xsl:template match="@*|node()">
    <xsl:copy>
      <xsl:apply-templates select="@*|node()"/>
    </xsl:copy>
  </xsl:template>

</xsl:stylesheet>
```

This merely copies the entire document from the input to the output. You then modify this basic stylesheet with a few extra rules to make the changes you desire. For example, suppose you want to change all the deprecated <i> elements to <em> elements. You would add this rule to the stylesheet:

```
<xsl:template match='html:i'>
  <em>
    <xsl:apply-templates select="@*|node()"/>
  </em>
</xsl:template>
```

Notice that the XPath expression in the match attribute must use a namespace prefix, even though the element it's matching uses the default namespace. This is a common source of confusion when transforming XHTML documents. You always have to assign the XHTML namespace a prefix when you're using it in an XPath expression.

Note

Several good introductions to XSLT are available in print and on the Web. First, I'll recommend two I've written myself. Chapter 15 of *The XML 1.1 Bible* (Wiley, 2003) covers XSLT in depth and is available on the Web at www.cafeconleche.org/books/bible3/chapters/ch15.html. *XML in a Nutshell,* 3rd Edition, by Elliotte Harold and W. Scott Means (O'Reilly, 2004), provides a somewhat more concise introduction. Finally, if you want the most comprehensive coverage available, I recommend Michael Kay's *XSLT: Programmer's Reference* (Wrox, 2001) and *XSLT 2.0: Programmer's Reference* (Wrox, 2004).

Chapter 3
Well-Formedness

The very first step in moving markup into modern form is to make it well-formed. Well-formedness is the basis of the huge and incredibly powerful XML tool chain. Well-formedness guarantees a single unique tree structure for the document that can be operated on by the DOM, thus making it the basis of reliable, cross-browser JavaScript. The very first thing you need to do is make your pages well-formed.

Validity, although important, is not nearly as crucial as well-formedness. There are often good reasons to compromise on validity. In fact, I often deliberately publish invalid pages. If I need an element the DTD doesn't allow, I put it in. It won't hurt anything because browsers ignore elements they don't understand. If I have a blockquote that contains raw text but no elements, no great harm is done. If I use an HTML 5 element such as m that Opera recognizes and other browsers don't, those other browsers will just ignore it. However, if the page is malformed, the consequences are much more severe.

First, I won't be able to use any XML tools, such as XSLT or SAX, to process the page. Indeed, almost the only thing I can do with it is view it in a browser. It is very hard to do any reliable automated processing or testing with a malformed page.

Second, browser display becomes much more unpredictable. Different browsers fill in the missing pieces and correct the mistakes of malformed pages in different ways. Writing cross-platform JavaScript or CSS is hard enough without worrying about what tree each browser will construct from ambiguous HTML. Making the page well-formed makes it a lot more likely that I can make it behave as I like across a wide range of browsers.

What Is Well-Formedness?

Well-formedness is a concept that comes from XML. Technically, it means that a document adheres to certain rigid constraints, such as every start-tag has a matching end-tag, elements begin and end in the same parent element, and every entity reference is defined.

Classic HTML is based on SGML, which allows a lot more leeway than does XML. For example, in HTML and SGML, it's perfectly OK to have a `<br>` or `<li>` tag with no corresponding `</br>` and `</li>` tags. However, this is no longer allowed in a well-formed document.

Well-formedness ensures that every conforming processor treats the document in the same way at a low level. For example, consider this malformed fragment:

```
<p>The quick <strong>brown fox</p>
jumped over the
<p>lazy</strong> dog.</p>
```

The `strong` element begins in one paragraph and ends in the next. Different browsers can and do build different internal representations of this text. For example, Firefox and Safari fill in the missing start- and end-tags (including those between the paragraphs). In essence, they treat the preceding fragment as equivalent to this markup:

```
<p>The quick <strong>brown fox</strong></p>
<strong>jumped over the </strong>
<p><strong>lazy</strong> dog.</p>
```

This creates the tree shown in Figure 3.1.

By contrast, Opera places the second p element inside the `strong` element which is inside the first p element. In essence, the Opera DOM treats the fragment as equivalent to this markup:

```
<p>The quick
  <strong>brown fox jumped over the
    <p>lazy dog.</p>
  </strong>
</p>
```

This builds the tree shown in Figure 3.2.

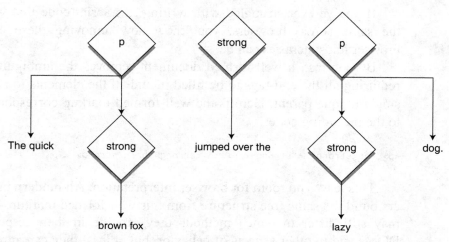

FIGURE 3.1 An overlapping tree as interpreted by Firefox and Safari

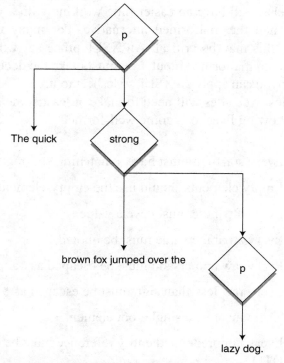

FIGURE 3.2 An overlapping tree as interpreted by Opera

If you've ever struggled with writing JavaScript code that works the same across browsers, you know how annoying these cross-browser idiosyncrasies can be.

By contrast, a well-formed document removes the ambiguity by requiring all the end-tags to be filled in and all the elements to have a single unique parent. Here is the well-formed markup corresponding to the preceding code:

```
<p>…foo<strong>…</strong></p> <p><strong>…bar</strong> </p>
```

This leaves no room for browser interpretation. All modern browsers build the same tree structure from this well-formed markup. They may still differ in which methods they provide in their respective DOMs and in other aspects of behavior, but at least they can agree on what's in the HTML document. That's a huge step forward.

Anything that operates on an HTML document, be it a browser, a CSS stylesheet, an XSL transformation, a JavaScript program, or something else, will have an easier time working with a well-formed document than the malformed alternative. For many use cases such as XSLT, this may be critical. An XSLT processor will simply refuse to operate on malformed input. You must make the document well-formed before you can apply an XSLT stylesheet to it.

Most web sites will need to make at least some and possibly all of the following fixes to become well-formed.

- Every start-tag must have a matching end-tag.

- Empty elements should use the empty-element tag syntax.

- Every attribute must have a value.

- Every attribute value must be quoted.

- Every raw ampersand must be escaped as &.

- Every raw less-than sign must be escaped as <.

- There must be a single root element.

- Every nonpredefined entity reference must be declared in the DTD.

In addition, namespace well-formedness requires that you add an `xmlns="http://www.w3.org/1999/xhtml"` attribute to the root `html` element.

Although it's easy to find and fix some of these problems manually, you're unlikely to catch all of them without help. As discussed in the preceding chapter, you can use xmllint or other validators to check for well-formedness. For example:

```
$ xmllint --noout --loaddtd http://www.aw.com
http://www.aw-bc.com/:118: parser error : Specification
mandate value for attribute nowrap
<TD class="headerBg" bgcolor="#004F99" nowrap align="left">
                                        ^
http://www.aw-bc.com/:118: parser error : attributes construct error
<TD class="headerBg" bgcolor="#004F99" nowrap align="left">
                                        ^
http://www.aw-bc.com/:118: parser error : Couldn't find end
of Start-tag TD line 118
<TD class="headerBg" bgcolor="#004F99" nowrap align="left">
                                        ^
...
```

TagSoup or Tidy can handle many of the necessary fixes automatically. However, they don't always guess right, so it pays to at least spot-check some of the problems manually before fixing them. Usually it's simplest to fix as many broad classes of errors as possible. Then run xmllint again to see what you've missed.

The following sections discuss the mechanics and trade-offs of each of these changes as they usually apply in HTML.

Change Name to Lowercase

Make all element and attribute names lowercase. Make most entity names lowercase, except for those that refer to capital letters.

```
<BLOCKQUOTE CITE=
  'http://www.gutenberg.org/dirs/etext00/dvlft10.txt'>
<P>
```

(continued)

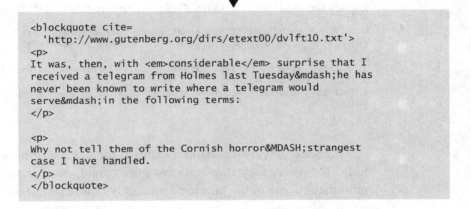

```
It was, then, with <EM>considerable</EM> surprise that I
received a telegram from Holmes last Tuesday&MDASH;he has
never been known to write where a telegram would
serve&MDASHin the following terms:
</P>

<P>
Why not tell them of the Cornish horror&MDASH;strangest
case I have handled.
</P>
</BLOCKQUOTE>
```

```
<blockquote cite=
  'http://www.gutenberg.org/dirs/etext00/dvlft10.txt'>
<p>
It was, then, with <em>considerable</em> surprise that I
received a telegram from Holmes last Tuesday&mdash;he has
never been known to write where a telegram would
serve&mdash;in the following terms:
</p>

<p>
Why not tell them of the Cornish horror&MDASH;strangest
case I have handled.
</p>
</blockquote>
```

Motivation

XHTML uses lowercase names exclusively. All elements and attributes
are written in lowercase. For example, `<table>` is recognized but not
`<TABLE>` or `<Table>`. In XHTML mode, lowercase is required.

Entity Names

Entity names are sometimes case-sensitive, even in classic HTML.
For instance, é resolves to é, but É resolves to É.
It's important to get these right, too, as an XHTML browser will rec-
ognize é and É but not &EAcute; or &EACUTE;.
Even a browser operating in HTML mode can guess wrong if you
don't have the right case in the entity reference.

Generic XML tools don't care about case but do care that it matches. That is, a `<table>` start-tag is closed by a `</table>` end-tag but not by `</TABLE>` or `</Table>`. The `id` attribute has the type ID as defined in the XHTML DTD and can be used as a link anchor. However, the `id` attribute does not and cannot.

Potential Trade-offs

There are relatively few trade-offs for converting to lowercase. All modern browsers support lowercase tag names without any problems. A few *very* old browsers that were never in widespread use, such as HotJava, only supported uppercase for some tags. The same is true of early versions of Java Swing's built-in HTML renderer. However, this has long since been fixed.

It is also possible that some homegrown scripts based on regular expressions may not recognize lowercase forms. If you have any scripts that screen-scrape your HTML, you'll need to check them to make sure they're also ready to handle lowercase tag names. Once you're done making the document well-formed, it may be time to consider refactoring those scripts, too, so that they use a real parser instead of regular expression hacks. However, that can wait. Usually it's simple enough to change the expressions to look for lowercase tag names instead of uppercase ones, or to not care about the case of the tag names at all.

Mechanics

The first rule of well-formedness is that every start-tag has a matching end-tag. The *matching* part is crucial. Although classic HTML is case-insensitive, XML and XHTML are not. `<DIV>` is not the same as `<div>` and a `</div>` end-tag cannot close a `<DIV>` start-tag.

For purely well-formedness reasons, all that's needed is to normalize the case. All tags could be capitalized or not, as long as you're consistent. However, it's easiest for everyone if we pick one case convention and stick to it. The community has chosen lowercase for XHTML. Thus, the first step is to convert all tag names, attribute names, and entity names to lowercase. For example:

- `<P>` to `<p>`
- `<Table>` to `<table>`
- `</DIV>` to `</div>`
- `<BLOCKQUOTE CITE="http://richarddawkins.net/ article,372,n,n">` to `<blockquote cite="http:// richarddawkins.net/article,372,n,n">`
- `&COPY;` to `&copy;`

There are several ways to do this.

The first and the simplest is to use TagSoup or Tidy in XHTML mode. Along with many other changes, these tools will convert all tag and attribute names to lowercase. They will also change entity names that need to be in lowercase.

You also can accomplish this with regular expressions. Because HTML element and attribute names are composed exclusively of the Latin letters *A* to *Z* and *a* to *z,* this isn't too difficult. Let's start with the element names. There are likely to be thousands, perhaps millions, of these, so you don't want to fix them by hand.

Tags are easy to search for. This regular expression will find all start-tags that contain at least one capital letter:

```
<[a-zA-Z]*[A-Z]+[a-zA-Z]*
```

This regular expression will find all end-tags that contain at least one capital letter:

```
</[a-zA-Z]*[A-Z]+[a-zA-Z]*>
```

Entities are also easy. This regular expression finds all entity references that contain a capital letter other than the initial letters:

```
&[A-Za-z][A-Za-z][A-Z]+[A-Za-z]*;
```

I set up the preceding regular expression to find at least three capital letters to avoid accidentally triggering on references such as `&Omega;` that should have a single initial capital letter and on references such as

Æ that have two initial capital letters. This may miss some cases, such as &Amp; and &AMp;, but those are rare in practice. Usually entity references are either all uppercase or all lowercase. If any such mixed cases exist, we'll find them later with xmllint and fix them by hand.

Attributes are trickier to find because the pattern to find them (=name) may appear inside the plain text of the document. I much prefer to use Tidy or TagSoup to fix these. However, if you know you have a large problem with particular attributes, it's easy to do a search and replace for individual ones—for instance, HREF= to href=. As long as you aren't writing about HTML, that string is unlikely to appear in plain text content.

Sometimes your initial find will discover that only a few tags use uppercase. For instance, if there are lots of uppercase table tags, you can quickly change <TD> to <td>, </TD> to </td>, <TR> to </tr>, and so forth without even using regular expressions. If the problem is a little broader, consider using Tidy or TagSoup. If that doesn't work, you'll need a tool that can replace text while changing its case. jEdit can't do this. However, Perl and BBEdit can. Use \L in the replacement pattern to convert all characters to lowercase. For example, let's start with the regular expression for start-tags:

```
(<[a-zA-Z]*[A-Z]+[a-zA-Z]*)
```

This expression will replace it with its lowercase equivalent:

```
\L\1
```

Quote Attribute Value

Put quotes around all attribute values.

```
<div id=speech1>
<span class=speaker>PROSPERO</span>
<blockquote cite=
http://www-tech.mit.edu/Shakespeare/tempest/tempest.4.1.html>
```

(continued)

```
<span class=verse id=a4s1v1>If I have too austerely
punish'd you,</span>
<span class=verse id=a4s1v2>Your compensation makes amends,
for I</span>
<span class=verse id=a4s1v3>Have given you here a third
of mine own life,</span>
<span class=verse id=a4s1v4>Or that for which I live;
who once again</span>
<span class=verse id=a4s1v5>I tender to thy hand:
all thy vexations</span>
<span class=verse id=a4s1v6>Were but my trials of
 thy love and thou</span>
<span class=verse id=a4s1v7>Hast strangely stood the
 test here, afore Heaven,</span>
</blockquote>
</div>
```

```
<div id="speech1">
<span class="speaker">PROSPERO</span>
<blockquote cite=
  "http://www-tech.mit.edu/Shakespeare/tempest/tempest.4.1.html">
<span class="verse" id="a4s1v1">If I have too austerely
punish'd you,</span>
<span class="verse" id="a4s1v2">Your compensation makes amends,
for I</span>
<span class="verse" id="a4s1v3">Have given you here a third
of mine own life,</span>
<span class="verse" id="a4s1v4">Or that for which I live;
who once again</span>
<span class="verse" id="a4s1v5">I tender to thy hand:
all thy vexations</span>
<span class="verse" id="a4s1v6">Were but my trials of
 thy love and thou</span>
<span class="verse" id="a4s1v7">Hast strangely stood the
 test here, afore Heaven,</span>
</blockquote>
</div>
```

Motivation

In XHTML, all attribute values are quoted, even those that don't contain whitespace.

Potential Trade-offs

Absolutely no browsers are in the least bit confused by a properly quoted attribute value.

This can add roughly two bytes per attribute value to the file size. If you're Google and are counting every byte on your home page because you serve gigabytes per second, this may matter. This should not concern anybody else.

Mechanics

Manually, all you have to do is type a single or double quote before and after the attribute value. For example, consider this start-tag:

```
<a class=q href=http://www.example.com>
```

You simply turn that into this:

```
<a class="q" href="http://www.example.com">
```

Or this:

```
<a class='q' href='http://www.example.com'>
```

There's no reason to prefer single or double quotes. Use whichever one you like. Mechanically, both Tidy and TagSoup will fill these quotes in for you. It's probably easiest to let them do the work.

Regular expressions are a little tricky because you also need to consider the case where there's whitespace around the equals sign. For instance, you don't just have to handle the preceding examples. You have to be ready for this:

```
<a class = q href = http://www.example.com>
```

And even this:

```
<a class=
    q href
    = http://www.example.com>
```

Finding the cases without whitespace is not too hard. This will do it:

```
[a-zA-Z]+=[^'"><\s]+
```

However, the preceding code snippet will also find lots of false positives. For instance, it will find this tag because of `item=15314` in the query string:

```
<a href="http://www.cybout.com/cgi-bin/product_info?item=15314">
```

We can improve this a little bit by requiring whitespace before the name, like so:

```
\w+[a-zA-Z]+=[^'"><\s]+
```

You may discover a few cases where the attribute value contained whitespace and was not quoted. Similarly, you may find a few places where the initial quote is present but the closing quote is not. These are problematic, and you need to fix them. Browsers do not always interpret these as you might expect, and different browsers handle them differently. What makes no difference in Internet Explorer may cause Firefox to hide content and vice versa.

Fill In Omitted Attribute Value

Add values to all valueless attributes.

```
<input type="radio" name="p" value="debit" checked></input>
<input name="generator" value="system78" readonly></input>
<input name="date" value="2007-12-17" disabled></input>
<a href="http://example.com/imagemap/library">
<img src="duane.png" ismap></a>
```

```
<input type="radio" name="p" value="debit" checked="checked" />
<input name="generator" value="system78" readonly='readonly' /
<input name="date" value="2007-12-17" disabled="disabled"></input>
<a href="http://example.com/imagemap/library">
<img src="duane.png" ismap="ismap"></a>
```

Motivation

XHTML does not support the attribute name-only syntax.

Potential Trade-offs

Minimal. Browsers are perfectly happy to read the values you supply.

Mechanics

Omitted attribute values are fairly rare in practice. The only place they're at all common is in forms and image maps. It may well be possible to manually fix all occurrences on a site without a great deal of effort. Alternatively, you can just use Tidy or TagSoup.

To fix one, just set the attribute value to the name. For example, change this:

```
<input type="radio" name="p" checked>
```

into this:

```
<input type="radio" name="p" checked='checked'>
```

Only a few elements and attributes support valueless attributes in the first place:

- input: checked, disabled, readonly, ismap
- optgroup: disabled
- option: selected, disabled
- textarea: disabled, readonly
- button: disabled
- script: defer
- img: ismap, controls
- area: nohref
- dl: compact
- ul: compact
- ol: compact
- ul: compact, plain

- `frame: noresize`
- `table: border`
- `marquee: truespeed`
- `link: disabled`
- `style: disabled`
- `applet: mayscript`
- `select: disabled, multiple`
- `object: declare`

Because many of the words involved can appear in plain text, it is not safe to use regular expressions to replace these. However, you can use a simple search to find them and then verify and fix them manually. For the attributes that aren't actually English words, such as `ismap` and `mayscript`, just search for those words. For the attributes that are, such as `border` and `compact`, use a regular expression such as this:

```
<.*\s+compact\s+.*>
```

Then search for the case where the valueless attribute is the last attribute:

```
<.*\s+compact\s*>
```

Replace Empty Tag with Empty-Element Tag

Change elements such as `<br>` to `<br class='empty' />`.

```
Polonius<hr>
You shall do marvelous wisely, good Reynaldo,<br>
Before you visit him, to make inquire<br>
Of his behavior.<br>
```

```
Polonius<hr class='empty' />
You shall do marvelous wisely, good Reynaldo,<br class='empty' />
Before you visit him, to make inquire<br class='empty' />
Of his behavior. <br class='empty' />
```

Motivation

XML parsers require that every start-tag have a matching end-tag. There can be no `<p>` without a corresponding `</p>`. Similarly, there can be no `<br>` without a corresponding `</br>`. Alternatively, you can use empty-element tag syntax, such as `<br/>` and `<hr/>`. This is usually simpler for elements that are guaranteed to be empty and more compatible with legacy browsers.

Potential Trade-offs

Although most modern browsers have no problem with empty-element tags, a few older ones you'll still find installed here or there, such as Netscape 3, do. For example, some will treat `<br/>` as an element whose name is `br/` and will not insert the necessary break. Others will take `<br></br>` as a double break, rather than a single break. The content will still be present, but it may not be styled properly.

Mechanics

Classic HTML defines 12 empty elements:

- `<br>`
- `<hr>`
- `<meta>`
- `<link>`
- `<base>`
- `<img>`
- `<embed>`
- `<param>`
- `<area>`
- `<frame>`
- `<col>`
- `<input>`

In addition, a few other elements from various proprietary browser extensions may also appear:

- `<basefont>`
- `<bgsound>`
- `<keygen>`
- `<sound>`
- `<spacer>`
- `<wbr>`

Although XML and XHTML allow these tags to be written either with a start-tag/end-tag pair such as `<br></br>` or with an empty-element tag such as `<br />`, the latter is much friendlier to older browsers and to human authors. There's little reason not to prefer the empty-element tag.

However, even an empty-element tag such as `<br/>` can confuse some older browsers that actually read this as an unknown element with the name `br/` instead of the known element `br`. Maximum compatibility is achieved if you add an attribute and a space before the final slash. The `class` attribute is a good choice. For example:

```
<br class="empty" />
<hr class="empty" />
```

I picked `empty` as the class to be clear why I inserted it. However, the value of the `class` attribute really doesn't matter. If you have reason to assign a different class to some or all of these elements, feel free.

TagSoup and Tidy will convert these elements as part of their fix-up. However, neither adds the `class="empty"` attributes. You can add those with an extra search and replace step at the end, or you can just make the entire change with search and replace. I would start with the `<br/>` element. You can simply search for all `<br>` tags and replace them with `<br class="empty" />`.

However, there are a few things to watch out for. The first is whether someone has already done this. Check to see whether there are any `</br>` elements in the source. If any appear, first remove them, as they're no longer necessary.

The remaining concern is br tags with attributes, such as `<br clear="all">`. You can find these by searching for "`<br.`"

If there aren't too many of these, I might just open the files and fix them manually. If there are a lot of them, you can automate the process, but this will require a slightly more complicated regular expression. The search expression is:

```
<br\s+([^>]*)=([^>]+[^/])>
```

The replace expression is:

```
<br \1=\2 />
```

When you're done, run your test suite to make sure all is well and you haven't accidentally broken something.

The hr element is handled almost identically. The meta and link elements are trickier because they almost always have attributes, so you need to use the more complicated form of the regular expressions. Of course, Tidy and TagSoup are also options.

Add End-tag

Close all paragraphs, list items, table cells, and other nonempty elements.

```
It is intended to include all the industries of the United
States concerned in French trade under the following
classifications:<p>

<ol>
<li>Machine-Tools, Wire, Transmission and Textiles
<li>Milling Machinery
<li>Electrical Apparatus
<li>Transportation
<li>Importers
<li>Synthetic Products based on chemical processes
```

(continued)

```
<li>Bankers
<li>Factory Architects, Engineers and Contractors
</ol>
```

```
<p>It is intended to include all the industries of the
United States concerned in French trade under the following
classifications:</p>

<ol>
<li>Machine-Tools, Wire, Transmission and Textiles</li>
<li>Milling Machinery</li>
<li>Electrical Apparatus</li>
<li>Transportation</li>
<li>Importers</li>
<li>Synthetic Products based on chemical processes</li>
<li>Bankers</li>
<li>Factory Architects, Engineers and Contractors</li>
</ol>
```

Motivation

The first motivation is simply XML compatibility. XML parsers require that each start-tag be matched by a corresponding end-tag.

However, there's a strong additional reason. Many documents do not display as intended in classic HTML when the end-tags are omitted. The problem is not that the browsers do not know how or where to insert end-tags. It's that authors often do not arrange the tags properly. All too often, the boundaries of an unclosed HTML element do not fall where the author expects. The result can be a document that appears quite different from what is expected. Indentation problems are the most common symptom (elements are not indented that should be, or elements are indented too far). However, all sorts of display problems can result. CSS is extremely hard to create and debug in the face of improperly closed elements.

Potential Trade-offs

Few and minimal. The resultant documents may be slightly larger. If you're not serving gigabytes per day, this is not worth worrying about.

Mechanics

Manually, you simply need to inspect each file and determine where the end-tags belong. For example, consider this table modeled after one in the HTML 4 specification:

```
<table>
<tr>
  <th rowspan="2">
  <th colspan="2">Average
  <th rowspan="2">Blond Hair
<tr><th>Height<th>Weight
<tr><th>Boys<td>1.4<td>58<td>28%
<tr><th>Girls<td>1.3<td>34.5<td>17%
</table>
```

Only the `</table>` end-tag is present. All the other end-tags are implied. A browser can probably figure this out. A human author might not and is likely to insert new content in the wrong place. Add end-tags after each element, like so:

```
<table>
  <tr>
    <th rowspan="2"></th>
    <th colspan="2">Average</th>
    <th rowspan="2">Blond Hair</th>
  </tr>
  <tr>
    <th>Height</th>
    <th>Weight</th>
  </tr>
  <tr>
    <th>Boys</th>
    <td>1.4</td>
    <td>58</td>
    <td>28%</td>
  </tr>
  <tr>
    <th>Girls</th>
    <td>1.3</td>
    <td>34.5</td>
    <td>17%</td>
  </tr>
</table>
```

Paragraphs are worth special attention here. When paragraph tags are omitted, the `<p>` start-tag usually serves as an end-tag rather than a start-tag. You'll commonly see content such as this tidbit from *Through the Looking Glass:*

```
Alice didn't like this idea at all: so, to change the
subject, she asked 'Does she ever come out here?'
<p>

'I daresay you'll see her soon,' said the Rose.  'She's one
of the thorny kind.'
<p>

'Where does she wear the thorns?' Alice asked with some
curiosity.
<p>
```

When encountering text such as this, you'll want to turn each `<p>` into a `</p>`, and then add the missing start-tags like so:

```
<p>Alice didn't like this idea at all:  so, to change the
subject, she asked 'Does she ever come out here?'
</p>

<p>'I daresay you'll see her soon,' said the Rose.
'She's one of the thorny kind.'
</p>

<p>'Where does she wear the thorns?' Alice asked with some
curiosity.
</p>
```

Tidy and TagSoup can fix this. However, they usually incorrectly guess the proper location of the start-tag and produce markup such as this:

```
Alice didn't like this idea at all:  so, to change the
subject, she asked 'Does she ever come out here?'
<p>

'I daresay you'll see her soon,' said the Rose.
'She's one of the thorny kind.'
</p>

<p>'Where does she wear the thorns?' Alice asked with some
curiosity.
</p>
<p>
</p>
```

Tidy doesn't add the closing empty paragraph, but it still fails to find the start of the first paragraph. You can tell Tidy to wrap paragraphs around orphan text blocks using the `--enclose-block-text` option with the value y:

```
$ tidy -asxhtml --enclose-block-text y  endtag.html
```

This doesn't matter for basic browser display, but it matters a great deal if you've assigned any specific CSS style rules to the p element. Furthermore, it can apply special formatting intended for the first paragraph of a chapter or section to the second instead.

Usually this happens only to the first paragraph in a section. However, if the runs of paragraphs are interrupted by a div, table, blockquote, or other element, there is likely such a block after each such block-level element.

Consequently, after running TagSoup over a page, search for empty paragraphs. Anytime you find one, it means there's probably a paragraph-less block of text earlier in the document that you should enclose in a new p element. However, this is tricky because often the start-tag and end-tag are on different lines. The following regular expression will find most occurrences:

```
<p>\s*</p>
```

This expression will find any empty paragraphs that have attributes:

```
<p\s[^>]*>\s*</p>
```

However, such paragraphs weren't created by Tidy or TagSoup, so you'll probably want to leave them in.

Remove Overlap

Close every element within its parent element.

```
This is <strong><em>very important</strong></em>!
<p>Sarah answered, <q>I'm really not sure about this.</p>
<p>Maybe you should ask somebody else?</q> Then she
```

(continued)

```
sat down.
</p>
```

```
This is <strong><em>very important</em></strong>!
<p>Sarah answered, <q>I'm really not sure about this.</q>
</p>
<p><q>Maybe you should ask somebody else?</q> Then she
sat down.
</p>
```

Motivation

Different browsers do not build the same trees from documents containing overlapping elements. Consequently, JavaScript can work very differently than you expect between browsers.

Furthermore, small changes in a document with overlap can make radical changes in the DOM tree that even a single browser builds. Consequently, JavaScript built on top of such documents is fragile. CSS is likewise fragile. JavaScript, CSS, and other programs that read a document's DOM are hard to create, debug, and maintain in the face of overlapping elements.

Potential Trade-offs

Sometimes the nature of the text really does call for overlap—for instance, when a quote begins in one paragraph and ends in another. This comes up frequently in Biblical scholarship, for instance. Not all text fits neatly into a tree.

Unfortunately, HTML, XML, and XHTML cannot handle overlap in any reasonable fashion. If you're doing scholarly textual analysis, you may need something more powerful still. However, this is rarely a concern for simple web publication. You can usually hack around the problem well enough for browser display by using more elements than may logically be called for.

Mechanics

A validator will report all areas where overlap is a problem. However, overlap is so confusing to tools that they may not diagnose it properly or in an obvious fashion. Different validators will report problems in different locations, and a single validator may report several errors related to one occurrence. Sometimes the problem will be indicated as an unclosed element or an end-tag without a start-tag, or both. For example:

```
overlap.html:10: parser error : Opening and ending tag
mismatch: q line 10 and p
<p>Sarah answered, <q>I'm really not sure about this.</p>
                                                         ^
overlap.html:11: parser error : Opening and ending tag
mismatch: p line 11 and q
<p>Maybe you should ask somebody else?</q> Then she
```

Furthermore, an overlap problem may cause a parser to miss the starts or ends of other elements, and it may not be able to recover. It is very common for overlap to cause a cascading sequence of progressively more serious errors for the rest of the document. Thus, you should start at the beginning and fix one error at a time. Often, fixing an overlap problem eliminates many other error messages.

Repairing overlap is not hard. Sometimes the overlap is trivial, as when the end-tag for the parent element immediately precedes the end-tag for the child element. Then you just have to swap the end-tags. For example, change this:

```
<strong><em>very important</strong></em>
```

to this:

```
<strong><em>very important</em></strong>
```

If the overlap extends into another element, you close the overlapping element inside its first parent and reopen it in the last. For example, suppose you have these two paragraphs containing one quote:

```
<p>Sarah answered, <q>I'm really not sure about this.</p>
<p>Maybe you should ask somebody else?</q> Then she
sat down.</p>
```

Change them to two paragraphs, each containing a quote:

```
<p>Sarah answered,
  <q>I'm really not sure about this.</q>
</p>
<p>
  <q>Maybe you should ask somebody else?</q>
  Then she sat down.
</p>
```

If there are intervening elements, you'll need to create new elements inside those as well.

Tidy and TagSoup can fix technical overlap problems but not especially well, and the result is usually not what you would expect. For example, Tidy will not always reopen an overlapping element inside the next element. For instance, it turns this:

```
<p>Sarah answered, <q>I'm really not sure about this.</p>
<p>Maybe you should ask somebody else?</q> Then she
sat down.</p>
```

into this:

```
<p>Sarah answered, <q>I'm really not sure about this.</p>
<p>Maybe you should ask somebody else? Then she
sat down.</p>
```

It completely loses the quote in the second paragraph. TagSoup keeps the quote in the second paragraph but introduces a quote around the boundary whitespace between the two paragraphs:

```
<p>Sarah answered, <q>I'm really not sure about this.</p>
<q></q>
<p><q>Maybe you should ask somebody else?</q> Then she
sat down.</p>
```

Consequently, I prefer to fix these overlap problems by hand if there aren't too many of them. You're more likely to reproduce the original intent that way.

Convert Text to UTF-8

Reencode all text as Unicode UTF-8.

Motivation

Pages that use any content except basic ASCII have cross-platform display problems. Windows encodings are not interpreted correctly on the Mac and vice versa. Web browsers guess what encoding they think a page is in, but they often guess wrong.

UTF-8 is a standard encoding that works across all web browsers and is supported by all major text editors and other tools. It is reasonably fast, small, and efficient. It can support all Unicode characters and is a good basis for internationalization and localization of pages.

Potential Trade-offs

You need to be able to control your web server's HTTP response headers to properly implement this. This can be problematic in shared hosting environments. Bad tools do not always recognize UTF-8 when they should.

Mechanics

There are two steps here. First, reencode all content in UTF-8. Second, tell clients that you've done that. Reencoding is straightforward, provided that you know what encoding you're starting with. You have to tell Tidy that you want UTF-8, but once you do, it will do the work:

```
$ tidy -asxhtml -m --output-encoding utf8 index.html
```

TagSoup you don't have to tell. It just produces UTF-8 by default.

A number of command-line tools and other programs will also save content in UTF-8 if you ask, such as GNU recode (www.gnu.org/software/recode/recode.html), BBEdit, and jEdit. You should also set your editor of choice to save in UTF-8 by default.

The next step is to tell the browsers that the content is in UTF-8. There are three parts to this.

- Add a byte order mark.
- Add a meta tag.
- Specify the Content-type header.

The byte order mark is Unicode character 0xFEFF, the zero-width space. When this is the first character in a document, the browser should recognize the byte sequence and treat the rest of the content as UTF-8. This shouldn't be necessary, but Internet Explorer and some other tools are more reliable if they have it. Some editors add this automatically and some require you to request it.

The second step is to add a meta tag in the `head`, such as this one:

```
<meta http-equiv="Content-Type"
    content="text/html; charset=UTF-8" />
```

The `charset=UTF-8` part warns browsers that they're dealing with UTF-8 if they haven't figured it out already.

Finally, you want to configure the web server so that it too specifies that the content is UTF-8. This can be tricky. It requires access to your server's configuration files or the ability to override the configuration locally. This may not be possible on a shared host, but it should be possible on a professionally managed server. On Apache, you can do this by adding the following line to your httpd.conf file or your .htaccess file within the content directory:

```
AddDefaultCharset utf-8
```

You really shouldn't have to do all three of these. One should be enough. However, in practice, some tools recognize one of these hints but not the others, and the redundancy doesn't hurt as long as you're consistent.

I do not recommend adding an XML declaration. XML parsers don't need it, and it will confuse some browsers.

Escape Less-Than Sign

Convert < to <.

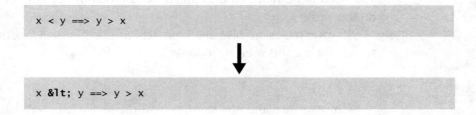

```
x < y ==> y > x
```

```
x &lt; y ==> y > x
```

Motivation

Although some browsers can recover from an unescaped less-than sign some of the time, not all can. An unescaped less-than sign is more likely than not to cause content to be hidden in the browser. Even if you aren't transitioning to full XHTML, this one is a critical fix.

Potential Trade-offs

None. This change can only improve your web pages. However, you do need to be careful about embedded JavaScript within pages. In these cases, sometimes the less-than sign cannot be escaped. You can either move the script to an external document where the escaping is not necessary or reverse the sense of the comparison.

Mechanics

Because this is a real bug that does cause problems on pages, it's unlikely to show up in a lot of places. You can usually find all the occurrences and fix them by hand.

I don't know one regular expression that will find all cases of these. However, a few will serve to find most. The first thing to look for is any less-than sign followed by whitespace. This is never legal in HTML. This regular expression will find those:

```
<\s
```

If you're not using any embedded JavaScript, you can search for <(\s) and replace it with <\1. However, if you're using JavaScript, you need to be more careful and should probably let Tidy or TagSoup do the work.

If your pages involve mathematics at all, it's also worth doing a search for a < followed by a digit:

```
<\d
```

However, a validator such as xmllint or HTML Validator should easily find all cases of these, along with a few cases the simple search will mix.

Embedded JavaScript presents a problem here. JavaScript does not recognize < as a less-than sign. Inside JavaScript, you have to use the literal character. A less-than sign can usually be recast as a greater-than sign with arguments reversed. For example, instead of writing

```
if (x < 7)
```

you write

```
if (7 > x)
```

However, I normally just rely on placing the script in an external file or an XML comment instead:

```
<script type="text/javascript" language="javascript">
<!--
if (location.host.toLowerCase().indexOf("example.com") < 0 &&
location.host.toLowerCase().indexOf("example.org") <= 0) {
    location.href="http://www.example.org/";
}// -->
</script>
```

This is a truly ugly hack and one I cringe to even suggest, but it is what seems to work and what browsers expect and deal with, and it is well-formed.

A lot of these problems can spread out across a site when the site is dynamically generated from a database and the scripts or templates that generate it do not sufficiently clean the data they're working with. A typical SQL database has no trouble storing a string such as x > y in a VARCHAR field. However, when you take data out of a database you have to clean it first by escaping any such characters. Most major templating languages have functions for doing exactly this. For instance, in PHP the `htmlspecialchars` function converts the five reserved characters (>, <, &, ', and ") into the equivalent entity references. Just make sure you use it. Even if you think there's no possible way the data can contain reserved characters such as <, I still recommend cleaning it. It doesn't take long, and it can plug some nasty security holes that arise from people deliberately injecting weird data into your system.

Note

You do not need to escape greater-than signs, although you can. The only situation where this is mandatory is when the three-character string]]> appears in regular content. This is likely to happen only if you're writing an XML tutorial. (That's the CDATA section closing delimiter.) Nonetheless, if you're worried about someone attempting to inject bad data into your system, you can use a similar approach to change > to >.

Escape Ampersand

Convert & to &.

```
<a href="/discipline/470.html">Health & Kinesiology</a>
<img src="text.gif" alt="Texts & Technology" />
```

```
<a href="/discipline/470.html">Health &amp; Kinesiology</a>
<img src="text.gif" alt="Texts &amp; Technology" />
```

Motivation

Although most browsers can handle a raw ampersand followed by whitespace, an ampersand not followed by whitespace confuses quite a few. An unescaped ampersand can hide content from the reader. Even if you aren't transitioning to full XHTML, this refactoring is an important fix.

Potential Trade-offs

None. This change can only improve your web pages.

However, you do need to be careful about embedded JavaScript within pages. In these cases, the ampersand usually cannot be escaped. Sometimes you instead can use an external script where the escaping is not necessary. Other times, you can hide the script inside comments where the parser will not worry about the ampersands.

Mechanics

Because this is a bug that results in visible problems, there usually aren't many cases of this. You can typically find all the occurrences and fix them by hand.

I don't know one regular expression that will find all unescaped ampersands. However, a few simple expressions will usually sniff them all out. First, look for any ampersand followed by whitespace. This is never legal in HTML. This regular expression will find those:

```
&\s
```

If the pages don't contain embedded JavaScript, simply search for &(\s) and replace it with \&\1. A validator such as xmllint or HTML Validator will easily find all cases of these, along with a few cases the simple search will mix. However, if pages do contain JavaScript, you must be more careful and should let Tidy or TagSoup do the work.

Embedded JavaScript presents a special problem here. JavaScript does not recognize & as an ampersand. JavaScript code must use the literal & character. I normally place the script in an external file or an XML comment instead:

```
<script type="text/javascript" language="javascript">
<!--
if (location.host.toLowerCase().indexOf("example.com") < 0 &&
location.host.toLowerCase().indexOf("example.org") <= 0) {
    location.href="http://www.example.org/";
}// -->
</script>
```

If a site is dynamically generated from a database, this problem can become more frequent. A SQL database has no trouble storing a string such as "A&P" in a field, and indeed it is the unescaped string that should be stored.

When you receive data from a database or any other external source, clean it first by escaping these ampersands. For example, in a Java environment, the Apache Commons library includes a `String-EscapeUtils` class that can encode raw data using either XML or HTML rules.

Do not forget to escape ampersands that appear in URL query strings. In particular, a URL such as this:

```
http://example.com/search?name=detail&uid=165
```

must become this:

```
http://example.com/search?name=detail&amp;uid=15
```

This is true even inside `href` attributes of a elements:

```
<a href=
"http://example.com/search?name=detail&amp;uid=16">
 Search</a>
```

Escape Quotation Marks in Attribute Values

Convert " to " or ' to ' in attribute values.

```
<blockquote cite='Jane's Fighting Ships 2007-2008,
  Stephen, R.N. Saunders, p. 32'>
<a title="How the Supreme Court "elected"
  George W. Bush president">
```

```
<blockquote cite='Jane&apos;s Fighting Ships 2007-2008,
  Stephen, R.N. Saunders, p. 32'>
<blockquote cite="Jane's Fighting Ships 2007-2008,
  Stephen, R.N. Saunders, p. 32">
<a title='How the Supreme Court "elected" George W. Bush'>
<a title="How the Supreme Court &quot;elected&quot;
  George W. Bush president">
```

Motivation

A quotation mark that appears inside an attribute value delimited with the same style of quotation mark prematurely closes the value. Different browsers deal differently with this situation, but the result is almost never anything you want. Even if you aren't transitioning to full XHTML, this refactoring is an important fix.

Potential Trade-offs

None. This change can only improve your web pages.

Mechanics

Because this is a real bug that does cause problems on pages, it's unlikely to show up in a lot of significant places. You can usually fix all the occurrences by hand fairly easily.

Because the legality or illegality of any one quote mark depends on others, it's not easy to check for this problem using regular expressions. However, well-formedness testing will find this problem. Indeed, you may need to fix this one before fixing other, lesser problems because it's likely to hide other errors.

As with < and &, this problem is most often caused by blindly copying data from a database or other external source without first scanning it for reserved characters. Be sure to clean the data using a function such as PHP's htmlspecialchars to convert quotation marks and apostrophes into the equivalent entity references before inserting them into attribute values.

Contrary to popular belief, you do not need to escape all quotation marks, only those inside attribute values. You can escape quote marks in plain text if you want to, but this is superfluous. I usually don't bother. Even inside attribute values, you only need to escape the kind of quote that delimits the attribute value. Because different authors, editors, and tools differ in whether they prefer single or double quote marks, I usually escape both to be safe.

Tidy and TagSoup cannot reliably fix quotation marks inside attribute values. For example, Tidy turned this:

```
<blockquote cite='Jane's Fighting Ships 2007-2008,
  Stephen, R.N. Saunders, p. 32'>
```

into this:

```
<blockquote cite='Jane' s="" fighting="" ships=""
  r.n.="" p.="">
```

You shouldn't encounter a lot of these problems, though, so it's best to fix them by hand once a validator points them out.

Introduce an XHTML DOCTYPE Declaration

Insert an XHTML DOCTYPE declaration at the start of each document.

```
<html xmlns="http://www.w3.org/1999/xhtml">
```

↓

```
<!DOCTYPE html
     PUBLIC "-//W3C//DTD XHTML 1.0 Transitional//EN"
     "DTD/xhtml1-transitional.dtd">
<html xmlns="http://www.w3.org/1999/xhtml">
```

Motivation

The DOCTYPE declaration points to the DTD that is used to resolve
entity references. Without it, the only entity references you can use are
&, <, >, ', and ". Once you've added it, though,
you can use the full set of HTML entity references: ©, ,
é, and so forth.

The DOCTYPE declaration will also be important in the next chapter when we begin to make documents valid, not merely well-formed.

Potential Trade-offs

Adding an XHTML DOCTYPE declaration has the side effect of turning off quirks mode in many browsers. This can affect how a browser
renders a document. In general, this is a good thing, because nonquirks
mode is much more interoperable. However, if you have old stylesheets
that depend on quirks mode for proper appearance, adding a DOC-
TYPE may break them. You might have to update them to be standards
conformant first. This is especially true for stylesheets that do very
precise layout calculations.

Mechanics

You can use three possible DTDs for XHTML: frameset, transitional, and strict.

- The frameset DTD allows pages to contain frames.
- The transitional DTD retains deprecated presentational elements such as i, b, u, iframe, and applet.
- The strict DTD removes all deprecated presentational elements and attributes that should be replaced with CSS. It also tightens up the content model of many elements. For instance, in strict XHTML, blockquotes and bodies cannot contain plain text, only other block-level elements.

These are indicated by one of the following three DOCTYPE declarations:

```
<!DOCTYPE html
 PUBLIC "-//W3C//DTD XHTML 1.0 Strict//EN"
 "http://www.w3.org/TR/xhtml1/DTD/xhtml1-strict.dtd">

<!DOCTYPE html
 PUBLIC "-//W3C//DTD XHTML 1.0 Transitional//EN"
 "http://www.w3.org/TR/xhtml1/DTD/xhtml1-transitional.dtd">

<!DOCTYPE html
 PUBLIC "-//W3C//DTD XHTML 1.0 Frameset//EN"
 "http://www.w3.org/TR/xhtml1/DTD/xhtml1-frameset.dtd">
```

In the short run, it doesn't matter which you pick. In the long run, you'll probably want to migrate your documents to the strict DTD, but for now you can use the frameset DTD on any pages that contain frames and the transitional DTD for other documents.

Browsers look at the public identifier to determine what flavor of HTML they're dealing with. However, they will not actually load the DTD from the specified URL. In essence, they already know what's there and don't need to load it every time.

Other, non-HTML-specific tools such as XSLT processors may indeed load the DTD. In this case, you may wish to replace the remote URLs with local copies. For example:

```
<!DOCTYPE html
 PUBLIC "-//W3C//DTD XHTML 1.0 Strict//EN"
 "dtd/xhtml1-strict.dtd">

<!DOCTYPE html
 PUBLIC "-//W3C//DTD XHTML 1.0 Transitional//EN"
 "dtd/xhtml1-transitional.dtd">

<!DOCTYPE html
 PUBLIC "-//W3C//DTD XHTML 1.0 Frameset//EN"
 "dtd/xhtml1-frameset.dtd">
```

As long as the public identifiers are the same, the browsers will still recognize these.

Some documents on a site may already have DOCTYPE declarations, either XHTML or otherwise. Many tools have added these by default over the years, even though browsers never paid much attention to them. Thus, the first step is to find out what you've already got. Do a multifile search for `<!DOCTYPE`. Unless you're writing HTML or XML tutorials, any hits you get are almost certain to be preexisting DOCTYPE declarations. In most cases, though, they will not be the right one. Usually, there are only a few variants, so you can do a constant string multifile search and replace to upgrade to the newer XHTML DOCTYPE. Any that don't fit the pattern can be fixed by hand.

Documents that don't have a DOCTYPE are also easy to fix. The DOCTYPE always goes immediately before the `<html>` start-tag. Thus, all you have to do is search for `<html\w` and replace it with the following:

```
<!DOCTYPE html
 PUBLIC "-//W3C//DTD XHTML 1.0 Strict//EN"
 "dtd/xhtml1-strict.dtd">
<html
```

You should also take this opportunity to configure your authoring tools to specify the XHTML DOCTYPE by default. Often it's a simple checkbox in a preference pane somewhere.

```
$ tidy -asxhtml --doctype strict file.htmlTagSoup does not add DOCTYPE
declarations. You'll need to insert these by hand. Tidy adds a
transitional DOCTYPE by default. However, you can request strict instead
with the --doctype strict option:
```

Terminate Each Entity Reference

Place semicolons after entity references.

```
&copy 2007 TIC Corp.
if (i &lt 7) {
Ben &amp Jerry's Ice Cream
```

↓

```
&copy; 2007 TIC Corp.
if (i &lt; 7) {
Ben &amp; Jerry's Ice Cream
```

Motivation

XML requires that each entity reference end with a semicolon.

Web browsers can usually work around a missing semicolon, but only if the entity name is followed by whitespace. For instance, most browsers can handle "Ben &amp Jerry's" but not "A&ampP".

Potential Trade-offs

None. All browsers recognize entity references that end with semicolons.

Mechanics

To find cases such as this, search for any entity reference where whitespace precedes the next semicolon:

```
&[^;]*\s
```

Because the next character after the entity reference is unpredictable, you're better off replacing it manually or letting Tidy or TagSoup do the work. They can both fix most of these problems.

This search will also find a number of purely unescaped ampersands. This is especially common in two places: JavaScript and URLs.

Validation should find any remaining cases, and you can fix those by hand. Sometimes manual inspection is necessary to see exactly where the entity boundary lies.

Replace Imaginary Entity References

Make sure all entity references used in the document are defined.

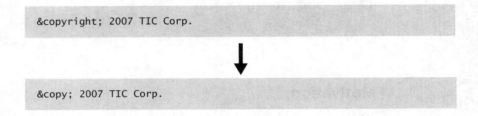

```
&copyright; 2007 TIC Corp.
```

```
&copy; 2007 TIC Corp.
```

Motivation

Occasionally, authors begin to use entity references that simply don't exist. Sometimes it's a simple typo, such as &apm; instead of &. Sometimes it's misremembered code, such as &tm; instead of ™ or &copyright; instead of ©. Either way, this causes display problems for all browsers and should be fixed.

Potential Trade-offs

None. This is only good.

Mechanics

The hardest problem is finding these imaginary entity references, because there's not necessarily any rhyme or reason to them. Often, the first time you realize there's a problem is while browsing your site. If you're lucky it will appear in the plain text like this:

```
&copyright; 2007 TIC Corp.
```

If not, the browser will just drop it out completely:

```
2007 TIC Corp.
```

The same mistakes do tend to repeat themselves, so once you've noticed a problem, a straight search and replace will usually find and fix all other occurrences.

Otherwise, validation (or at least well-formedness checking) is necessary to identify these issues. Once a validator finds such imaginary entity references, you can fix them by hand if they aren't too numerous, or with a targeted search and replace if they are.

Occasionally, you'll find someone has invented an entity reference that perhaps should exist but doesn't: ¥ for ¥ or &bet; for the Hebrew letter ב. Although it's theoretically possible to define new entity references such as these in the internal DTD subset or external DTD, I do not recommend this. XML parsers can handle this, but browsers cannot. Either replace the references with the actual characters (especially if you already reencoded the document in UTF-8) or use a numeric character reference such as ¥ or ב.

Introduce a Root Element

Make sure every document has an `html` root element.

Motivation

XML requires every document to have a single root element. XHTML requires that this element be `html`.

Browsers interpret html-less (and headless and bodyless) documents differently. Adding the proper root element will synchronize their behavior.

Potential Trade-offs

None.

Mechanics

Search for documents that don't contain <html. Because of DOCTYPE declarations, comments, whitespace, and byte order marks, this often isn't exactly the first thing in the document, but it's usually pretty near the start. It's very unusual to find this string in any document that doesn't have an html root element.

This problem isn't a common one, but I have seen it more frequently than I'd expect. Fixing it is straightforward: Just put <html> at the start (though after the DOCTYPE) and </html> at the end.

Documents that are missing html tags are often missing head and/or body elements, too. You may need to add these as well. The head is not technically required, but you really want to have one with at least a title. The body element is required if you have any content at all: text, paragraphs, tables, anything.

Introduce the XHTML Namespace

Add an xmlns="http://www.w3.org/1999/xhtml" attribute to every html element.

```
<html>
```

↓

```
<html xmlns="http://www.w3.org/1999/xhtml">
```

Motivation

XSLT and other XML-based tools can treat the same element differently, depending on its namespace. XML-based XHTML tools expect to find HTML elements in the XHTML namespace and will usually not function correctly if they are in no namespace instead.

Furthermore, many browser extensions such as XForms, SVG, and MathML operate correctly only when embedded inside a properly namespaced XHTML document.

Potential Trade-offs

None. This will not affect browser display.

Mechanics

This can mostly be fixed with search and replace. The most common `html` start-tag is simply `<html>` with no attributes. Without even using regular expressions, you can do a multifile search and replace that converts this into `<html xmlns="http://www.w3.org/1999/xhtml">`.

However, you may also encounter some other additional attributes on the `html` element. The `lang` attribute is particularly common, but other possibilities include `id` and `dir`. For example:

```
<html lang='en-UK'>
```

Thus, as a first step, I suggest searching for `<html\s`—that is, `<html` followed by any whitespace character. If there are a few of them, you can fix them manually. If there are a lot of them, most likely some person, tool, or program made a common practice of adding some particular attribute to the `html` start-tag. If so, this is likely to be consistent across the site. For example, you may need to search for `<html lang='en'>` instead of just `<html>`.

The only thing you need to be careful of is that no one has already changed some (but not all) of the HTML documents to use the

XHTML namespace. You may wish to do a search for this first. Thus, the order is

1. Search for `http://www.w3.org/1999/xhtml`. If no results are found, continue. Otherwise, exclude the files containing this string from future replacements.

2. Search for `"<html\s"` and replace it with `"<html xmlns='http://www.w3.org/1999/xhtml' "`.

3. Search for `<html>` and replace it with `<html xmlns=' http://www.w3.org/1999/xhtml'>`.

When you're done, set your validator to check for XHTML specifically. It should warn you of any lingering problems that you missed.

Chapter 4
Validity

Validity goes beyond mere well-formedness to ensure that a document is not merely syntactically correct but semantically correct. It promises that only elements and attributes defined in the HTML specification appear so that browsers aren't taken by surprise. It also promises that they appear only in certain places where their meaning is well defined. For example, in a valid document you won't find a table in the head or a blockquote in a paragraph.

Validity offers many advantages to site authors and even more advantages to site consumers. First, valid sites are predictable. They show the same content to users with different browsers. Although details regarding font size and positioning can vary from one browser to another, valid pages are more likely to look reasonably similar from one browser to the next.

Valid pages convey the same information to different readers, even readers that use such widely varying interfaces as a graphical browser, an Atom feed reader, or a screen reader. Valid pages are more device-independent.

Because valid pages are more predictable, you waste less time debugging cross-browser idiosyncrasies. Valid pages are much easier to make work reliably.

Valid pages are also more future-proof. They are more likely to work reliably in tomorrow's browsers, not just today's. Weird hacks designed for particular browsers sometimes stop working with a new browser release. Invalid pages often depend on the subtle bugs and quirks of a particular browser version. Valid pages are more predictable in browsers you can't even test yet.

In brief, validity is a solid base for future development. Making a site valid will almost always improve a site's usability, accessibility, speed, and reliability. Most important, it improves a site's *maintainability*. Valid pages are easier to upgrade, easier to style, and easier to improve than invalid pages. Valid pages are simply more robust.

What is true for validity is doubly true for strict validity. Strict validity goes beyond mere validity to also insist that content be separated from presentation. This makes pages smaller, simpler, and more understandable. Furthermore, it enables you to use far more powerful CSS techniques to style pages that go well beyond what you can achieve with simple font tags, spacer GIFs, and table layout.

Validity is not always required. Browsers do build consistent DOMs from merely well-formed documents, and XML tools can still parse an invalid but well-formed document. However, validity does increase the predictability of browser display. Just because you can put a table in the head doesn't mean you should.

There are, however, times when you need to violate validity. For instance, if you're adding markup from other applications such as XForms, MathML, or Scalable Vector Graphics (SVG) to your documents, those documents will not be valid. The HTML DTDs do not recognize these elements, but you can use them nonetheless. Similarly, if you're experimenting with HTML 5, the standard DTDs and browsers won't recognize your new elements. And there are other reasons you might choose to introduce invalid markup.

That being said, if you can make your documents valid, you should. Valid XHTML will help browsers more closely reflect the author's intent. If you absolutely must publish invalid documents, I suggest that you carefully control and limit the invalidity. First, make a valid document that leaves out the invalid pieces; then add the minimum number of invalid pieces you need to accomplish your goals.

As a practical matter, you should usually start by making a document well-formed before making it valid. Often the distinction is a little fuzzy. For instance, normalizing the case of all tags to lowercase improves both well-formedness (because start-tags now match end-tags) and validity (because only lowercase element names are valid). Adding a DOCTYPE declaration is optional for well-formedness, but it is required for validity. You can even have valid HTML (though not

XHTML) that is not well-formed. In general, though, it is simplest if validity builds on well-formedness.

A document can be invalid in an infinite number of ways. In this chapter, I'll focus on some of the most common problems you're likely to need to fix. Once you have valid pages, you will be ready to move on to the next steps, and you can begin to work on improving the appearance, accessibility, and usability of your site.

Introduce a Transitional DOCTYPE Declaration

Insert the XHTML transitional DOCTYPE declaration at the start of each document.

```
<html xmlns="http://www.w3.org/1999/xhtml">
```

↓

```
<!DOCTYPE html
    PUBLIC "-//W3C//DTD XHTML 1.0 Transitional//EN"
    "DTD/xhtml1-transitional.dtd">
<html xmlns="http://www.w3.org/1999/xhtml">
```

Motivation

The transitional DTD enables you to validate the document while not immediately requiring fully semantic markup. It still allows documents to include deprecated presentational elements such as i, b, and center. Thus, you can find and fix any serious structural problems before moving on to improving the semantics of your document.

Potential Trade-offs

Browsers that use the presence or absence of a DOCTYPE to select quirks mode may format the document somewhat differently after you've added the DOCTYPE. Although changes should not be major, you should manually inspect pages to make sure nothing too serious has changed. The most likely things to break are any browser-specific hacks you've installed, especially ones intended for Internet Explorer.

Mechanics

The first step to making a document valid is to add a document type definition, or DTD. Technically, you don't add the DTD itself to the document. Rather, you add a DOCTYPE declaration that points to the document type definition. The DOCTYPE declaration will be the first item in the document, even before the root element. For example:

```
<!DOCTYPE html PUBLIC
"-//W3C//DTD XHTML 1.0 Transitional//EN"
"http://www.w3.org/TR/xhtml1/DTD/xhtml1-transitional.dtd">
<html xmlns="http://www.w3.org/1999/xhtml">
```

In practice, browsers never actually read the DTD that the DOC-TYPE declaration references. They simply check the public identifier to see which variant of HTML they're dealing with. Thus, you don't need to worry that this points to an external file on an external server. This will not slow down document display in the browser.

XML parsers and other XML tools do read the DTD, though. If you're using any of these, you may wish to point to a local copy of the DTD instead. For example, this DOCTYPE asserts that the transitional DTD can be found at the root of the current server in the dtds directory:

```
<!DOCTYPE html PUBLIC
"-//W3C//DTD XHTML 1.0 Transitional//EN"
"/dtds/xhtml1-transitional.dtd">
```

You can download the DTDs from the W3C at www.w3.org/TR/2002/REC-xhtml1-20020801/xhtml1.zip and install them wherever convenient. That archive contains the entire XHTML spec. You'll find the DTDs in the DTD folder.

Pages that define framesets should use the frames DTD instead:

```
<!DOCTYPE html PUBLIC
"-//W3C//DTD XHTML 1.0 Transitional//EN"
```

```
"http://www.w3.org/TR/xhtml1/DTD/xhtml1-frameset.dtd">
<html xmlns="http://www.w3.org/1999/xhtml">
```

This is not necessary for pages that merely use an `iframe` for an ad or two. The transitional DTD works fine for those.

You can automate these fixes fairly easily. TagSoup does not add DOCTYPE declarations, but Tidy does. Unless asked otherwise, it defaults to the transitional DTD when run in XHTML mode.

This is also fairly easy to fix with multifile search and replace. Search for an `html` start-tag at the beginning of a document, like this:

```
\A<html
```

You may want to allow for whitespace in front of the start-tag, too:

```
\A\s*<html
```

Then replace that with the desired DOCTYPE followed by `<html`.

Once you've added the DOCTYPE, validate all your documents, as discussed in Chapter 2. This will reveal a number of problems to fix. I'll detail some of the most common problems in subsequent sections in this chapter.

Remove All Nonexistent Tags

Eliminate bogons.

Motivation

Modern browsers do not support a lot of the old, deprecated, vendor-proprietary tags such as `marquee` and `multicol` introduced in the wild and wooly early days of the Web. If still relevant, these should be replaced by standard tags and CSS stylesheets. If not, they should be deleted to save space and simplify documents.

Potential Trade-offs

Older browsers that actually depend on these tags may see a slightly less formatted page. For example, old versions of Netscape will no longer see two columns on a page after you replace a `multicol` element with CSS. However, today many more browsers don't support the `multicol` element than do. You'll improve the experience for a lot more people than you'll degrade it.

Regardless of what changes you make, all the actual content of the page should still be present and accessible. It may just be formatted a little differently. This will be improved with CSS later.

Mechanics

Chances are there aren't a lot of bogons in your documents. However, if one does show up, it's worth searching for it across more of the site. You'll usually find the first one by validation. For example, here's xmllint complaining about an unrecognized `multicol` element:

```
$ xmllint --valid --noout document.html
valid.html:18: element multicol: validity error : No
declaration for element multicol
</p></multicol>
                ^
valid.html:20: element body: validity error : Element body
content does not follow the DTD, expecting (p | h1 | h2 | h3 | h4 | h5 |
h6 | div | ul | ol | dl | pre | hr |
blockquote | address | fieldset | table | form | noscript
| ins | del | script)*, got (h1 multicol )
</body></html>
      ^
```

Notice that it complains twice: once to tell you that there's no declaration for the `multicol` element and once to tell you that `multicol` is not a legal child of its parent body element.

Where there's one bogon, there are usually more. Once I noticed that someone had added `multicol` elements to one page, I'd do a quick search for `<multicol` across the entire document tree. Any pages where that phrase pops up are worth a closer look. In this case, there's no good CSS equivalent for multicolumn layouts, so we'll probably just remove the tags. (They haven't worked in most browsers for years anyhow.) Just replace `<multicol>` and `</multicol>` with the empty string.

If the `multicol` elements have attributes, you can search for the regular expression `<multicol\s*[^>]*>` instead.

Here are some other elements you may find in your documents that you'll want to do away with:

- `marquee`
- `blink`
- `xmp`
- `basefont`
- `bgsound`
- `keygen`
- `sound`
- `spacer`
- `app`
- `comment`
- `htmlplus`
- `layer`
- `hype`
- `wbr`

This isn't an exhaustive list. There was a time when browser vendors were competing in terms of how many weird tags they could add to HTML. A surprising number of those are still floating around unnoticed on web pages.

A few of these may still work in some browsers. For instance, Firefox supports both `marquee` and `blink`. However, neither scrolling nor blinking text is a good idea in the first place. These elements were left out of the official HTML specs for good reason, and you should leave them out of your sites, too. You may want to look at individual occurrences to see what more static styles you might replace these with.

`xmp` is another bogon that may actually have a *raison d'être* on your site, especially if the site is dedicated to HTML tutorials or markup languages. It functions much like an XML CDATA section. That is, it interprets everything inside the text as plain text, not markup. You could replace <xmp> with <![CDATA[and </xmp> with]]>. However, legacy browsers don't recognize CDATA sections, so you're better off just removing the xmp tags and manually escaping everything between them.

You may also occasionally encounter a misspelled tag. For example, you could see <tabel> instead of <table> or <dvi> instead of <div>. These are worth a closer look to figure out just what was intended in the first place. However, because they had no actual effect, you can probably take them out without breaking anything.

Add an alt Attribute

Add an alt attribute to every img tag that doesn't have one.

```
<img src="right_arrow.gif" width="100" height="50"/>
<img src="integral.png" width="75" height="65" />
<img src="logo.png" width="42" height="42" />
```

↓

```
<img src="right_arrow.gif" width="100" height="50" alt="next"/>
<img src="integral.png" width="75" height="65"
    alt="The definite integral of x squared
          between 1 and 2 equals seven thirds."/>
<img src="logo.png" width="42" height="42" alt=""/>
```

Motivation

The primary reason to add alt text is to assist visually impaired users. Although currently this is a relatively small number of people with visual handicaps, in the near future this class is likely to grow quickly as audio browsers become embedded in cell phones, cars, MP3 players, and other devices aimed at people who may need to keep their visual attention elsewhere.

The second reason is for search engine optimization. Google, especially Google image search, pays a disproportionate amount of attention to the text in `alt` attributes. If your content is visual—photographs, maps, diagrams, and so forth—you can get quite a bit more high-quality traffic by tagging your images accurately.

Potential Trade-offs

Adding `alt` text requires a lot of time and human intelligence. There are few shortcuts. That being said, the improvements are linear. You can make some of the changes and get some of the return. You don't have to do it all at once.

Mechanics

Finding images with no `alt` attributes is straightforward. XHTML requires an `alt` attribute so that the validator will report all `img` elements that do not have an `alt` attribute. You can also do a quick search with a regular expression that matches `img` tags and all their possible attributes except `alt`:

```
<img\s+((height|width|border|class|align|id|src|usemap|hspace|vspace)\s
*=\s*("[^"]+"|'[^']+')\s*)*>
```

This does not match `img` tags that contain `alt` attributes and does match every other likely `img` tag.

However, filling in the missing attributes is not so trivial, and it requires some consideration and human intelligence.

Every image that is part of the content should have a text description that *substitutes* for the image when used by a screen reader. Sometimes this is simply a description of the image itself. For example, when I posted the picture in Figure 4.1 as part of a story, I used the `alt` text "30 White Ibis walking across the street in front of a stop sign."

Or perhaps you've embedded a PNG of the equation in a mathematical paper, like so:

$$\int_1^2 x^2\,dx = \frac{7}{3}$$

FIGURE 4.1   A content picture

The correct `alt` text for this would be "The definite integral of *x* squared between 1 and 2 is seven thirds."

However, many times the image is not really content. It is iconographic. In this case, choose your words so that the meaning is conveyed rather than the description. For example, on many web sites you'll see something like this:

```
<a href="slide67.html">
  <img src="right_arrow.gif" width="100" height="50"/>
</a>
```

The correct `alt` text here is not "blue arrow facing right". Instead, it is simply the word *Next*. This conveys the meaning of the image better than a description could.

Finally, many images are simply decorations with no real content at all. These should have empty `alt` attributes. That is, they should look like this:

```
<img src="bookcover.png" width="90" height="150" alt=""/>
```

Consider what happens when every image on your page is replaced with its `alt` text, because this is exactly what happens for a blind user. The page is likely to be imperfect under these conditions, but try to make it as sensible as possible.

Browsing the Web with a screen reader is challenging at best. Try it sometime yourself if you possibly can. Recruit some blind people to user-test your site while you watch. One thing you can do to improve the experience is remove the number of images whose `alt` text must be read. Even things that are logically content, such as corporate logos, product photos, and book covers, should often have empty `alt` text if seeing them is not essential to grasp the content of the page. It takes longer to hear a page than to read it, so anything you can do to compress the page for blind users is appreciated.

There is one trick you can play to speed up the process and reduce the effort of adding `alt` text. Many images, especially decorative and functional ones, are reused on multiple pages. This makes it possible to do a quick search and replace to add the same `alt` text to many pages. For example, if you know the file right_arrow.gif is used throughout the site to point to the next page, you can search for `src="right-arrow.gif"` and replace it with the following:

```
src="right-arrow.gif" alt="next"
```

You may even want to just search for `right-arrow.gif"` and `right-arrow.gif'` to account for tags in different directories that use different paths to that same file. Literal search is usually sufficient here. You don't need regular expressions.

Replace embed with object

Change all `embed` elements to `object` elements.

```
<embed src="banner.swf" quality="high" bgcolor="#006699"
  width="160" height="600" name="banner"
  align="middle" allowScriptAccess="sameDomain"
```

(continued)

```
type="application/x-shockwave-flash"
  pluginspage="http://www.macromedia.com/go/getflashplayer" />
<embed src="quicktime_example.mov" width="640" height="480"
    autoplay="true" controller="false"
    pluginspage="http://www.apple.com/quicktime/download/"
/>
<embed src="wicked.rpm" width='200' height='134' />
```

```
<object type="application/x-shockwave-flash"
        width="160" height="600" id="banner">
  <param name="allowScriptAccess" value="sameDomain" />
<param name="movie" value="banner.swf" />
  <param name="quality" value="high" />
  <param name="bgcolor" value="#006699" />
</object>
<object width="640" height="480"
    classid="clsid:02BF25D5-8C17-4B23-BC80-D3488ABDDC6B"
    codebase="http://www.apple.com/qtactivex/qtplugin.cab">
    <param name="src" value="quicktime_example.mov">
    <param name="controller" value="false">
    <param name="autoplay" value="true">
</object>
<object id='media23'
  clasid="clsid:CFCDAA03-8BE4-11cf-B84B-0020AFBBCCFA"
  width='200' height='125'>
    <param name='src' value='wicked.rpm'/>
</object>
```

Motivation

Netscape invented the embed element to reference any sort of content that would be handled by external plug-ins rather than the browser itself: Flash, RealMedia, QuickTime, PDF, and so on. If this tag were invented today, namespaces would be used, but back then elements were just added to HTML willy-nilly. Netscape figured that one tag for 100 formats would be better than 100 tags for 100 different formats, and they were almost right. However, it did allow the embed element to have an indefinite number of undefined attributes, which makes it impossible to validate.

Consequently, despite its broad adoption and support, embed has never been a part of any HTML specification. However, because it is a nonstandard extension, browser support is inconsistent, even to the level of which attributes browsers recognize and what they mean.

The `object` element is better documented, more consistently supported in modern browsers, and more agnostic about just what kind of content it loads and who renders it. Most important, whereas `embed` can have an infinite number of possible attributes, `object` has just a few. Plug-in-specific parameters can be passed through `param` child elements, each of which has just two attributes—`name` and `value`—to identify the parameter being set. This means `object` can be validated in a way `embed` never could be.

Potential Trade-offs

Some older browsers, including Netscape 4 and earlier and Internet Explorer for the Mac, do not recognize the `object` tag. To work around this you can include an `embed` element inside the `object` element like so:

```
<object type="application/x-shockwave-flash"
        width="160" height="600" id="banner">
  <param name="allowScriptAccess" value="sameDomain" />
  <param name="movie" value="banner.swf" />
  <param name="quality" value="high" />
  <param name="bgcolor" value="#006699" />
  <embed src="banner.swf" quality="high" bgcolor="#006699"
         width="160" height="600" name="banner"
         align="middle" allowScriptAccess="sameDomain"
         type="application/x-shockwave-flash"
  pluginspage="http://www.macromedia.com/go/getflashplayer" />
</object>
```

Browsers that don't recognize `object` will use the `embed` element. Browsers that do recognize `object` will ignore it. Such documents are not valid. However, they do work well in browsers. In fact, this is close to what the Flash authoring environment exports.

A somewhat more serious concern is that Internet Explorer will not stream Flash animations embedded like this. It will download and play them, but that can take awhile for a large file. The trick here, named Flash Satay by its discoverer Drew McLellan, is to embed an initial small Flash file whose only purpose is to load and stream the second, actual Flash animation. The minimum you need in the loader movie is this ActionScript on the first frame:

```
_root.loadMovie(_root.path,0);
```

The URL to the second, actual animation is in the `path` variable of the first animation's query string. Thus, your `object` element will look like this:

```
<object type="application/x-shockwave-flash"
   data="first.swf?path=second.swf"
   width="300" height="300">
  <param name="movie" value="first.swf?path=second.swf" />
</object>
```

Another noticeable trade-off is one of developer education and convenience. The Flash authoring program generates HTML for authors to include in web pages. However, this HTML is nonstandard and ugly. Using clean, standard markup requires editing a lot of this by hand.

Mechanics

Because the `embed` element has never been officially included in HTML (though it has been widely supported), any level of validation will find it. Alternatively, you can just do a quick search for `<embed` to find all the places you have to fix.

Embedded Flash animations usually have the offending `embed` element wrapped in an `object` element, because that's what the Flash authoring environment generates. However, this `object` element only works for some browsers, and you'll need to modify it to make it work for all of them.

Usually the `object` tag you start with looks like this:

```
<object
  classid="clsid:d27cdb6e-ae6d-11cf-96b8-444553540000"
codebase="http://fpdownload.macromedia.com/pub/shockwave/cabs/flash/
swflash.cab#version=8,0,0,0"
width="160" height="600" id="banner" align="middle">
  <param name="allowScriptAccess" value="sameDomain" />
  <param name="movie" value="banner.swf" />
  <param name="quality" value="high" />
  <param name="bgcolor" value="#006699" />
</object>
```

This is suitable for Internet Explorer but not for most other browsers. To make it work elsewhere you need to make these changes.

- Add a `type="application/x-shockwave-flash"` attribute.
- Add a `data` attribute that points to the movie—for example, `data="banner.swf"`.
- Remove the `codebase` attribute.
- Remove the `align` attribute. Use CSS `float` properties instead. Add an `id` attribute for this property to attach to.

The result looks like this:

```
<object id="flash23"
  classid="clsid:d27cdb6e-ae6d-11cf-96b8-444553540000"
  type="application/x-shockwave-flash"
  width="160" height="600" id="banner">
  <param name="allowScriptAccess" value="sameDomain" />
  <param name="movie" value="banner.swf" />
  <param name="quality" value="high" />
  <param name="bgcolor" value="#006699" />
</object>
```

Other embedded content, such as QuickTime movies, may not be so conveniently wrapped. In this case, you will need to construct your own equivalent `object` element to replace it. Some of the attributes of the `embed` element map more or less directly to attributes of the `object` element or to CSS properties, as shown in Table 4.1.

However, the `embed` element uses different attributes for different types of content. Embedding a QuickTime movie has one set of attributes. Embedding a Flash animation has a different set of attributes. Embedding a Windows Media Player movie has still another. For example, consider this element that embeds a QuickTime movie:

```
<embed src="quicktime_example.mov" width="640" height="480"
    autoplay="true"
    controller="false"
    pluginspage="http://www.apple.com/quicktime/download/"
    playeveryframe="true"
    loop="true"
    showlogo="false"
/>
```

TABLE 4.1 Converting Embed to Object

embed Attribute	object Attribute	CSS Property
hidden		display: hidden
border		border
frameborder		border
pluginurl	codebase	
pluginspage	codebase	
type	type	
src	data	
width	width	
height	height	
align	align	float
hspace	hspace	padding-left, padding-right
vspace	vspace	padding-top, padding-bottom

When changing embed to object, all attributes except width, height, id, and archive become param elements. The name of each param is the name of the attribute, and the value of the param is the value of the attribute:

```
<object width="640" height="480"
  classid="clsid:02BF25D5-8C17-4B23-BC80-D3488ABDDC6B"
  codebase="http://www.apple.com/qtactivex/qtplugin.cab">
  <param name="src" value="quicktime_example.mov">
  <param name="controller" value="false">
  <param name="autoplay" value="true">
  <param name="loop" value="true">
  <param name="showlogo" value="false">
</object>
```

Introduce a Strict DOCTYPE Declaration

Insert the XHTML strict DOCTYPE declaration at the start of each document.

```
<!DOCTYPE html
    PUBLIC "-//W3C//DTD XHTML 1.0 Transitional//EN"
    "DTD/xhtml1-transitional.dtd">
```

```
<!DOCTYPE html
    PUBLIC "-//W3C//DTD XHTML 1.0 Strict//EN"
    "DTD/xhtml1-strict.dtd">
```

Motivation

The strict DTD removes deprecated presentational elements such as b, i, and center. You can replace these with semantic elements such as em and strong and CSS styles. This will make your meaning clearer.

It also enables you to move the style information fully into CSS. This reduces bandwidth and makes it much easier to lay out a page, because the markup is not competing with the stylesheet.

Potential Trade-offs

The strict DTD is extremely limiting. *A lot* of elements and attributes you've been accustomed to using are no longer allowed. Some changes that may be required involve substantial manual effort.

The counterbalance is that web browsers do not require validity. It is OK to serve documents with the strict DTD even if they still use deprecated elements such as b, i, and iframe. It is OK to have text that is not enclosed in a paragraph. Such documents are not valid, but browsers can handle them. You can gradually increase your conformance by making a series of small changes as time permits.

Mechanics

The first change you need to make is to point to the strict DTD from the DOCTYPE declaration:

```
<!DOCTYPE html PUBLIC
"-//W3C//DTD XHTML 1.0 Strict//EN"
"http://www.w3.org/TR/xhtml1/DTD/xhtml1-strict.dtd">
```

If you've already made your documents valid against the transitional DTD, this is a simple search and replace. Search for `-//W3C//DTD XHTML 1.0 Transitional//EN` and replace it with `-//W3C//DTD XHTML 1.0 Strict//EN`. Then search for `xhtml1-transitional.dtd` and replace it with `xhtml1-strict.dtd`.

Tidy defaults to the transitional DTD when run in XHTML mode, but you can ask it for strict instead using the `--doctype` option:

```
$ tidy -asxhtml --doctype strict example.html
```

Once you've added the strict DOCTYPE, validate all your documents once more, as discussed in Chapter 2. This will reveal a number of problems to fix. I'll detail some of the most common problems in subsequent sections in this chapter.

Replace center with CSS

Change all `center` elements into `div`s or the equivalent semantic element; then apply the CSS `text-align` property.

```
<h1><center>Martians Invade!</center></h1>
```

```
<h1 style="text-align: center">Martians Invade!</h1>

or

h1 {text-align: center; }
…
<h1>Martians Invade!</h1>
```

Motivation

XHTML strict does not allow the `center` element because centering is about appearance, not meaning. Centering is not possible in non-GUI browsers such as Lynx or screen readers. It should be replaced by more descriptive semantic markup.

Because centering is so purely presentational, it's often a candidate for style changes when a site is redesigned. If the styles are extracted out into external CSS stylesheets, the updates associated with a redesign are much simpler and faster to implement.

Potential Trade-offs

Very old browsers may not recognize the CSS rules, so a few details may not come across, but we're talking truly ancient browsers here.

Mechanics

In CSS, centering is accomplished by the `text-align` property with the value `center`. You can apply this property to all elements of a specific type. For instance, you can center all level 1 headings:

```
h1 {text-align: center; }
```

Or you can apply it to all elements of a specific class, such as `booktitle`:

```
*.booktitle {text-align: center; }
```

You also can center one specific element by referencing its ID:

```
*#bt1 { text-align: center; }
```

You can apply this rule in one of three places:

- A `style` attribute on the element itself
- A `style` element in the document's head
- An external CSS stylesheet

The last option is usually the best. It enables you to share styles across documents, which maintains a consistent look and feel for the site as well as reducing bandwidth requirements. However, we'll often use the first two as intermediate steps while working up to fully external stylesheets. Furthermore, I will sometimes demonstrate a technique with an inline style here just to keep the examples reasonably short.

Tidy will define replacement CSS classes and rules if you ask it to with the `-clean` option. Then it will put them in the head. For example, it changes this:

```
<html>
<head>
    <title>Wet Willy's Wonderland!</title>
</head>
<body>

<h1><center>Wet Willy's Wonderland!</center></h1>
```

into this:

```
<html xmlns="http://www.w3.org/1999/xhtml">
<head>
<title>Wet Willy's Wonderland!</title>

<style type="text/css">
/*<![CDATA[*/
 div.c1 {text-align: center}
/*]]>*/
</style>
</head>
<body>
<div class="c1">
<h1>Wet Willy's Wonderland!</h1>
</div>
```

However, the names it chooses aren't especially meaningful, and it can't distinguish among different reasons for the center element. Furthermore, it may introduce unnecessary divs, as it did here. What you'd really like in this case is something more like this:

```
<html xmlns="http://www.w3.org/1999/xhtml">
<head>
<title>Wet Willy's Wonderland!</title>

<style type="text/css">
/*<![CDATA[*/
```

```
h1 {text-align: center}
/*]]>*/
</style>
</head>
<body>
<h1>Wet Willy's Wonderland!</h1>
```

In fact, even this rule should really go into an external stylesheet. Consequently, you'll probably want to clean up Tidy's output by hand.

Replace font with CSS

Change all font elements into div, span, or the equivalent semantic element; then apply CSS font properties.

```
<font face="Tahoma" size="+3" >
  Camp Edgewood in the Sunny Pines
</font>
<p><font face="Arial">
  Where every boy deserves a week of summer camp.
  <font size="1">(Not responsible for leeches.)</font>
</font>
</p>
```

```
h1 { font-family: Tahoma; }
p#motto { font-family: Arial; }
*.disclaimer { font-size: small }
…
<h1>Camp Edgewood in the Sunny Pines</h1>
<p id='motto'>
  Where every boy deserves a week of summer camp.
  <span class="disclaimer">
  (Not responsible for leeches.)
  </span>
</font>
</p>
```

Motivation

XHTML strict does not allow the font element because fonts describe appearance, not meaning. They are deprecated in XHTML transitional and even HTML 4. They are the poster child of presentational markup. They do not work in non-GUI browsers such as Lynx or screen readers. In many environments such as screen readers, the whole notion of a font may be meaningless. They should be replaced by more descriptive markup. This can take the form of semantic elements such as cite or h1, or span elements with descriptive class names.

Because fonts are purely presentational, they are frequently changed when a site is redesigned. If the styles are extracted out into external CSS stylesheets, the updates associated with a redesign are much simpler and faster to implement.

Because this refactoring removes elements, your pages will likely be smaller and load faster without font elements, especially if your stylesheets are externalized.

Furthermore, the DOM built for these pages is smaller and simpler. This may improve JavaScript execution speed. It will certainly improve the ease with which you can write JavaScript programs that use the browser's DOM.

Potential Trade-offs

Very old browsers may not recognize the CSS rules, but we're talking truly ancient browsers here. Even the first and buggiest third-generation browsers that supported CSS at all supported this much.

Mechanics

Finding font elements is simple. Strict validation will sniff them all out, or you can just search for <font or </font>. Once you've found them, convert their attributes to CSS properties, as shown in Table 4.2.

The values for face and color attributes are also legal values for the font-family and color properties, respectively. However, for size, one additional change is needed. CSS uses keywords where font uses

TABLE 4.2 Fonts

HTML Font Attribute	CSS Property
size	font-size
face	font-family
color	color

numbers. Table 4.3 shows the mappings between font numbers and CSS keywords.

You're likely to encounter two kinds of font tags: those that are nestled snug against other tags and those that appear in the middle of text. The first case is more common. Typically it looks something like this:

```
<h3><font size="-1">Random Sites Around the Web</font></h3>
```

TABLE 4.3 Font Sizes

HTML size Attribute Value	CSS font-size Property Value
1	xx-small
2	x-small
3	small
4	medium
5	large
6	x-large
7	xx-large
-3	59% (approximate)
-2	70% (approximate)
-1	smaller
+1	larger
+2	144% (approximate)
+3	172% (approximate)

Sometimes the `font` element is wrapped around another element instead of inside it:

```
<font size="-1"><h3>Random Sites Around the Web</h3></font>
```

In either case, you simply assign an ID to the semantic element (`h3` in this example) and then add a rule to your stylesheet that applies the same style to that ID:

```
h3#randomsites { font-size: smaller; }
...
<h3 id="randomsites">Random Sites Around the Web</h3>
```

It's not uncommon to discover the same font applied to several related elements on the page. For instance, if several H3 headers are styled as `<font size="-1">` you define a class that all these elements can share and apply the style to that:

```
h3#sites { font-size: smaller; }
...
<h3 class="sites">Intranet Sites</h3>
<h3 class="sites">Random Sites Around the Web</h3>
```

Less commonly, the `font` element encloses several elements, so you use `class` and/or `id` to apply the style to them too.

On occasion, you may find a `font` element that neither immediately encloses another element nor is immediately closed inside one. For example:

```
<p>Sincerely yours,<br />
<font face='Lucida Handwriting'>
  Harry W. Wacker
</font></p>
```

In this case, you can simply replace the `font` element with a `span` or `div` element, assign an `id` and/or `class` to that `span` or `div`, and then apply the styling to it.

```
span#signer { font-family: "Lucida Handwriting"; }
...
<p>Sincerely yours,<br />
<span id='signer'>
  Harry W. Wacker
</span></p>
```

Font choices do sometimes convey meaning. For instance, in the preceding fragments, a handwriting font indicates the correspondent's signature. If this is the case, define a class name that indicates that meaning and use it to attach the equivalent CSS rule. For example:

```
*.signature { font-family: "Lucida Handwriting"; }
…
<p>Sincerely yours,<br />
<span class='signature'>
  Harry W. Wacker
</span></p>
```

The mechanics for replacing font with CSS are much the same as the mechanics for replacing center with CSS. The key difference is that font is an inline element, whereas center is a block element. Thus, if you need to insert an extra element to which to attach the CSS rule, it will be a span rather than a div.

Used with the -clean option, Tidy fixes up font tags as it does center tags. It replaces the font tags with span tags and adds CSS rules to the document's header to indicate the changes. This comes with the same caveats as it does for center: The names it chooses aren't especially meaningful, and Tidy can't distinguish among different reasons for different font elements. Furthermore, it may introduce unnecessary spans when the font is nested directly against an enclosing element. I prefer not to use Tidy for this fix.

Replace i with em or CSS

Change all i elements into em, span, or the equivalent semantic element.

```
<i>Literally</i> should <i>not</i> be used to emphasize a
phrase. (<i>Strunk and White, Elements of Style,
p. 52</i>).
```

```
<span class="wordasword">Literally</span> should
<em>not</em> be used to emphasize a phrase.
(<cite>Strunk and White, Elements of Style, p. 52</cite>).
```

Motivation

The i element is not allowed in XHTML strict. It describes appearance, not meaning, and it does not work in non-GUI browsers such as Lynx or screen readers. It should be replaced by more descriptive semantic markup. Sometimes that's an em element, but surprisingly often it's something else.

Potential Trade-offs

The very oldest browsers may not recognize the CSS rules. However, even the first and buggiest browsers that supported CSS at all supported this much. The em element is supported by all browsers back to Mosaic 1.0.

Mechanics

Simple validation with the strict DTD will locate all the i elements. That's not hard. Alternatively, you can just do a quick search for </i> to find them all.

If you're willing to assert that the only reason you ever used the i element was for emphasis, you can just replace these with em tags. However, that's actually not common.

Many sites use the i element purely as a presentational effect, without meaning a whole lot. If this is the case, replace it with CSS. For example, change this:

```
<li><i>JavaOne</i></li>
```

into this:

```
<li style="font-style: italic">JavaOne</li>
```

You may wish to use a class or id attribute so that you can place the style information in an external stylesheet instead:

```
<li class="conference" id="javaone07">JavaOne</li>
```

If necessary, you can introduce an extra `span` element to hold the `style`, `class`, and/or `id` attributes:

```
<span class="conference" id="javaone07">JavaOne</span>
```

Often the `i` element means something, but not emphasis. One common use is to indicate the title of something: a book, a newspaper, an article, and so on. This is better handled in strict HTML with the underused `cite` element. For example:

```
<cite>My Sister Eileen, pg. 9</cite>
```

Most graphical browsers style the `cite` element as italic.

Another common use of italics is to indicate foreign words in English text. These can be noted in HTML with the `lang` or `xml:lang` attribute. For example:

```
I greeted Pierre with a hearty
<span xml:lang="fr">Bon jour!</span>
```

There are many other uses of italics in text. Some of the more common include the following.

- Names of legal cases, for example, *Eldred v. Ashcroft*
- Epigraphs at the heads of book chapters
- Words used as words: It's hard to spell *necessarily*
- Words that imitate sounds: *D'oh!*
- Genus and species, for example, *Aix sponsa*
- The words *see* and *see also* in cross references and indexes for example, *see also* the Chicago Manual of Style, Section 17.18.

HTML does not have individual elements representing these uses. Instead, they should be indicated by a `span` or `div` element whose `class` attribute indicates the reason for formatting the text as italic:

```
The drake Wood Duck
(<span class="species">Aix sponsa</span>) is
the prettiest waterfowl.
```

Similar techniques should be used for nontraditional uses of italics, such as the earlier conference example or indicating the external links on a page. Indeed, it's even more important to use external CSS for these elements because you're even more likely to want to change the style as part of a redesign. If you later decide that conference names should be colored red instead of italicized, it's relatively hard to find all the conferences in your site. It's relatively easy to change the one line in a CSS stylesheet that formats elements with `class="conference"`.

Replace b with strong or CSS

Change all b elements into `strong` elements or `span` elements.

```
I'm <b>very</b> certain of this.
The triangle inequality states that
||<b>x</b> + <b>y</b>||   ||<b>x</b>|| + ||<b>y</b>||
```

↓

```
I'm <strong>very</strong> certain of this.
The triangle inequality states that
||<span class='vector'>x</span>
+ <span class='vector'>y</span>||
  ||<span class='vector'>x</span>||
+ ||<span class='vector'>y</span>||
```

Motivation

The b element is not allowed in XHTML strict. It describes appearance, not meaning, and it does not work in non-GUI browsers such as Lynx or screen readers. It should be replaced by more descriptive semantic markup. Usually that's a `strong` element, but on occasion it's something else.

Potential Trade-offs

Very old browsers may not recognize the CSS rules. However, even the first and buggiest third-generation browsers that supported CSS at all supported this much. All browsers back to Mosaic 1.0 support the `strong` element.

Mechanics

Simple validation with the strict DTD will locate all the b elements. Alternatively, a quick search for `</b>` will find them all.

If you're willing to assert that the only reason you ever used the b element was to emphasize something, you can just replace these with `strong` tags.

However, many sites use the b element as a fairly presentational effect, without meaning a whole lot. If this is the case, replace it with CSS. For example, change this:

```
<a href="72.html"><b>Next Page</b></a>
```

into this:

```
<a style="font-weight: bold" href="72.html">Next page</a>
```

You may wish to use a `class` or `id` attribute so that you can place the style information in an external stylesheet instead:

```
<a class="navigation" id="nextlink" href="72.html">Next page</a>
```

If necessary, you can introduce an extra `span` element to hold the `style`, `class`, and/or `id` attributes.

Sometimes the b element does mean something, but what it means is not important. In particular, headlines are often listed in bold, sometimes with accompanying font tags as well. These should be replaced by the appropriate level of header: `h1` to `h6`, and CSS used to reapply the styles. For example, suppose you had this *New York Post* classic at the top of the page:

```
<b>Headless Body Found in Topless Bar</b>
```

This should become

```
<h1>Headless Body Found in Topless Bar</h1>
```

Other cases you should watch out for where bold may not mean importance include

- Vector quantities in mathematics, physics, and engineering
- Page numbers of drawings in book indexes

These uses are uncommon, and you can usually ignore them. However, if you encounter any of these cases, turn them into `class` attributes. For example:

```
span.vector {font-weight: bold }
…
||<span class='vector'>x</span>
+ <span class='vector'>y</span>||
 ||<span class='vector'>x</span>||
+ ||<span class='vector'>y</span>||
```

Replace the color Attribute with CSS

Move all descriptions of color out of the HTML document and into the CSS stylesheet.

```
<body bgcolor="#FFFFFF" text="#000000">
<h2><font color="#AA0000">Today's News</font></h2>
```

```
body {color: black;
      background-color: white; }
h2#today { color: #AA0000; }
…
<body>
<h2 id="today">Today's News</h2>
```

Motivation

Color attributes are not allowed in XHTML strict. They describe appearance, not meaning, and they do not work in non-GUI browsers such as Lynx or screen readers. They should be replaced by semantic `class` attributes mapped to CSS rules.

CSS will make it much easier to maintain a consistent color scheme across a site. It will also make it much easier to update and experiment with new color schemes. In addition, it enables you to provide different but equivalent noncolor styles to be used when the document is printed on a black-and-white printer.

Potential Trade-offs

Very old browsers may not recognize the CSS rules, so a few details may not come across, but we're talking truly ancient browsers here. Even the first and buggiest third-generation browsers that supported CSS at all supported this much.

Mechanics

Moving color from HTML into CSS differs from the last few refactorings because color is always specified with an attribute rather than a specific element. With the partial exception of `font`, usually an element is already present in an obvious location to which you can attach the styles. At most, you should just have to add an `id` or `class` attribute to it so that you can address it from CSS. Sometimes you don't even have to do that.

Table 4.4 lists the various color attributes you may encounter and the CSS equivalents.

The most common place to see colors set is on the `<body>` start-tag. For example, some pages specify black text on a white background:

```
<body bgcolor="#FFFFFF" text="#000000">
```

TABLE 4.4   Colors

HTML Attribute	Used On	CSS Property
color	font, basefont	color
bgcolor	body, table, tr, th, td	background-color
text	body	color
vlink	body	a:visited {color: *value*;}
alink	body	a:active {color: *value*;}
link	body	a:link {color: *value*;}
background	body	background-image

This is easily replaced with this CSS rule:

```
body { color: #000000;
       background-color: #FFFFFF; }
```

CSS supports the same hexadecimal values for color properties as HTML does, so you can just copy the old HTML attribute values into the CSS properties. Of course, if you like, feel free to upgrade to HTML 4/CSS named colors instead. For example:

```
body { color: black;
       background-color: white; }
```

You also can specify the vlink, alink, and link attributes of the body element in CSS using the same color property. You simply apply the color to the pseudoclasses :visited, :active, and :link instead of to an element. For example:

```
*:vlink { color: green; }
*:alink { color: red; }
*:link  { color: yellow;  }
```

However, in this case I'll make a strong suggestion that you simply delete these attributes without replacing them in CSS. Standard colors that don't change from one site to the next help users to recognize links. Changing link colors makes your site harder to navigate. A discontinuity in color schemes between the link colors and everything else on your site is a small price to pay for assisting users with navigating your site.

If a font element specifies the colors, you may need to replace that element with a span element to have someplace to put the color. Follow the instructions in the previous section.

When invoked with the -clean option, Tidy will define replacement CSS classes and insert matching rules in a style element in the head. For example, it changes this:

```
<body bgcolor="#FFFFFF" text="#000000">
<h2><font color="#AA0000">Today's News</font></h2>
```

into this:

```
<style type="text/css">
/*<![CDATA[*/
 body {
  background-color: #FFFFFF;
  color: #000000;
 }
 h2.c1 {color: #AA0000}
/*]]>*/
</style>
</head>
<body>
<h2 class="c1">Today's News</h2>
```

However, the names Tidy chooses aren't especially meaningful, and it can't determine the reasons for the color element. Furthermore, the rules should really go into an external stylesheet. If possible, clean up Tidy's output by hand.

Convert img Attributes to CSS

Remove the `align`, `border`, `hspace`, and `vspace` attributes from `img` elements. Replace them with CSS rules.

```
<img src="/images/newicon.png" alt="New!"
     width="90" height="54"
     hspace="5" vspace="5" border="0" align="left" />
```

```
<img src="/images/newicon.png" alt="New!"
 width="90" height="54"
 style="border: 0; float: left; padding-right: 5px;
 padding-left: 5px; padding-top: 5px; padding-bottom: 5px;"
 />
```

Motivation

XHTML strict moves much of the style for `img` elements such as `align`, `vspace`, `hspace`, and `border` into CSS.

Making this change is especially important if you're doing heavy CSS layout. Adding layout attributes such as these to `img` elements can interfere with the layout described in the external CSS stylesheet. It's easier to debug CSS layouts when all the relevant details are in one place, rather than spread out across different files and locations.

Potential Trade-offs

As usual, moving the presentation into CSS does cause cosmetic problems in older browsers, and in this case maybe they're not quite as ancient. However, it's still true that all current browsers should work just fine with strict markup, and older ones won't be shut out. They'll just see a less attractive page.

Mechanics

Validation will find the `img` elements you need to fix. From that point, though, it's a bit of a slog. Tidy and TagSoup will not help. Furthermore, many of these attributes have values specific to just one image, so you'll need to assign an ID to each image and write some rules just for it. Consequently, this is one of the few places where I suspect it often does make sense to use `style` attributes and inline CSS rather than an external stylesheet.

Table 4.5 lists the attributes you'll need to change and the CSS properties you'll replace them with.

For `hspace` and `vspace`, notice that CSS gives you more control. You can set the right padding separately from the left padding and the top padding separately from the bottom. When converting to CSS, you'll need to copy the values from `hspace` into both `padding-left` and `padding-right`. You'll also need to copy the values from `vspace` into both `padding-top` and `padding-bottom`.

If you've modified `align`, you should also look for any `<br clear="all"/>` tags that may be lying around. These make sure that the image doesn't go too far down the screen when the line width is larger than expected. The `br` element is allowed in strict XHTML, but the `clear` attribute is not. Instead, you assign the `br` element a CSS `clear` property with the value `left`, `right`, or `both`. There's not a lot

TABLE 4.5   IMG Attributes

IMG Attribute	*CSS Property*
`align`	`float`
`border`	`border`
`hspace`	`padding-left`, `padding-right`
`vspace`	`padding-top`, `padding-bottom`

of semantics involved here, so I usually just identify these as classes.
For example:

```
br.left   { clear: left; }
br.right  { clear: right; }
br.all    { clear: both; }
...
<br class="left" />
<br class="right"/>
<br class="all" />
```

Tidy will not help with these. You're on your own.

Replace applet with object

Change all `applet` elements to `object` elements.

```
<applet code="com.example.Bullseye" codebase="/applets"
        width="100" height="100" align="left"
        alt="Bullseye!" name="bullseye">
  <param name="rings" value="8" />
  <param name="outer" value="red" />
  <param name="inner" value="white" />
  <p>Bullseye!</p>
</applet>
```

```
<object code="com.example.Bullseye" codebase="/applets"
        classid="clsid:8AD9C840-044E-11D1-B3E9-00805F499D93"
codebase="http://java.sun.com/products/plugin/1.4/jinstall-
14-win32.cab#Version=1,4,0,mn"
        width="100" height="100" align="left"
        alt="Bullseye!" name="bullseye">
  <param name="codebase" value="/applets" />
  <param name="rings" value="8" />
  <param name="rings" value="8" />
  <param name="outer" value="red" />
  <param name="inner" value="white" />
  <p>Bullseye!</p>
</object>
```

Motivation

XHTML strict does not allow `applet`. Instead, it uses the `object` element. The `applet` element was removed because it only handles Java applets, not Flash, PDF, HTML, QuickTime, or many other formats authors want to insert in web pages. The `object` element is simply more generically useful.

In some browsers, the `applet` element is handled by an outdated Java virtual machine bundled with the browser. However, the `object` element is handled by the more up-to-date virtual machine in the Java plug-in. Furthermore, the `object` element allows for near-automatic installation of the current version of Java, whereas the `applet` element does not.

Potential Trade-offs

No one object syntax works for all browsers. To work around this you can nest `object` elements inside each other and use conditional comments to keep Internet Explorer from seeing the second `object` element:

```
<object width="300" height="300"
  classid="clsid:8AD9C840-044E-11D1-B3E9-00805F499D93"
codebase="http://java.sun.com/products/plugin/1.4/jinstall-
14-win32.cab#Version=1,4,0,mn">
  <param name="codebase" value="/applets">
  <param name="archive" value="foo.jar">
  <param name="code" value="com.example.applets.BugView">
<!--[if !IE]> -->
  <object classid="com.example.applets.BugView"
          archive="BugView.jar"
          type="application/x-java-applet"
          width="300" height="300">
    <param name="codebase" value="/applets">
  </object>
<!-- <![endif]-->
</object>
```

Browsers fall through these until they find one they recognize. However, IE's must-ignore behavior is nonconformant, so we have to use special comments to hide markup from it. This is ugly and large, but it is technically valid, and it does seem to work in all modern browsers.

Mechanics

Strict validation will find and report all `applet` elements that you need to fix. Alternatively, you can just do a quick search for `<applet`.

You need to change this twice, once for IE and once for other browsers. The IE-specific `object` element wraps the other `object` element. We use IE conditional comments to hide the inner `object` element from IE.

For the outer element:

- Change `applet` to `object` in both the start- and end-tags.

- If the value of the `code` attribute ends in `.class`, remove `.class`. The value of the code attribute should be the fully package-qualified name of the applet, nothing more or less.

- Add a `classid="clsid:8AD9C840-044E-11D1-B3E9-00805F499D93"` attribute.

- Move the `codebase` attribute (if any) into a `param` child element with a `name="codebase"` attribute. The `value` attribute of this `param` element should have the actual codebase as its value.

- Add a new `codebase` attribute

- Move the `archive` attribute (if any) into a `param` child element with a `name="archive"` attribute. The `value` attribute of this `param` element should have the value of the old `archive` attribute as its value.

- Change the `object` attribute (if any) to a `data` attribute with the same value.

- Add a `codebase` attribute pointing to the version of the Java plug-in you want to use—for instance, `http://java.sun.com/products/plugin/1.4/jinstall-14-win32.cab#Version=1,4,0,mn` for Java 1.4.

Other attributes and child elements can remain in place.

The resulting object will work in Internet Explorer, but not in most other browsers. For that, we need a second `object` element. To prevent IE from seeing it and becoming confused, we first have to wrap it in IE conditional comments:

```
<!--[if !IE]> -->
<object …>
…
</object>
<!-- <![endif]-->
```

In this `object` element we make the following changes:

- Change `applet` to `object` in both the start- and end-tags.

- Remove the `code` attribute.

- Add a `classid="java:`*fully.package.qualified.classname*`"` attribute.

- Add a `type="application/x-java-applet"` attribute.

- Move the `codebase` attribute (if any) into a `param` child element with a `name="codebase"` attribute. The `value` attribute of this `param` element should have the actual codebase as its value.

- Remove the `codebase` attribute.

- Change the `object` attribute (if any) to a `data` attribute with the same value.

Finally, put the non-IE `object` element inside the IE `object` element and use this to replace the `applet` element.

This has focused on the Java-specific changes. You may also need to move some presentational attributes into CSS. In particular, the `align` attribute turns into a CSS `float` property, and the `hspace` and `vspace` attributes are replaced by `padding` properties. Table 4.6 summarizes.

TABLE 4.6   Converting applet to object

applet Attribute	object Attribute	CSS Property
codebase	`<param name="codebase" value="url"/>`	
	`codebase="plugin URL"`	
code="name"	`classid="java:name"`	
	`<param name="code" value="name">`	
name	name	
object	data	
	`codetype="application/java"`	
archive	archive	
width	width	
height	height	
align	align	float
hspace	hspace	padding-left, padding-right
vspace	vspace	padding-top, padding-bottom

Replace Presentational Elements with CSS

Remove all big, small, strike, s, tt, and u elements and insert equivalent CSS or semantic elements.

```
<big>All Items A Fraction of Their Usual Price!</big>
<small>That fraction is 7/3.</small>
<strike>Pick up laundry.</strike>
<s>Walk dog.</s>
<tt>$ ls *.txt</tt>
<u>The Lord of The Rings</u>
```

```
*.announce {font-size: 64pt; }
*.legal    {font-size: 6pt }
```

```
*.done      {text-decoration: line-through }
*.announce  {font-size: 64pt; }
*.legal     {font-size: 6pt }
*.done      {text-decoration: line-through }
cite        {text-decoration: underline}
...
<strong class="announce">
  All Items A Fraction of Their Usual Price!
</strong>
<span class="legal">That fraction is 7/3.</span>
<span class="done">Pick up laundry.</span>
<del>Walk dog.</del>
<samp>$ ls *.txt</samp>
<cite>The Lord of The Rings</cite>
```

Motivation

XHTML strict does not allow any of these elements either. Usually there's a good semantic reason for these styles that you can capture with specific elements, such as `cite`, or with a `class` attribute.

Potential Trade-offs

Very old browsers may not recognize the CSS rules, so a few details may not come across, but we're talking truly ancient browsers here. Even the earliest browsers that supported CSS at all supported this much.

Mechanics

Validation against the strict DTD finds all of these. Alternatively, you can search for the start-tags `<big`, `<small`, `<strike`, and so on. These elements aren't as commonly used, so there aren't likely to be quite as many of them as `i` and `b`.

Sometimes these elements are purely presentational. In this case, replace them with a `span` and attach the necessary CSS to reproduce the styles. The one I'd make an exception for is the u element. Underlining is almost never appropriate for anything except links. It's used to simulate italics on typewriters, but it has little place in print or on the Web.

Many times, however, these elements do have semantic meaning, and it's worth capturing that. For example:

- `<tt>` is sometimes used to mark up code. If so, replace it with `<code>`.
- `<tt>` is sometimes used to mark up sample output. If so, replace it with `<samp>`.
- `<big>` is often used for important (`<strong>`) or headline (`<h1>`–`<h6>`) text.
- `<s>` and `<strike>` are used to indicate deleted text. If so, replace them with `<del>`.

Of course, HTML doesn't have elements for all the uses to which you might have put these styles. For instance, `<small>` often indicates legal fine print. You can mark this up with CSS and a semantic class:

```
<span class="legal">
  All users of this web site agree to turn over
  their first-born children. All legal disputes will be
  resolved by binding arbitration overseen by an impartial
  panel chosen from the Board of Directors' spouses,
  children, and other immediate family members.
</span>
```

Table 4.7 lists the remaining, less common deprecated elements from classic HTML that you'll want to replace with CSS.

TABLE 4.7   CSS Equivalents for Presentational Elements

HTML Attribute	CSS Property
big	font-size: large
small	font-size: small
tt	font-family: monospace
u	text-decoration: underline
s	text-decoration: line-through
strike	text-decoration: line-through

The mechanics of fixing them are much the same as for fixing b and i. If you know that all the occurrences of one of these styles are for the same reason, you can just do a quick regular expression search and replace. However, if they've been used inconsistently, you'll need to inspect them manually. This isn't as much of a problem here as with the more common b and i tags, though.

Nest Inline Elements inside Block Elements

Give every inline element a block-level parent, and remove all block-level elements from paragraphs.

```
Do you like this picture?<br />
<img src="file.gif" alt="Goose" width='100' height='100'/>
I think it's really <em>neat</em>.<br />
```

```
<p>Do you like this picture?</p>
<div>
 <img src="file.gif" alt="Goose" width='100' height='100'/>
</div>
<p>I think it's really <em>neat</em>.</p>
```

Motivation

To be valid, it is not sufficient that all the elements in a document be legal XHTML strict elements. They must also have the right relationships to each other. Browsers and other programs depend on correct placement. For instance, an li element must always be a child of a ul or ol element, and each ul or ol element must have at least one li child. Blockquotes can contain paragraphs, but paragraphs can't contain blockquotes.

Although browsers will display documents that violate these structure rules, they may interpret them differently. Furthermore, this sort of invalidity can even more seriously confuse editors and other non-browser tools that attempt to work with the HTML. For instance, as I write this, some people are having problems because WordPress is rewriting their markup in unexpected ways to try to fix blockquote/paragraph nesting issues.

When paragraphs or block-level elements are not found where they're expected, browsers and other tools guess where they should insert extra content to make them fit. They don't always guess right, and they don't always guess the same. This causes problems designing cross-browser CSS and JavaScript. Nesting your elements correctly helps browsers and tools to process a document consistently.

Potential Trade-offs

None. Browsers deal inconsistently with poorly structured pages. Reorganizing them will give much more consistent behavior across browsers.

Mechanics

The main body of an HTML page consists of several kinds of elements plus text:

- Paragraphs: `p`, `pre`
- Block-level elements: `address`, `blockquote`, `center`, `dir`, `div`, `dl`, `fieldset`, `form`, `h1`, `h2`, `h3`, `h4`, `h5`, `h6`, `hr`, `noscript`, `ol`, `table`, `ul`
- Inline elements: `a`, `abbr`, `acronym`, `b`, `bdo`, `br`, `cite`, `code`, `dfn`, `em`, `img`, `input`, `label`, `q`, `samp`, `select`, `span`, `strong`, `sub`, `sup`, `textarea`, `var`
- Miscellaneous elements: `button`, `del`, `iframe`, `ins`, `map`, `object`, `script`
- Context-limited elements: `li`, `dt`, `dd`, `tr`, `th`, `td`, `tbody`, `input`, `select`
- Raw text; a.k.a. PCDATA

A block element represents a distinct section that is separated from the elements that precede and follow it. In visual renderings, this separation usually takes the form of a hard line break. In strict XHTML, the body of the page can only contain block elements.

Most block elements can nest. That is, a block can contain other blocks. However, there are a couple of notable exceptions: p and pre.

A p element represents a paragraph. However, unlike other block-level elements, a p may not contain another p or another block element such as blockquote. It can only contain plain text and inline elements. It is in some sense the lowest block-level element.

The pre element is also special in this way. It can contain inline elements, but not other block elements.

Inline elements such as span, strong, img, and a are contained within some block. In transitional XHTML, this block may be implicit, but in strict XHTML, this block must be an explicit block-level element. Inline elements can usually contain other inline elements (though there are exceptions), but they may not contain block elements. Inline elements may wrap from one line to the next, but they do not cause line breaks as long as there's space left on the current line.

A few miscellaneous elements such as object and ins can be used as either inline or block elements. However, if they're used as inline elements (i.e., they're inside a paragraph or pre), they cannot contain a block element.

Finally, a few context-sensitive elements appear in certain parent elements but not others. For instance, an li element must be a child of a ul or ol element. An li element anywhere else is invalid. A td element must be a child of a tr element, which must itself be a child of a tbody or table element. These elements may not appear outside their defined parent elements.

If any elements appear where they don't belong, the validator will tell you about them. There are actually two styles of error message you may see. Some validators tell you that the parent element has the wrong child. For example, xmllint provides this error message:

```
example.html:12: element p: validity error : Element div is
not declared in p list of possible children
```

Others tell you that the child has the wrong parent. A few may tell you both. Either way the meaning is the same.

The most common variation of this problem is an inline element without a parent—in particular, raw text that is an immediate child of the body element:

```
<body>
<h1>Welcome to Acme!</h2>
Your one-stop source for rockets, explosives, anvils,
and portable holes.
```

In this case, just wrap the excess text in a paragraph or a div as appropriate:

```
<body>
<h1>Welcome to Acme!</h2>
<p>
Your one-stop source for rockets, explosives, anvils,
and portable holes.
</p>
```

Another element that often surprises is img. This is an inline element, and it should be wrapped in a div or possibly a paragraph. For instance, change this:

```
<img src="cup.gif" width="89" height="67" alt="Cup" />
```

to this:

```
<div>
  <img src="cup.gif" width="89" height="67" alt="Cup"/>
</div>
```

figure Element

HTML 5 may add a figure element specifically for block-level images:

```
<figure>
  <img src="cup.gif" alt="Cup"
      width="89" height="67"/>
</figure>
```

It is also a validity error if a p element contains another p or block element. The paragraph is the lowest block-level element. Although a div, blockquote, or table can contain a paragraph, the reverse is not true. For example, this is a problem:

```
<p>Once upon a time someone famous said,
  <blockquote cite="Percy Bysshe Shelley, Ozymandias">
    <p>My name is Ozymandias, king of kings</p>
    <p>Look on my works, ye mighty, and despair!</p>
  </blockquote>
but who it was that said that, I cannot say. He has been
forgotten.
</p>
```

The usual way to fix it is to make two paragraphs—one before the blockquote and one after, like so:

```
<p>Once upon a time someone famous said,</p>
  <blockquote cite="Percy Bysshe Shelley, Ozymandias">
    <p>My name is Ozymandias, king of kings</p>
    <p>Look on my works, ye mighty, and despair!</p>
  </blockquote>
<p>
but who it was that said that, I cannot say. He has been
forgotten.
</p>
```

Similar fixes work for tables, lists, and other block elements you may find in a paragraph.

Blockquotes in Paragraphs

The prohibition on blockquotes within paragraphs is somewhat controversial. Irrespective of HTML, many style manuals do recognize the presence of blockquotes within single paragraphs, and they do treat a construct such as the preceding example as one paragraph that contains a blockquote rather than as a sequence of paragraph-blockquote-paragraph. XHTML 2 has proposed to make it possible to embed blockquotes within paragraphs.

Tidy can fix this if you use the --enclose-block-text yes option:

```
$ tidy -asxhtml -c --enclose-block-text yes example.html
```

Chapter 5
Layout

Well-formedness and validity check basic syntactic constraints. The next step is to make sure the semantics are appropriate. Each element should be used for its intended purpose: `ul` for unordered lists, `ol` for numbered lists, `table` for tabular data, `blockquote` for quotations, `h1`–`h6` for headings, and so forth. Using the proper semantics for each element renders pages more intelligible to screen readers, and makes sure they can be displayed properly on different platforms. As you'll see, proper semantics have a number of other beneficial characteristics as well.

Many good semantic elements, such as `ul`, `blockquote`, and `table`, have been abused to achieve particular layout effects. The goal of this abuse is to produce a very particular appearance for a page. However, that appearance rarely extends across browsers, almost never across platforms, and often not anywhere beyond the designer's own computer. Proper HTML can account for this, but you have to stop thinking about what the page *looks like* and start thinking about what it *means*.

Of course, we do want our pages to have pleasing appearances. We want them to stand out from the competition. It is possible to achieve this by placing all the presentation information in a separate CSS stylesheet. The CSS describes what the page looks like. However, browsers are free to use a different or modified stylesheet if they choose. Indeed, you are free to send different stylesheets to different browsers, tailored to each one's unique capabilities.

In modern browsers, CSS enables much greater control over the appearance of a page. It's not merely that the fanciest sites can be duplicated in CSS. They can *only* be designed in CSS. Creating a modern page requires moving away from tabular layout and font tags to XHTML cleanly separated from CSS.

Replace Table Layouts

Remove all table layouts and replace them with `div` elements that linearize the content. Then use a CSS stylesheet to position the `divs` in the form you want.

```
<html xmlns="http://www.w3.org/1999/xhtml">
<head>
    <title>3 Column Page</title>
</head>
<body>

<table>
<tr>
<td valign="top" id="Left">
Left column content
</td>

<td valign="top" id="Center">
Center column content
</td>

<td valign="top" id="Right">
Right column content
</td>
</tr>
</table>

</body>
</html>
```

```
<blockquote cite=
   'http://www.gutenberg.org/dirs/etext00/dvlft10.txt'>
<p>
It was, then, with <em>considerable</em> surprise that I
received a telegram from Holmes last Tuesday&mdash;he has
```

```
<html xmlns="http://www.w3.org/1999/xhtml">
<head>
    <title>3 Column Page</title>
    <link rel="stylesheet" href="threecolumns.css"
          type="text/css" />
</head>
<body>

<div id="Left">
Left column content
</div>

<div id="Center">
Center column content
</div>

<div id="Right">
Right column content
</div>

</body>
</html>
```

Motivation

CSS layouts are more powerful and more accessible than table layouts. They work better across a broader variety of devices, such as PDAs and audio browsers. They are more understandable to machines and thus enable better processing of content, including somewhat enhanced search engine optimization. Finally, they make it easier to edit and update pages both because the pages are simpler and because the style and content are separated so that designers don't step on authors' toes and vice versa.

CSS-based pages are smaller and simpler than table-based pages. This makes them easier to edit and easier to author. It also makes them faster to download. All those <td> and <tr> tags add up. A kilobyte here, a kilobyte there, and pretty soon you're talking about real bandwidth. High-volume sites such as Slashdot can save gigabytes per day and thousands of dollars in bandwidth costs per year by moving to CSS. Although the CSS files themselves take some bandwidth, they can be cached and reused. They do not need to be downloaded with every page.

Potential Trade-offs

CSS layouts do tend to fix sizes more than table layouts do. For example, with tables it is possible to define a three-column layout in which each column is as big as it needs to be, with any extra space distributed among the columns. You can specify widths for the columns, but you don't have to. With CSS, you usually need to specify widths for at least one of the columns.

Older browsers may not work as well with the CSS versions of a page as they do with the table layouts. However, they will still see the complete content of the page, and given the minuscule market share of browsers that don't support CSS, that's good enough.

Although the overall site may download faster and perform better with external CSS stylesheets, that is likely not true for the first such page visited. The first time a browser loads the external CSS stylesheet two HTTP connections will be needed. Over a fast connection, this is negligible, but it can cause temporary problems for dial-up clients and slow servers. I still tend to think that the speedups on second and subsequent pages more than outweigh this, though.

Laying out pages with CSS absolutely has a steeper learning curve than laying out pages with tables. This is very much a technique for full-time professionals. Amateurs should either use professionally designed templates or stick to simple, linear pages with browser default layouts.

Even for professionals, CSS layouts are much harder to implement and debug, especially across browsers, than table-based layouts. You have to invest more time and effort upfront. The saving grace is that not too many layouts are needed. Probably less than a dozen basic layouts account for 99% of all web pages, and almost all of these are simple variations of one to three columns with optional headers and footers in varying widths and heights. Consequently, you can copy preexisting CSS layouts and make slight modifications, rather than reinventing each layout from scratch every time.

Mechanics

No one layout works for every site and no one recipe fits all needs. However, certain common layouts appear frequently enough to be worthy of special notice. Mastering the techniques involved in these layouts will enable you to customize them for many other cases. In particular, three layouts are among the most common on the Web today:

- Two columns, with a fixed-width sidebar on the left and a liquid content column on the right
- Two columns, with a fixed-width sidebar on the right and a liquid content column on the left
- Three columns, with fixed-width sidebars on the right and left and content in the middle

Layouts with fixed-width content columns are also common. However, fixed-width content is almost always a bad idea. Users have different screen sizes, browser widths, font choices, and more. Some users maximize their browser windows and some don't. (Windows users are much more likely to maximize their browser windows than Mac users are, even on identically sized monitors.) One size does not fit all.

These layouts may or may not have headers and footers. Usually, the header and footer belong to the main content column. However, they can also precede or follow all three columns, in which case they usually extend across the full width of the browser window. A header that precedes all three columns is a little more common than a footer that follows all three. The problem with a footer that is below all three is that it may show up far underneath the main column if the main content is short.

Usually the column heights are determined naturally by the amount of content they contain. Occasionally, the columns may be set at a fixed height to guarantee equal widths. However, this is problematic for content-heavy sites because the content of the individual columns is by no means guaranteed to match up. It works a little better for short pages consisting of no more than one screen of text.

The Content

Arranging the HTML itself is the easiest part. Divide each separate section into its own `div` element. Give the `div` element a unique `id` attribute by which it can be addressed. These `div`s can be nested if necessary. Ideally, the main content `div` should appear before any sidebars, headers, or footers. This way, screen readers that access the page linearly will start with the most important content on the page. So will search engine robots that often assign a higher priority to content that appears earlier in the page.

Listing 5.1 demonstrates a typical two-column HTML page. There are two divs: Pages and Content. The main content contains the first page from Bram Stoker's *Dracula*. The left-hand column contains links to other pages in this book. I've abridged the text somewhat for printing in this book, but this should give you an idea of the structure we'll be dealing with. In the following sections, we'll style this page.

LISTING 5.1   A Two-Column HTML Page

```
<!DOCTYPE html PUBLIC "-//W3C//DTD XHTML 1.0 Strict//EN"
        "http://www.w3.org/TR/xhtml1/DTD/xhtml1-strict.dtd">
<html xmlns="http://www.w3.org/1999/xhtml">
<head>
  <title>Dracula, Page 1</title>
</head>
<body>

<div id="Content">
<h1>Jonathan Harker's Journal</h1>
<p>
3 May. Bistritz.--Left Munich at 8:35 P.M., on 1st May,
arriving at Vienna early next morning; should have arrived
at 6:46, but train was an hour late.  Buda-Pesth seems a
wonderful place, from the glimpse which I got of it from the
train and the little I could walk through the streets.  I feared
to go very far from the station, as we had arrived late and would
start as near the correct time as possible.
</p>

<p>
The impression I had was that we were leaving the West and
entering the East; the most western of splendid bridges over
the Danube, which is here of noble width and depth, took us
among the traditions of Turkish rule.
</p>

<p>...</p>

</div>

<div id="Pages">

<ul>
<li><a href='page1.html'>Page 1</a></li>
<li><a href='page2.html'>Page 2</a></li>
```

```
<li><a href='page3.html'>Page 3</a></li>
<li>...</li>
<li><a href='page291.html'>Page 291</a></li>
<li><a href='page292.html'>Page 292</a></li>
<li><a href='page293.html'>Page 293</a></li>
</ul>

</div>
</body>
</html>
```

It's worth noting that even if there's no CSS or further styling, this page works. The user can read all the content and then find the navigation. It's not ideal, but it's adequate. This is an important consideration that's especially crucial for cell phone browsers, screen readers, robots, and other renderers that are never going to show a two-dimensional layout no matter how it's implemented, with tables or CSS.

Two Columns, Sidebar on Left

Once you've done a few of these layouts, you'll usually just copy and paste some standard layouts. However, for learning it's helpful to build up the stylesheet in stages. The first step is to assign different background colors to the individual divs so that you can see where the boxes are going.

Coloring the divs

It's often helpful to add borders and different background colors to the individual column divs when designing a new layout, just so that you can see where things are going. For example, I used these styles when working on this section:

```
div#Content {
  background: red;
  border: solid;
}

div#Pages {
  background: green;
  border: solid;
}
```

Then I took them out when I was satisfied with the results.

Chris Pederick's Web Developer extension for Firefox is also an invaluable tool, especially it's Outline Block-level Elements and Outline Positioned Elements commands. It's usually easiest to make a layout work in Firefox first, and then to figure out what hacks you need to add to make it look decent in Internet Explorer. Most of the time layouts that work in Firefox work without further changes in Safari and Opera.

To create a columnar layout, we have to float at least one of the columns to the right or left. Because we'd like the content to come first, we need to float both. Therefore, both will need a specified width. (Floats simply don't work if the widths aren't specified. I can't justify this fact, but it is the way it is.) There are three possibilities for the width:

1. Fixed width for both columns

2. Fixed width for the left column; percentage width for the content column

3. Percentage widths for both columns

Option 1 is the most common choice, but I rather prefer option 3, though option 2 is sometimes a nice compromise. The problem with fixing the width is that it's almost guaranteed to be too small for some users and too large for others. If it's too large, a reader has to scroll horizontally to view the content, and horizontal scrolling makes text very hard to read. If it's too small, too little text will fit on each line, making for frequent eye movement and hard-to-read text. Columns that are too small are better than columns that are too large, but there's simply no way to design one fixed-width layout that suits everyone. It simply cannot be done. At the very least, the main content column should resize to fit the window width.

The stylesheet to accomplish this is simple and appears in Listing 5.2. It places the sidebar on the left and the content on the right. Figure 5.1 shows the rendered document.

LISTING 5.2   Liquid-Width, Two-Column Layout, Sidebar on Left

```
#Content {
    float: right;
    width: 80%;
}

#Pages {
    float: left;
    width: 18%;
}
```

This should be enough, but we actually need to add one more rule to work around Internet Explorer 6 bugs:

```
* html {
    left: 18%;
}
```

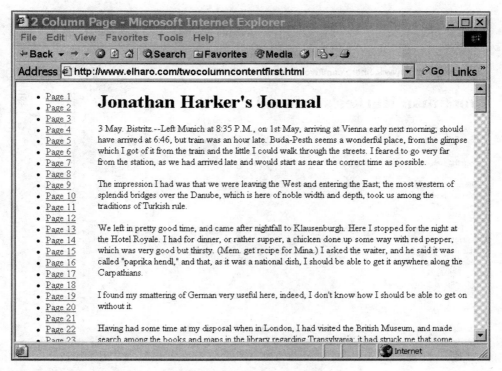

FIGURE 5.1   A liquid two-column layout with a left sidebar

Of course, this is a very bare-bones stylesheet. You'll likely want to adjust the fonts, borders, margins, padding, and more. That's straightforward once you have the layout in place.

Two Columns, Sidebar on Right

Moving the sidebar to the right is easy. Simply swap `float: left` and `float: right` in the two rules as demonstrated in Listing 5.3. Figure 5.2 shows the outcome. If you've used an external stylesheet, you don't need to change one bit of the HTML file to change from a left to a right sidebar. That's the power of CSS and separation of presentation from content.

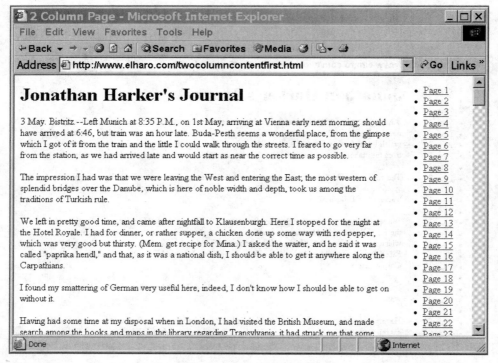

FIGURE 5.2   A liquid two-column layout with a right sidebar

LISTING 5.3 Liquid-Width, Two-Column Layout, Sidebar on Right

```
#Content {
    float: left;
    width: 80%;
}

#Pages {
    float: right;
    width: 18%;
}
```

In this case, because the sidebar follows the content in the text, rather than merely on the screen, you actually don't need the extra rule for IE.

Three Columns, Sidebar on Left and Right

Three-column layouts are trickier. In fact, they're so tricky that it took many smart people quite a few years of experimentation to develop the technique I show here. In fact, so many people searched for this while believing that it didn't actually exist that this technique goes under the name "The Holy Grail." The goal is simple: two fixed-width columns on the left and right and a liquid center for the content in the middle. (That something so frequently needed was so hard to invent doesn't speak well of CSS as a language, but it is the language we have to work with.)

Listing 5.4 demonstrates a typical three-column HTML layout. Now there are three divs: Pages, Content, and Books. The main content contains the first page from *Dracula*. The left-hand column contains links to other pages in this book. The right-hand column contains links to other books. Once again, the content comes first.

LISTING 5.4 A Three-Column HTML Page

```
<!DOCTYPE html PUBLIC "-//W3C//DTD XHTML 1.0 Strict//EN"
        "http://www.w3.org/TR/xhtml1/DTD/xhtml1-strict.dtd">
<html xmlns="http://www.w3.org/1999/xhtml">
<head>
  <title>Dracula, Page 1</title>
</head>
<body>
```

```
<div id="Content">
<h1>Jonathan Harker's Journal</h1>
<p>
3 May. Bistritz.--Left Munich at 8:35 P.M., on 1st May,
arriving at Vienna early next morning; should have arrived at
6:46, but train was an hour late.  Buda-Pesth seems a wonderful
place, from the glimpse which I got of it from the train and
the little I could walk through the streets.  I feared to go
very far from the station, as we had arrived late and would
start as near the correct time as possible.
</p>

<p>
The impression I had was that we were leaving the West and
entering the East; the most western of splendid bridges over
the Danube, which is here of noble width and depth, took us
among the traditions of Turkish rule.
</p>

<p>...</p>

</div>

<div id="Pages">

<ul>
<li><a href='page1.html'>Page 1</a></li>
<li><a href='page2.html'>Page 2</a></li>
<li><a href='page3.html'>Page 3</a></li>
<li>...</li>
<li><a href='page291.html'>Page 291</a></li>
<li><a href='page292.html'>Page 292</a></li>
<li><a href='page293.html'>Page 293</a></li>
</ul>

</div>

<div id="Books">

<ul>
<li><a href="/book97/">Flatland: a romance of many
                            dimensions</a></li>
<li><a href="/book604/">Gulliver of Mars</a></li>
<li><a href="/book1607/">A journey in other worlds<br />
A romance of the future</a></li>
<li><a href="/book7052/">Dr. Heidenhoff's Process</a></li>
...
<li><a href="/book12163/">The Sleeper Awakes<br /></li>
<li><a href="/book8968/">The World Set Free</a></li>
<li><a href="/book20553/">Out Around Rigel</a></li>
</ul>
</div>

</body>
</html>
```

Let's suppose we want the left column to be 10 ems wide and the right column to be 20 ems wide. We set up three columns, one for each `div`. Each `div` is positioned relative and floated to the left. The left and right columns have fixed widths and the center column is set to 100% width. Then margins are used to keep the columns from laying on top of each other. To be specific:

- Left column:

  Position is relative.

  Float is left.

  Width is a fixed value you choose.

  The right position is equal to the width of the column plus the left padding plus the right padding plus the left padding of the center column plus the right padding of the center column.

  The left margin is −100%.

- Right column:

  Position is relative.

  Float is left.

  Width is a fixed value you choose.

  The right position is equal to the width of the column plus the left padding plus the right padding.

  The right margin is −100%.

- Center column:

  Position is relative.

  Float is left.

  Width is 100%.

- Body:

  Margin is 0.

  Left padding is equal to the full width of the left column, including left and right padding.

Right padding is equal to the full width of the right column, including left and right padding.

Minimum width is equal to the full width of the left column plus the full width of the center column, including the left and right padding of both.

The template in Listing 5.5 should make this clearer. The rules in the Fixed Values section should be copied directly into your stylesheet without change, aside from the IDs of the columns. Then you can set the values in the Chosen Values section to your liking. I've used em measurements here, but pixels, inches, and other length units work as well. Finally, you calculate the values in the Calculated Values section based on the specified formulas and the numbers you entered in the second section.

This would be somewhat easier if CSS supported variables and simple calculations. However, it doesn't, so you have to determine the right sizes by hand using these formulas. Then insert the relevant literal values in your stylesheet.

LISTING 5.5 Three-Column Stylesheet with Fixed-Width Left and Right Columns, Liquid Center Column

```
/* Fixed Values */
body {
    margin: 0;
}

#Content {
    width: 100%;
    position: relative;
    float: left;
}

#Pages {
    margin-left: -100%;
    position: relative;
    float: left;
}

#Books {
    margin-right: -100%;
    position: relative;
    float: left;
}
```

```
/* Chosen Values */
#Content {
    padding-right: 2em;
    padding-left:  2em;
}
/*
LC = Left column
RC = Right column
CC = Center column
*/
#Pages {
    width: 9em;              /* LC width */
    padding-right: 1em;      /* LC right padding */
    padding-left: 1em;       /* LC left padding */
}

#Books {
    width: 15em;             /* RC width */
    padding-right: 1em;      /* RC right padding */
    padding-left:  1em;      /* RC left padding */
}

/* Calculated Values */
body {
    padding-left: 11em;      /* LC width + LC right padding
                                + LC left padding */
    padding-right: 22em;     /* RC width + RC right padding
                                + RC left padding + CC left padding
                                + CC right padding */
    min-width: 15em;         /* LC width + LC right padding
                                + LC left padding + CC left padding
                                + CC right padding */
}

#Pages {
    right: 15em;             /* LC width + LC right padding
                                + LC left padding
                              + CC left padding + CC right padding */
}
```

IE 6 has some problems with this technique. To work around them, we add this rule:

```
html #left {
 left: 17em; /* RC width + RC right padding + RC left padding*/
}
```

What's especially annoying about this technique is that it's very easy to get the widths a little off. They are calculated based on each other, but they are defined as static constants in the CSS file. However, once you get this right, it does work, and it works reasonably well across modern browsers.

Replace Frames with CSS Positions

Convert framesets to single pages.

```
<frameset cols="20%,80%">
  <frame frameborder="1" src="navframe.html" name="navframe"
         scrolling="auto" />
  <frame frameborder="1" src="contentframe.html"
         name="contentframe"
         scrolling="auto" />
  <noframes>
    <body>
      <p>
       Go away! We don't want your kind here.
      </p>
    </body>
  </noframes>
</frameset>
```

```
<div id="outer">
  <div id="nav" style="border: 1; overflow: scroll; width: 20%">
    navigation links here…
  </div>
  <div id="content"
       style="border: 1; overflow: scroll; width: 80%">
    <p>
      Howdy neighbor! Come on in.
    </p>
  </div>
</div>
```

Motivation

Frames were a bad idea that hasn't improved in the ten years since they were invented. They are a usability disaster. They make it extremely hard to bookmark or return to a particular page. They make it hard to save a page or print it. They break the connection between the URL displayed in the title bar and the content on the page. They take control away from the user, because frame sizes are set by the page author. Users cannot resize individual frames to fit their needs. Scroll bars take up valuable screen real estate.

Frames confuse search engines and reduce your Google rank. Furthermore, when users do find a relevant framed page with a search engine, they're likely to come into the framed page directly, rather than the frameset, thus completely bypassing your carefully designed frame layout.

Browsers have partially compensated for some of these flaws with tools such as the This Frame context menu in Firefox. However, this is still a limited solution. Furthermore, when users take advantage of such functionality, they may well break a site that depends on having all frames in a set visible at once. Critical navigation or other content can be missed when a reader sees only part of a frameset.

Potential Trade-offs

The techniques outlined here will not work quite as well in older browsers that are rarely used anymore. However, the content will still be accessible to them. It just won't be as pretty. In modern browsers, by contrast, it should be both more attractive and more usable.

The individual nonframe pages may require more bandwidth than the frame equivalents. That's because the frame content will need to be served to the client on each page.

Mechanics

Frames were a hack in the very early days of the Web before browsers supported CSS or servers supported sophisticated include schemes. Today a combination of both of these is preferred to achieve a much nicer frame effect with greater usability.

There are actually two reasons that sites use frames:

- To include static content on all pages, without separately editing each page
- To present a multicolumn appearance

Although these are legitimate goals, in 2008 neither of them requires the use of frames. You already saw in the preceding section that it's not hard to create multicolumn layouts with CSS.

It is very common for web sites to have navigation bars or other content that remains the same or almost the same from page to page. For example, in Java API documentation there are two frames on the left-hand side that contain a list of all packages and all classes in the current package. The main content frame is on the right. This is shown in Figure 5.3.

This actually works fairly well, and it is one of the better uses of frames. Let's see how we might replace it with CSS. The key is to set up three divs, one for each frame. The content of each div is taken from the body of each framed document. These divs are then positioned using the same CSS properties described in the preceding sec-

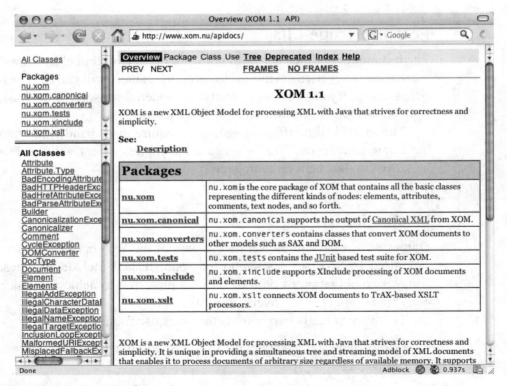

FIGURE 5.3 Javadoc frame layout

tion. However, this time we'll add one more piece. We'll make them individually scrollable using the overflow property.

Listing 5.6 shows the original document.

LISTING 5.6 The Framed Page

```
<!DOCTYPE html PUBLIC "-//W3C//DTD XHTML 1.0 Frameset//EN"
"http://www.w3.org/TR/2000/REC-xhtml1-20000126/DTD/xhtml1-
frameset.dtd">
<html xml:lang="en-US" xmlns="http://www.w3.org/1999/xhtml">
 <head>
  <title>XOM 1.1 API</title></head>
  <frameset cols="20%,80%">
    <frameset rows="30%,70%">
      <frame frameborder="1" src="overview-frame.html"
      name="packageListFrame" title="All Packages"
      scrolling="auto" />
      <frame frameborder="1" src="allclasses-frame.html"
name="packageFrame" title="All classes and interfaces
  (except non-static nested types)" scrolling="auto" />
    </frameset>
    <frame frameborder="1" src="overview-summary.html"
         name="classFrame" scrolling="auto"
         title="Package, class and interface descriptions"  />
    <noframes><body><h2>
Frame Alert</h2>
<p>
This document is designed to be viewed using the frames feature.
If you see this message, you are using a non-frame-capable web
client.
<br clear="none"></br>
Link to<a shape="rect" href="overview-summary.html">Non-frame
version.</a>
</p></body></noframes>
</frameset>
</html>
```

The first thing you can do is take out the noframes element. We won't need this anymore. The nonframe version should work with any browser. This gives us the simpler Listing 5.7, though this is just an intermediate step we won't actually publish.

LISTING 5.7 Removing noframes

```
<!DOCTYPE html PUBLIC "-//W3C//DTD XHTML 1.0 Frameset//EN"
"http://www.w3.org/TR/2000/REC-xhtml1-20000126/DTD/xhtml1-
frameset.dtd">
<html xml:lang="en-US" xmlns="http://www.w3.org/1999/xhtml">
 <head>
```

```
<title>XOM 1.1 API</title></head>
<frameset cols="20%,80%">
  <frameset rows="30%,70%">
    <frame frameborder="1" src="overview-frame.html"
     name="packageListFrame" title="All Packages"
     scrolling="auto" />
    <frame frameborder="1" src="allclasses-frame.html"
     name="packageFrame" title="All classes and interfaces
     (except non-static nested types)" scrolling="auto" />
  </frameset>
  <frame frameborder="1" src=" overview-summary.html"
   name="classFrame"
   title="Package, class and interface descriptions"
   scrolling="auto" />
</frameset>
</html>
```

Next, change each frameset and frame into a div, as shown in List-
ing 5.8. The name attributes will need to be changed into id attributes.
Also, add a body element. Finally, change the DOCTYPE to the
XHTML strict DOCTYPE.

LISTING 5.8   Replacing Frames with divs

```
<!DOCTYPE html PUBLIC "-//W3C//DTD XHTML 1.0 Strict//EN"
        "http://www.w3.org/TR/xhtml1/DTD/xhtml1-strict.dtd">
<html xml:lang="en-US" xmlns="http://www.w3.org/1999/xhtml">
<head>
<title>XOM 1.1 API</title></head>
<body>

<div cols="20%,80%">
  <div rows="30%,70%">
    <div frameborder="1" src="overview-frame.html"
     id="packageListFrame" title="All Packages"
     scrolling="auto">
  <div frameborder="1" src="allclasses-frame.html"
      id="packageFrame" scrolling="auto" title=
 "All classes and interfaces (except non-static nested types)"
     />
</div>
  <div frameborder="1" src="overview-summary.html"
      id="classFrame" scrolling="auto"
  title="Package, class and interface descriptions" />
</div>
</body>
</html>
```

Now change the cols and rows attributes into CSS width and height
values. This is tricky because frames put these values on the container

(the outer div), whereas CSS puts them on the contained item (the inner div). For example, the 20% col from the top div becomes a 20% width on its first child div, and the 80% col from the top div becomes an 80% width on its second child div, as shown in Listing 5.9.

LISTING 5.9   Replacing cols and rows with CSS Width and Height

```
<!DOCTYPE html PUBLIC "-//W3C//DTD XHTML 1.0 Strict//EN"
        "http://www.w3.org/TR/xhtml1/DTD/xhtml1-strict.dtd">
<html xml:lang="en-US" xmlns="http://www.w3.org/1999/xhtml">
<head>
<title>XOM 1.1 API</title></head>
<body>

<div>
  <div style="width: 20%;">
    <div style="height: 30%;" frameborder="1"
      src="overview-frame.html" scrolling="auto"
      id="packageListFrame" title="All Packages"  />
    <div style="height: 70%" frameborder="1"
      src="allclasses-frame.html" id="packageFrame"
      title="All classes and interfaces
    (except non-static nested types)" scrolling="auto" />
  </div>
  <div style="width: 80%" src="overview-summary.html"
      id="classFrame" title="Package, class and interface
            descriptions" scrolling="auto" />
</div>
</body>
</html>
```

We also need to change the frameborder attributes into CSS border properties. We replace the scrolling attribute with the CSS overflow property. Listing 5.10 shows this step.

LISTING 5.10   Replace Scrolling with CSS Overflow

```
<!DOCTYPE html PUBLIC "-//W3C//DTD XHTML 1.0 Strict//EN"
        "http://www.w3.org/TR/xhtml1/DTD/xhtml1-strict.dtd">
<html xml:lang="en-US" xmlns="http://www.w3.org/1999/xhtml">
<head>
<title>XOM 1.1 API</title></head>
<body>

<div>
  <div style="width: 20%;">
    <div style="height: 30%; border: solid; overflow: scroll;"
         src="overview-frame.html" id="packageListFrame"
         title="All Packages" />
```

```
    <div style="height: 70%; border: solid; overflow: scroll;"
       src="allclasses-frame.html" id="packageFrame"
       title="All classes and interfaces
    (except non-static nested types)" />
  </div>
  <div style="width: 80%; border: solid; overflow: scroll"
       src="overview-summary.html" id="classFrame"
       title="Package, class and interface descriptions" />
</div>
</body>
</html>
```

The next step is to copy the text from the body elements in the framed documents into the new source document. This text can, of course, be rather long, so in Listing 5.11, I've just filled in some dummy text. This is now a valid XHTML strict document.

LISTING 5.11   The Finished Frame-Free Document

```
<!DOCTYPE html PUBLIC "-//W3C//DTD XHTML 1.0 Strict//EN"
        "http://www.w3.org/TR/xhtml1/DTD/xhtml1-strict.dtd">
<html xml:lang="en-US" xmlns="http://www.w3.org/1999/xhtml">
<head>
<title>XOM 1.1 API</title></head>
<body>

<div id="outer">
  <div id="leftFrame" style="width: 20%;">
    <div style="height: 30%"
      id="packageListFrame" title="All Packages" >
      Package list goes here
    </div>
    <div style="height: 70%"
      id="packageFrame" title="All classes and interfaces
    (except non-static nested types)" >
      Class list goes here
    </div>
  </div>
  <div style="width: 80%;"
      id="classFrame" title="Package, class and interface
            descriptions"  >
   Summary details go here
  </div>
</div>
</body>
</html>
```

Of course, if we stopped here we'd have a technically valid but rather ugly and hard-to-use document. The final step is to reproduce the original layout with CSS instead of frames. The techniques are much the same as used in earlier sections for eliminating table layouts. The details will vary depending on the frame-based layouts you're replacing. Simple sidebar and navigation layouts can be handled using the stylesheets presented earlier. For the Javadoc layout demonstrated here, Listing 5.12 shows a CSS stylesheet that does the job. Figure 5.4 shows the finished document.

LISTING 5.12 A CSS Stylesheet for Javadoc Layout

```
#outer { position: relative; }

#leftFrame {
  position: fixed;
  height: 100%;
  width: 20%;
  top: 0;
}

#classFrame {
  position: absolute;
  left: 21%;
  width: 77%;
}

#packageListFrame{
  position: static;
  height: 200px;
  overflow: scroll; }

#packageFrame {
  position: static;
  height: 70%;
  overflow: scroll;
}
```

The problem with this technique is that it violates the DRY (Don't Repeat Yourself) principle. Although it's fine for one page, the same content is repeated on page after page after page, often with simple, small variations. Repetitive content is usually a code smell, and one that you should pay attention to. Frames do avoid needless repetition in a way that static, frameless HTML does not. That would almost be enough to convince me they're not so bad if only they weren't such a problem for users. I advocate clean, maintainable code, but not at the expense of the user interface. If forced to choose between ugly code and an ugly user interface, I'll pick the ugly code every time. Frame code is cleaner, but frame interfaces are not.

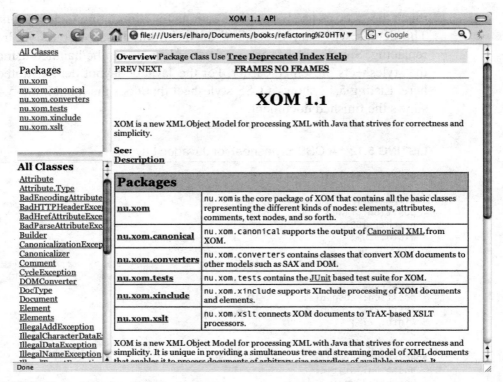

FIGURE 5.4   Javadoc CSS layout

More static sites that are not generated by code, databases, or CMSs should consider using some form of server-side include technology to manage repetitive content. This is transparent to the user but a big help to the author. For example, the Apache 2.0 web server provides the `mod_include` module. You can include repetitive static content in many pages simply by using comments such as `<!--#include virtual="/header.html" -->`, as shown in Listing 5.13. However, maybe we don't have to make that choice. Although the raw HTML shown in the last few examples is repetitive, that is not necessarily the code we edit. The example developed here—Javadoc—is automatically generated from Java source code. The HTML is more akin to compiled assembly code than source code. The real source is the Java code from which the Javadoc is extracted and the HTML is generated.

By modifying the doclet that generates the HTML, we could switch all the Javadoc to frameless XHTML without changing a line of the actual source. Wikis, blogs, content management systems (CMSs), and more can all easily duplicate the authoring convenience of frames without the user-facing problems they cause.

LISTING 5.13   Apache Server-Side Includes

```
<html xmlns="http://www.w3.org/1999/xhtml">
<head>
<title>On Iterators and Indexes</title>
</head>
<body>

 <!--#include virtual="/header.html" -->
<div id="Content">
<h1>On Iterators and Indexes</h1>
<p>
Here's a neat little trick Wolfgang Hoscheck <a href="http://
lists.ibiblio.org/pipermail/xom-interest/2004-November/
001501.html">showed me</a>… </p>
</div>
 <!--#include virtual="/footer.html" -->
 <!--#include virtual="/sidebar.html" -->

</body>
</html>
```

Customarily, files that contain server-side includes end with .shtml to tell the server to parse them and resolve the includes before sending them to clients. Although `mod_include` is compiled into Apache by default, it may not be enabled for all directories. You need to add these three configuration directives for each directory that uses server-side includes, either in the main Apache config file or in an .htaccess file:

```
AddType text/html .shtml
AddOutputFilter INCLUDES .shtml
Options +Includes
```

PHP has similar functionality accessed via the `include` function, as demonstrated in Listing 5.14.

LISTING 5.14   PHP Includes

```
<html xmlns="http://www.w3.org/1999/xhtml">
<head>
<title>On Iterators and Indexes</title>
</head>
<body>

<?php
   include("header.html");
?>
<div id="Content">
<h1>On Iterators and Indexes</h1>
<p>
Here's a neat little trick Wolfgang Hoscheck <a href="http://
lists.ibiblio.org/pipermail/xom-interest/2004-November/
001501.html">showed me</a>… </p>
</div>
<?php
   include("footer.html");
   include("sidebar.html");
?>

</html>
```

I wouldn't recommend switching to PHP just for server-side includes, but if you're already using PHP, as so many sites are, this is very convenient.

These are just a couple of common examples. All but the most basic web servers support some form of server-side include functionality.

Performance may be marginally slower with server-side includes of various stripes than with static files, but not usually significantly slower. CPU and local disk speed are rarely the limiting factors on even the highest-volume web sites today.

Move Content to the Front

When reading the raw HTML from start to finish, the main content of the page should be the very first thing encountered. Sidebars, headers, footers, navigation, and such should follow.

```
<div id="left">Left sidebar</div>
<div id="content">Page content</div>
<div id="right">Right sidebar</div>
```

```
<div id="content">Page content</div>
<div id="left">Left sidebar</div>
<div id="right">Right sidebar</div>
```

Motivation

Search engines often treat content earlier in the page as more important than content later in the page. You usually want the unique content on the page, not the navigation, advertisements, logos, and other froufrou.

Putting content first is extremely important for accessibility. Screen readers see the page as a linear sequence that starts at the beginning and continues to the end. Pages laid out as two-dimensional columns are big problems for blind readers. For these readers, especially, it's really important to put the crucial content upfront rather than making them wade through several dozen irrelevant links first.

Potential Trade-offs

Insisting on having the content first does make designing CSS stylesheets with positioning more difficult. You'll likely need to modify any such stylesheets to account for the new content order.

Mechanics

To the extent that static content such as headers, footers, navigation, ads, and sidebars are repeated from page to page, there's usually some constant string you can search for, such as id="sidebar". If your

pages are structured very consistently, you may even be able to automate moving the secondary content after the main content. More
often, though, you'll need to find these issues manually unless all the
pages are generated out of a CMS or database of some kind. If that's
the case, you just need to update the template.

The biggest problem is likely to be reorganizing the CSS stylesheet
to support the new content order. CSS is not as independent of content order as one would like it to be. However, the techniques given in
the first section in this chapter for converting from a table-based layout apply here as well. There is one common problem I did not address
in that section: putting the header after the main content. This is
tricky, though it can be done. If you don't want to update the stylesheets
just yet, you should at least install skip links, as discussed in the next
chapter.

However, if you do want to go whole-hog, the trick is to absolutely
position the header at the top of the page and then give the content and
sidebars enough of a top margin to slide out of its way. This is not a
perfect solution. It does tend to let the main content bleed over the
header at very large font sizes, but it's adequate for most sites.

Imagine we've added new divs for headers and footers, as shown
in Listing 5.15. The footer is actually inside the content, so it will
show up at the bottom. The header appears at the very end, after all the
other content. Nonetheless, we want it to appear at the top of the page.

LISTING 5.15   A Three-Column HTML Page with Header and Footer

```
<!DOCTYPE html PUBLIC "-//W3C//DTD XHTML 1.0 Strict//EN"
      "http://www.w3.org/TR/xhtml1/DTD/xhtml1-strict.dtd">
<html xmlns="http://www.w3.org/1999/xhtml">
<head>
  <title>Dracula, Page 1</title>
</head>
<body>

<div id="Content">
<h1>Jonathan Harker's Journal</h1>
<p>
3 May. Bistritz.--Left Munich at 8:35 P.M., on 1st May,
arriving at Vienna early next morning; should have arrived
at 6:46, but train was an hour late.  Buda-Pesth seems a
wonderful place, from the glimpse which I got of it from the
train and the little I could walk through the streets. I feared
to go very far from the station, as we had arrived late and
```

```
would start as near the correct time as possible.
</p>
<p>...</p>

<div id="Footer">
  <p>The text is in the public domain and courtesy of
     <a href="http://www.gutenberg.org/">Project Gutenberg</a>.
  </p>
</div>

</div>

<div id="Pages">
<ul>
<li><a href='page1.html'>Page 1</a></li>
<li><a href='page2.html'>Page 2</a></li>
<li>...</li>
<li><a href='page292.html'>Page 292</a></li>
<li><a href='page293.html'>Page 293</a></li>
</ul>
</div>

<div id="Books">
<ul>
<li><a href="/book97/">Flatland: a romance
                            of many dimensions</a></li>
...
<li><a href="/book20553/">Out Around Rigel</a></li>
</ul>
</div>

<div id="Authors">
Edward Bellamy | Marion Zimmer Bradley | Edgar Rice Burroughs
| John W. Campbell | Lester Del Rey | Cory Doctorow
| Arthur Conan Doyle | H. Beam Piper | Robert Sheckley
| E. E. Smith | Jules Verne | H. G. Wells
</div>

</body>
</html>
```

Although the Authors header is at the end of the document, we can still move it to the visual top of the page by absolutely positioning it with this rule:

```
#Header {
  position: absolute;
  top: 1ex;
  margin:10px 10px 2ex 10px;
  padding-right: 17em;
  font-size: small;
}
```

Note that we had to set its right margin to keep it from overlapping the right sidebar containing the titles. We also need to push the main content down the page by setting Content's top margin like so:

```
#Content {
    top: 24ex;
}
```

You'll have to experiment to find the right size for the top of the main content. It will depend on how much text you put in the header, as well as how big the header font is. If you leave some extra whitespace, you can usually find a value that works for a wide range of user font sizes and browser widths. If the font gets really huge, there may be some overlap. However, I've been using layouts such as this for several years now, and so far no one has written me to complain that at 64 points or larger, the header starts to overlap the rest of the page.

The footer is actually quite easy to handle. Because that comes after the main content in both the logical and presentational flow of the document, it doesn't require nearly as much trickery as the header does. In fact, all you really have to do is place the footer div inside the main content div, rather than outside. That moves it to the bottom, and no extra CSS positioning is needed.

Mark Up Lists as Lists

Make sure any lists are marked up as ul elements, or, occasionally, as dl or ol elements.

```
<div id="Authors">
Edward Bellamy | Marion Zimmer Bradley | Edgar Rice Burroughs
| John W. Campbell | Lester Del Rey | Cory Doctorow
| Arthur Conan Doyle | H. Beam Piper | Robert Sheckley
| E. E. Smith | Jules Verne | H. G. Wells
</div>
```

```
<ul id="Authors">
<li>Edward Bellamy</li>
```

```
<li>Marion Zimmer Bradley</li>
<li>Edgar Rice Burroughs</li>
<li>John W. Campbell</li>
<li>Lester Del Rey</li>
<li>Cory  Doctorow</li>
<li>Arthur Conan Doyle</li>
<li>H. Beam Piper</li>
<li>Robert Sheckley</li>
<li>E. E. Smith</li>
<li>Jules Verne</li>
<li>H. G. Wells</li>
</ul>
```

Motivation

Identifying lists as lists improves accessibility. In particular, it enables the use of screen reader tools for skipping over and navigating through lists.

Potential Trade-offs

Most browsers assign very specific appearances to lists and list items, typically indented and bulleted, and you may not want this appearance. You can fix this easily with CSS in modern browsers. However, some older browsers do not support all the necessary properties and will display these pages in less-than-ideal fashion.

Mechanics

There's no simple way to find all the unidentified lists in a site. You'll just have to read the pages and look for lists. They can be marked up in dozens of different ways: as paragraphs, divs, tables, inline text separated by commas or other symbols, and more.

Once you've found a list, marking up the individual items is easy. Just use a ul, ol, or dl instead of the current wrapper element. Use the ordered list ol if the items are numbered. Use dl if the list takes the form name-description, name-description, name-description. Use ul for all other lists.

Although lists are extremely common in content, list elements are not. The reason is that browsers usually indent and bullet or number each separate item, as well as placing line breaks in between items; and this is not always desired. However, this is easy to fix with CSS. For example, to remove the bullets add this rule to the page's CSS stylesheet:

```
ul {
  list-style-type: none;
}
```

Or, instead of removing the bullet, you can add a custom bullet loaded from an image file with the list-style-image property like so:

```
ul li {
 list-style-image: url(images/star.gif)
}
```

To get rid of the indentation, add this rule:

```
ul {
  margin-left: 0px;
  padding-left: 0px;
}
```

Alternatively, you can set a different margin by increasing the value of these properties. If you like, you can also play with the text-indent property, which indents just the first line. Negative values create hanging indents.

To place the list items on a single line use this rule:

```
ul, li {
  display: inline;
  margin: 0px;
  padding: 0px;
}
```

To place a character such as a comma between list items add this rule:

```
ul li:after {
  content: ", ";
}
```

This actually puts a comma after each list item, including the last. To avoid that, assign a special class to the last item in the list, like so:

```
<li class="last">H.G. Wells</li>
```

Then add one extra rule just for this last item that overrides the earlier rule:

```
ul li.last:after {
  content: "";
}
```

Of course, you can use class or ID selectors to apply these rules to some lists and not others if you like.

Replace blockquote/ul Indentation with CSS

Change any blockquotes or ul elements used purely to indent their contents into divs, and assign CSS rules to the div that use the margin-left and margin-right properties to indent.

```
<blockquote>
The quick brown fox jumped over the lazy dog.
</blockquote>
```

```
<div id="i8" style="margin-left: 40px; margin-right: 40px">
The quick brown fox jumped over the lazy dog.
</div>
```

Motivation

blockquote should be reserved for quotations. ul should be reserved for lists.

CSS offers much greater control over exactly how far any given chunk of text is indented. You also have the option to set a right margin separately from the left margin, to indent the first line differently than the rest, to specify a hanging indent, or anything else you can imagine. CSS is simply a more powerful and precise means of indenting text than `blockquote` and `ul` ever were.

Potential Trade-offs

Minimal. Even if a browser cannot load the CSS stylesheet, the consequent lack of indentation has a very small effect on the overall appearance of the page.

Mechanics

Finding text improperly marked up with `blockquote` is tricky. On some sites, there are no real blockquotes, so a quick search for `<blockquote` will locate all the occurrences. However, if a site is using real blockquotes anywhere, you'll need to inspect each example.

To find places where `ul` (or, less commonly, `ol`) has been used to indent, first try validation. Even the transitional XHTML DTD requires all `ul` and `ol` elements to contain at least one `li` child element. Lists that don't contain any list items should pop right up with an error message such as this:

```
test.html:9: element ul: validity error : Element ul content
does not follow the DTD, expecting (li)+, got ()
</ul>
    ^
```

You can also use regular expressions to locate any item-less `ul` elements. Because these almost always extend across multiple lines, this is a little tricky, but it is doable:

```
<ul>([^<]|<[^l]|<l[^i])*?</ul>
```

Once you find one, change it into a `div`. Then set the `margin-left` and `margin-right` properties on the `div`. Forty pixels is a common value that many browsers use for blockquote indentation, so this rule would reproduce that:

```
<div style="margin-left: 40px; margin-right: 40px; ">
```

Of course, you could take this opportunity to choose a different size if you like, and you probably should place the style rule in an external stylesheet to allow for easier updates later.

If you like, you can also play with the `text-indent` property, which indents just the first line. Negative values create hanging indents. However, this is very different from the both-sides indentation that you get with a blockquote or a list.

Replace Spacer GIFs

Delete all spacer GIFs. Use CSS `margin`, `padding`, `position`, and `indent` properties as necessary to reproduce their effects.

```
<td>
  <img src="images/spacer.gif" hspace="10" vspace="1">
</td>
<p>foo</p>
<img src="images/spacer.gif" hspace="1" vspace="10">
<p>bar</p>
<img src="images/spacer.gif" hspace="1" vspace="10">
```

```
<td style="width: 10px;">
   
</td>
<p style="margin-bottom: 1ex;">foo</p>
<p style="margin-bottom: 1ex;">bar</p>
```

Motivation

Spacer GIFs were a really ugly hack from the days even before tables, much less CSS. They may have made sense in 1995 (barely), but they're in no way necessary today. It's shocking that these are still showing up on web sites, even new ones.

Spacer-GIF-based layouts are fragile and unreliable. They tend to break in modern browsers. They do not scale well with increased or decreased font sizes.

Spacer GIFs without `alt` attributes cause massive problems for screen readers.

Furthermore, many browsers and browser plug-ins today refuse to load single-pixel GIFs because they are commonly abused for user tracking.

Potential Trade-offs

None.

Mechanics

To find spacer GIFs, just search your web site for the word *spacer* (case-insensitive). Any hits on that string are a red flag. Of course, there's nothing magical about the name spacer, though it is by far the most common. Other names I've seen pop up more than once include transparent.gif, 1.gif, and 1x1.gif. If you discover any spacer GIFs using a different name, search for those too to see what other files they may be infecting. You may even find a few spacer "GIFs" that are actually JPEGs or PNGs, and of course, you should replace these as well.

Spacer GIFs can and should be replaced by CSS rules. Exactly which properties you replace them with will depend on the use to which the spacer GIF was put, but usually it's one or more of margin, padding, or position that's involved.

For example, this is an old attempt to indent a paragraph 20 pixels by prefixing it with a transparent spacer GIF:

```
<p>
 <img src="spacer.gif" width="20" height="1" />
I was not able to light on any map or work giving the exact
locality of the Castle Dracula, as there are no maps of this
country as yet to compare with our own Ordnance Survey Maps;
but I found that Bistritz, the post town named by Count Dracula,
is a fairly well-known place. I shall enter here some of my notes,
as they may refresh my memory when I talk over my travels
with Mina.
</p>
```

You can easily replace this with a `text-indent` CSS property with the value 20px:

```
<p style="text-indent: 20px">
I was not able to light on any map or work giving the
exact locality...
</p>
```

Better still, use a text relative unit of measure, such as ems, so that the indent will grow and shrink as necessary to match the browser's default font size:

```
<p style="text-indent: 4em">
I was not able to light on any map or work giving the
exact locality...
</p>
```

As always, this rule can and probably should be placed in an external stylesheet.

Add an ID Attribute

Assign each element a unique `id` by which it can be addressed.

```
<h2>Resources</h2>
  <ul>
    <li><a href="/faq.html">Frequently Asked Questions</a></li>
    <li><a href="/tutorial.html">Tutorial</a></li>
    <li><a href="/contact.html">Contact Us</a></li>
  </ul>
  <p>Are you <strong>really</strong> sure?</p>
```

```
<h2 id='resources'>Resources</h2>
  <ul id='resourcelist'>
    <li id='l1'><a id='a1' href="/faq.html">Frequently Asked
Questions</a></li>
    <li id='l2'>
      <a id='a2' href="/tutorial.html">Tutorial</a>
```

(continued)

```
<h2 id='resources'>Resources</h2>
  <ul id='resourcelist'>
    <li id='l1'><a id='a1' href="/faq.html">Frequently Asked
Questions</a></li>
      <li id='l2'>
        <a id='a2' href="/tutorial.html">Tutorial</a>
```

Motivation

ID attributes allow you to precisely target individual elements for styling with CSS, addressing with JavaScript, transforming with XSLT, and more. They make it much easier for programs to operate on the document.

ID attributes also make it easier for you and other people to link to and cite your content. Instead of referencing the entire page, they can now reference the individual paragraph, heading, table, or other content.

Potential Trade-offs

Adding ID attributes to every element can bloat file sizes by a noticeable amount. If bandwidth is a major concern, consider adding ID attributes to only some of the elements. In particular, it's usually enough to put an id on every p, table, blockquote, ul, ol, dl, and div.

Mechanics

The ID attribute is named id, and it must contain a single XML name. For example, consider this paragraph:

```
<p>Game over. Sony has
<a href=
 "http://www.sgknox.com/2007/01/11/no-porn-on-blu-ray/">
   forfeited</a>
and Blu-Ray has lost.</p>
```

You simply add an id attribute to each start-tag, like so:

```
<p id='p1'>Game over. Sony has
<a id='a1' href=
 "http://www.sgknox.com/2007/01/11/no-porn-on-blu-ray/">
   forfeited</a>
and Blu-Ray has lost.</p>
```

There are a few rules for the values of id attributes, but they're not especially onerous.

- The value must begin with a letter.
- The value must contain only letters and digits.
- Each value must be unique within the document where it appears.

The ID values do not have to have any particular system or meaning, though they can if that's convenient for you. Usually, however, they're pretty much arbitrary strings.

Assuming the documents are already well-formed, it's easy enough to automate this process. Listing 5.16 demonstrates a simple XSLT stylesheet that adds IDs to all elements in a document that don't already have them.

LISTING 5.16   An XSLT Stylesheet That Adds IDs to All Elements

```
<xsl:stylesheet xmlns:xsl='http://www.w3.org/1999/XSL/Transform'
  version='1.0'>

  <!-- match elements with IDs -->
  <xsl:template match='*[@id]' priority='1.5'>
    <xsl:copy>
      <xsl:apply-templates select="@*|node()"/>
    </xsl:copy>
  </xsl:template>

  <!-- match elements without IDs -->
  <xsl:template match='*' priority='1'>
    <xsl:copy>
      <xsl:attribute name='id'>
        <xsl:value-of select='generate-id()'/>
      </xsl:attribute>
      <xsl:apply-templates select="@*|node()"/>
    </xsl:copy>
  </xsl:template>

  <!-- match non-elements -->
  <xsl:template match='@*|node()' priority='0.5'>
    <xsl:copy>
      <xsl:apply-templates select="node()"/>
    </xsl:copy>
  </xsl:template>

</xsl:stylesheet>
```

Listing 5.17 modifies this slightly to add id attributes to only p, table, and div elements. You can easily adjust the list of elements you add ids to by changing the element names in the match pattern in the second template rule.

LISTING 5.17   An XSLT Stylesheet That Adds IDs to Particular Elements

```
<?xml version='1.0'?>
<xsl:stylesheet version='1.0'
  xmlns:xsl='http://www.w3.org/1999/XSL/Transform'
  xmlns:html='http://www.w3.org/1999/xhtml'>

  <!-- match elements that already have IDs -->
  <xsl:template match='html:*[@id]' priority='1.5'>
    <xsl:copy>
      <xsl:apply-templates select="@*|node()"/>
    </xsl:copy>
  </xsl:template>

  <!-- match elements we will add IDs to -->
  <xsl:template match='html:p | html:table | html:div'
                priority='1.25'>
    <xsl:copy>
      <xsl:attribute name='id'>
        <xsl:value-of select='generate-id()'/>
      </xsl:attribute>
      <xsl:apply-templates select="@*|node()"/>
    </xsl:copy>
  </xsl:template>

  <!-- match elements we're not going to add IDs to -->
  <xsl:template match='*' priority='1'>
    <xsl:copy>
      <xsl:apply-templates select="@*|node()"/>
    </xsl:copy>
  </xsl:template>

  <!-- match non-elements -->
  <xsl:template match='@*|node()' priority='0.5'>
    <xsl:copy>
      <xsl:apply-templates select="node()"/>
    </xsl:copy>
  </xsl:template>

</xsl:stylesheet>
```

Add Width and Height to an Image

Add `width` and `height` attributes to all `img` elements that don't have them.

```
<img src="winter.jpg" alt="Frozen river" />
```

```
<img src="winter.jpg" width='640' height='480'
alt="Frozen river" />
```

Motivation

`width` and `height` attributes enable a browser to format a page much more quickly and display it to the user sooner. This is especially critical on slow dial-up connections, which about 20% of web surfers still use.

Potential Trade-offs

If you change the size of the images, you'll also need to change the HTML. Otherwise, the pictures may be strangely compressed or expanded. If you're frequently changing images—for instance, while designing a page—you may wish to leave the insertion of widths and heights to the final prepublication stage.

Mechanics

The XHTML DTD does not require `width` and `height` attributes on `img` elements, so simple validation will not find the problem. However, a regular expression can find missing `width` attributes. The trick is to match all possible attributes except `width` and `height`, like so:

```
<img\s+((alt|border|class|align|id|src|usemap|hspace|vspace)
\s*=\s*("[^"]+"|'[^']+')\s*)*>
```

Only `img` tags that do not contain `width` and `height` attributes will match. (Here we're relying on the absence of weird, unexpected attributes. In essence, validity is a weak prerequisite for this search.)

If you think you might have remembered to add a `height` but not a `width` or vice versa, check these regular expressions:

```
<img\s+((width|alt|border|class|align|id|src|usemap
|hspace|vspace)\s*=\s*("[^"]+"|'[^']+')\s*)*>
```

```
<img\s+((height|alt|border|class|align|id|src|usemap
|hspace|vspace)\s*=\s*("[^"]+"|'[^']+')\s*)*>
```

That should sniff out all the missing sizes.

If you find only a few such elements, you might as well open the files, load the relevant images into a program that will tell you their size, and fix them manually. Firefox helpfully shows the image width and height when you open an image directly (as opposed to the HTML page in which the image is embedded).

However, if there are many such problems, you'll want to automate the process with a program that parses the documents and fills in the missing sizes. Randal Schwartz has published a Perl script called addsize that does this, which you can find at www.stonehenge.com/merlyn/WebTechniques/col36.html. It's a little old, but it's still functional. Marc Merlins has another at http://marc.merlins.org/linux/scripts/addsize that is based on ImageMagik. And Eric S. Raymond has written one called imgsizer in Python (www.catb.org/~esr/imgsizer/). None of them is perfect, but imgsizer is probably the most up-to-date and reliable. It should run on most UNIX/Linux variants fairly easily.

To update one file in place, just type:

```
$ imgsizer -n filename.html
```

To change all HTML files in a directory, use the -d option:

```
$ imgsizer -n -d /var/www/html
```

This program does not back up the files before changing them, and it can create malformed files in some cases. Be sure to make a backup before running it or any similar utility. Indeed, it's probably a good idea to run the tool on only a copy of your files and to verify the modified copy before proceeding.

Chapter 6
Accessibility

The Web has the potential to more fully integrate people with seeing, hearing, physical, learning, and other disabilities into society. By limiting the interaction necessary to communicate, as well as enabling delayed communications so that participants can move at their own pace, the Web has transformed our relationships with one another. Properly designed web pages neither know nor care whether you're reading them with a CRT or a screen reader. Properly designed forms neither know nor care whether you're inputting data with a keyboard, a mouse, or voice recognition software.

However, accessibility does not come automatically. Many pages are locked into one modality of use, most commonly visual. Many pages are designed with the assumption that the user will view the page in the same way the designer does. Such pages can lock out people with different levels of eyesight, attention, motor skills, and a dozen other characteristics.

Accessibility is not just about supporting people with extreme physical impairments such as blindness either. Ability and accessibility are both continuums. People don't merely see or not see. They see better or worse. Most of us see worse with age. By age 40, we've either discovered the Ctrl-+ keyboard shortcut for increasing the font size of our browser or we've begun to curse 20-something web designers as we surf (or both). The changes you make to improve accessibility don't just help people who meet the legal definition of *disabled*. They help everyone whose seeing, hearing, or motor skills are less than perfect. At least some of the time, that's all of us. If it isn't today, it will be tomorrow. As we age, eyesight and motor skills decline, and accessibility becomes more important. When I started on the web, college students represented a majority of the population on the Net. Today they're probably less than 10%, and they are vastly outnumbered by senior citizens.

Accessibility also improves your site for people accessing it with nontraditional devices. A 28-year-old Wall Street trader may prefer to view your news through the small screen of her BlackBerry. Even an airline pilot with 20/20 vision may as well be blind when listening to your page on his cell phone while jogging.

Of course, accessibility isn't just about supporting people with physical or device impairments. Wheelchair ramps are far more commonly used by parents with strollers, students with bicycles, and delivery people with hand trucks than they are by people in wheelchairs. When properly done, increasing accessibility for the disabled increases accessibility for everyone. That's as true on the World Wide Web as it is in the physical world.

In many jurisdictions, accessibility is not just a good idea. It's the law. In the United States, the Americans with Disabilities Act requires that all web sites built or procured by the federal government be accessible to users without regard for physical handicap. In the United Kingdom, the Disability Discrimination Act imposes similar requirements, and many other nations either already or soon will have equivalent laws.

If all that isn't enough to convince you that it's important to invest time and resources in making your pages accessible, consider this. The most profoundly disabled user of your page is going to be a search engine robot. Robots can't see, hear, touch, or think. They are unbelievably stupid. Although a person can eventually make sense out of a strange layout or text encoded in an image, a robot never will. Almost everything you do to make your pages more accessible to and usable by people will be paid back tenfold in search engine optimization.

Simply making documents valid XHTML makes documents a lot more accessible than they otherwise would be. Making them strict XHTML rather than transitional goes even further. Removing presentational elements such as b and replacing them with semantic elements such as `strong` helps a little. Separating the content from the presentation using CSS stylesheets helps a lot.

However, that's the beginning of accessibility, not the end. If you aren't careful, you can create completely valid but almost totally inaccessible pages. Validation is an automatic and unthinking process. It focuses purely on the syntax. It can't tell whether you've chosen green or red text that will be impenetrable to many color-blind visitors. It doesn't know that the first 20 KB of your page are advertising and navigation that blind users have to slog through before getting to the actual content. It can't distinguish between a well-designed data table containing monthly financials and a layout table that rearranges the linear flow of text into unintelligible gibberish.

Making web sites accessible requires applying human intelligence to recognize and then fix problems such as these. As usual, tools are available that can help. The W3C HTML validator discussed in Chapter 2 notes many accessibility problems as well as pure well-formedness and validity errors. Other tools are available that check more deeply for accessibility. The W3C maintains a list of many such tools at www.w3c.org/WAI/ER/tools/complete/. These tools are helpful, but they are relatively stupid. They may find problems a validator won't, such as green text on a red background, and they may suspect that certain tables are likely being used for layout. However, they don't know this, and there are many problems they will never find. You must spend some time looking at the site with accessibility in mind.

Accessibility is ultimately about people, not about following a fixed set of rules. If your site is open and accessible to all users, you've done your job, even if you've violated a rule here or there. If your site is confusing and hard to use, you haven't, even if it validates and passes all the automated checks. To really tell how well you've succeeded, you have to do user testing. Observe real people navigating your site. Watching even a single user will reveal problems you didn't know you had. Time and budget permitting, you should observe many people, and include users with different skill sets and abilities. Watching a senior citizen navigate your site will tell you very different things than watching a teenager. Watching a blind user navigate with a screen reader will reveal issues you won't encounter with a sighted user. Try to test as many different classes of users as you can. Even if your budget does not permit formal user testing, do some informal testing by recruiting your friends, family, and coworkers for simple tests.

Sometimes even seeing the difficulties other users experience isn't enough. We have to experience them for ourselves. If you do not have easy access to blind users, you can simulate their experience. First, try to surf your site through the text mode browser Lynx. Second, try using a voice browser. Turn off your monitor and surf your own site. If you use a Mac, VoiceOver is built in (though it does take some time to get used to). However, most blind users prefer the more powerful pay-ware Windows program, JAWS. Either one will give you a decent approximation of how a blind user views your site. Next, turn the monitor back on, disconnect the mouse and the keyboard, and try to navigate with voice recognition. This will help to teach you how some physically disabled people will approach the site and where their pain points are likely to be.

Web-site accessibility is still quite poor, and in 2008 there's no excuse for that. Most users are inconvenienced, some critically so. However, there are some simple changes and improvements you can make to the design of your sites to improve matters.

Convert Images to Text

Replace any images that contain text with the text they contain, along with the markup and CSS rules that mimic the styling.

```
<img src="logo.gif" width="200" height="200"
     alt="Welcome to TIC!" />
```

```
<h1 style="font-family: Verdana; font-size: 18pt;
           font-weight: bold">Welcome to TIC!</h1>
```

Motivation

Visually impaired users can't see images, but they can hear text with a screen reader or feel it with a Braille printer. An alt attribute helps, but it is not a substitute for real, marked-up text.

Converting images to text dramatically improves search engine optimization. Search engines pay a lot of attention to text and relatively little to images. They pay special attention to text that appears early in the document and in headings. Thus, it's particularly important to make sure that headings are real text, not images or word art.

Replacing images with text also improves web-site performance, especially over slow or overloaded connections. It will save you bandwidth costs and save your readers time.

Potential Trade-offs

The text will likely not look exactly like it was mocked up in Photoshop, even after you've styled it with CSS. Furthermore, its appearance is likely to change slightly from one person to the next depending on their operating system, fonts installed, default fonts chosen, and browser. Readers almost never care about this, but sometimes designers do.

This may also bother the company lawyers in the very specific case of trademarked logos. If the lawyers cannot be reasoned with, keep the logos as `img` elements (with appropriate `alt` attributes), but change all other text images to real text.

Mechanics

Begin by looking at your pages to see where text is hidden inside images. Start at the home page and work your way through the site. If you're uncertain whether something is or isn't text, try to select the individual letters. If you can, it's text. If you can't, it's an image. Alternatively, right-click on the suspect text and see whether you have an option to View Image, Save Picture As, or some such thing. If you can do this, it's a picture, not text.

Once you've ascertained that you're dealing with an image rather than text, you need to replace the image with text, while retaining as much of the formatting as possible. Fortunately, CSS gives you a lot of power. CSS can easily change the colors of the foreground and background of the text. Indeed, with a CSS background image you may be able to use the same background picture the text has. You'll also be able to adjust font styles and weights: Make the text bold or italic, and so forth. CSS can specify the same font that was used in the image, though not all browsers may have that font installed, and many readers may have to substitute a slightly different font.

For example, on the Addison-Wesley home page, I found the logo shown in Figure 6.1.

FIGURE 6.1   The Addison-Wesley logo

We can actually reproduce this fairly well using HTML+CSS, as shown in Listing 6.1.

LISTING 6.1   Addison-Wesley Logo in HTML and CSS

```
<div style="width: 84px; height: 64px;">
<div style="background-color: #3D468B;
            color: white;
            font-family: Helvetica, sans-serif;
            font-size: 10pt;
            text-align: center;
            padding-top: 4px;
            padding-bottom: 3px;
            border-bottom-style: solid;
            border-bottom-width: medium;
            border-bottom-color: #FBE537;
            letter-spacing: 0.08em">
PEARSON
</div>
<div style="background-color: #327BBF;
            color: white;
            padding-left: 0.5em;
            padding-top: 6px;
            font-family: Times, serif;
            font-size: 12pt;">
<div>
Addison
</div>
<div style="text-indent: 1.5em;
            padding-bottom: 5px;">
Wesley
</div>
</div>
</div>
```

Figure 6.2 shows the rendered result.

FIGURE 6.2   The Addison-Wesley logo re-created in HTML+CSS

We can do even better if we allow ourselves to use background images, as shown in Listing 6.2 and Figure 6.3. Now we get the swoosh and everything.

LISTING 6.2   Addison-Wesley Logo in HTML and CSS with Background Image

```
<div style="width: 84px; height: 64px;
            background-image: url('background-logo.gif')">
<div style="color: white;
            font-family: Helvetica, sans-serif;
            font-size: 10pt;
            text-align: center;
            padding-top: 4px;
            padding-bottom: 3px;
            letter-spacing: 0.08em">
PEARSON
</div>
<div style="color: white;
            padding-left: 0.5em;
            padding-top: 6px;
            font-family: Times, serif;
            font-size: 12pt;">
<div>
Addison
</div>
<div style="text-indent: 1.5em;
            padding-bottom: 5px;">
Wesley
</div>
</div>
</div>
```

Unlike the original img tag, the background image is purely presentational. Although I've included the style rules inline here for illustration, they should be moved into an external CSS stylesheet. The HTML document would then have pure content, no decoration. Nonetheless, the

FIGURE 6.3   The Addison-Wesley logo drawn in pure HTML, plus background image

result shown in Figure 6.3 is equally attractive. You'd really have to compare the two side by side to notice any difference at all.

Fancier tricks, such as running the text along a curve or making the type jump around like ransom notes, may not succeed. To be honest, though, I'm not sure I'd want that. Simpler is often better.

Machines cannot reliably read printed text, especially the heavily stylized text you find in images on many web sites. Thus, there's no way to fully and reliably automate this process. However, you easily can search through the site for the filename to find the pages where you'll need to replace an image with text. For example, on the Addison-Wesley home page, I noticed the image is in the file aw-logo.gif. Therefore, I would search for aw-logo.gif to find other HTML files where I need to make the same change.

Add Labels to Form Input

Make sure each nonhidden `input`, `textarea`, `select`, or other form element has an associated label.

```
Red-necked Grebe
<input name="rng" type="checkbox"/>
```

```
<label>Red-necked Grebe
  <input name="rng" type="checkbox"/>
</label>
```

Motivation

Visually impaired users with screen readers cannot always use the two-dimensional layout of a page to determine which labels go with which fields. It is important to explicitly tag each nonhidden field with a label so that it is properly identified by screen readers.

There are more visually impaired users than you might think. This includes not only physically blind users, but also people using cell phone browsers while driving, and others who may not be able to immediately look at the screen but can listen to it. This class of user is set to grow significantly over the next few years.

Adding explicit `label` elements, possibly with `id` and `class` attributes, will also make it easier to style the labels with CSS or provide additional hints with JavaScript or smarter browsers. For example, a browser might highlight the associated label when the user tabs or clicks into an input field.

Potential Trade-offs

None. This should not affect your existing layout for most users and will improve it for some.

Because you're introducing new elements and changing the parents of some elements, a few programs that access the DOM or use XPath may need to be updated. However, such programs are uncommon.

Mechanics

For every form `input`, `select`, or `textarea` element, there must be at least one `label` element. (I tend to think there should be exactly one, but multiple labels are allowed.) The `label` element can either enclose the input element or have a `for` attribute that contains the ID of the element it refers to.

Consider a typical login form:

```
<form action="login.php" method="post">
<p>Username:
  <input type="text" name="log" id="log" size="18" />
```

```
</p>
<p>Password:
  <input type="password" name="pwd" id="pwd" size="18" />
</p>
<p>
  <input name="stayloggedin" type="checkbox"
         id="stayloggedin" value="remember" />
  Remember me on this computer
</p>
<p class="submit">
  <input type="submit" name="submit" id="submit"
         value="Login" />
  <input type="hidden" name="redirect" value="admin.php" />
</p>
</form>
```

Some of the labels appear on the left, and some appear on the right. This is a very simple form with just four visible elements, so chances are a blind user could figure out which text labels go with which input fields. However, the more complex the form gets, the harder it becomes to match the text to the right elements. Indeed, if the form begins to depend too heavily on the layout of one particular browser at one screen size, it may become challenging even for fully sighted users. All too often, I've seen forms where the labels get pushed away from the fields they describe because my font size or window size isn't quite what the designers expected.

Fixing this is not hard. The simplest approach is merely to enclose each input field and its associated description in a `label` element, like so:

```
<form action="login.php" method="post">
<p><label>Username:
  <input type="text" name="log" id="log" size="18" />
</label></p>
<p><label>Password:
  <input type="password" name="pwd" id="pwd" size="18" />
</label></p>
<p><label>
  <input name="stayloggedin" type="checkbox"
         id="stayloggedin" value="remember" />
  Remember me on this computer</label>
</p>
<p class="submit">
  <input type="submit" name="submit" value="Login" />
</p>
</form>
```

You do not need to label hidden fields with predefined values, because these are not meant to be seen by anybody. However, you can if you wish.

Sometimes the descriptive text is not immediately next to the form field. In these cases, it's most important to label the field description. Each form field should have an `id` attribute by which it is uniquely identified. The `label` element can be placed in any convenient location in the document. Its `for` attribute points to the `id` of the associated field. For example, this form puts the labels in separate paragraphs so that they appear above their fields rather than adjacent to them:

```
<form action="login.php" method="post">
<p><label for="log">Username: </label></p>
<p><input type="text" name="log" id="log" size="18" /></p>
<p><label for="pwd">Password: </label></p>
<p><input type="password" name="pw" id="pw" size="8" /></p>
<p><label for="stayloggedin ">
Remember me on this computer</label></p>
<p><input name="stayloggedin" type="checkbox"
        id="stayloggedin" value="remember" /></p>
<p class="submit">
  <input type="submit" name="submit"
      id="submit" value="Login" />
</p>
</form>
```

Of course, you can do both—include the input field directly inside the `label` element and use a `for` attribute:

```
<form action="login.php" method="post">
<p><label for="log">Username:
  <input type="text" name="log" id="log" size="18" />
</label></p>
<p><label for="pwd">Password:
  <input type="password" name="pwd" id="pwd" size="18" />
</label></p>
<p><label for="stayloggedin ">
  <input name="stayloggedin" type="checkbox"
        id="stayloggedin" value="remember" />
  Remember me on this computer</label>
</p>
<p class="submit">
  <input type="submit" name="submit" id="submit" value="Login" />
</p>
</form>
```

I'm not sure this is really necessary, but it doesn't hurt, and it might help some tool somewhere.

Introduce Standard Field Names

Rewrite your forms and form processing scripts to use conventional names for conventional things such as e-mail addresses, credit card numbers, phone numbers, and so forth.

```
<form action="/register" method="post">

<p>Salutation:
<label><input type="radio" name="n1" value="m" />  Mr.</label>
<label><input type="radio" name="n2" value="f" />  Ms.</label>
</p>

<p><label>First Name:
<input type="text" name="n3" />
</label></p>

<p><label>Last Name:
<input type="text" name="n4" />
</label></p>

<p><label>E-Mail Address:
<input type="text" name="e1" />
</label></p>

<p><label>Password:
<input type="password" name="p1"  />
</label></p>

<p><label>Address Line 1:
<input type="text" name="a1"  />
</label></p>
<p><label>Address Line 2:
<input type="text" name="a2" />
</label></p>
<p><label>City:
<input type="text" name="a3" />
</label></p>
<p><label>State/Province:
<input type="text" name="a4" />
</label></p>
<p><label>ZIP/Postal Code:
<input type="text" name="a5" /></label></p>
```

```
<p><label>Voice:
<input type="text" name="t1" />
</label></p>
<p><label>Fax:
<input type="text" name="t2" />
</label></p>

<input type="submit" title="Register" />

</form>
```

```
<form action="/register" method="post">
<p>Salutation:
<label><input type="radio"
   name="Ecom_BillTo_Postal_Name_Prefix" value="m" />  Mr.</label>
<label><input type="radio"
   name="Ecom_BillTo_Postal_Name_Prefix" value="f" />  Ms.</label>
</p>

<p><label>First Name:
<input type="text" name="Ecom_ShipTo_Postal_Name_First" />
</label></p>

<p><label>Last Name:
<input type="text" name="Ecom_ShipTo_Postal_Name_Last" />
</label></p>

<p><label>E-Mail Address:
<input type="text" name="Ecom_ShipTo_Online_Email" />
</label></p>

<p><label>Password:
<input type="password" name="Ecom_User_Password"  />
</label></p>

<p><label>Address Line 1:
<input type="text" name="Ecom_ShipTo_Postal_Street_Line1"  />
</label></p>
<p><label>Address Line 2:
<input type="text" name="Ecom_ShipTo_Postal_Street_Line2" />
</label></p>
<p><label>City:
<input type="text" name="Ecom_ShipTo_Postal_City" />
</label></p>
<p><label>State/Province:
<input type="text" name="Ecom_ShipTo_Postal_StateProv" />
</label></p>
```

(continued)

```
<p><label>ZIP/Postal Code:
<input type="text" name="Ecom_ShipTo_Postal_PostalCode" />
</label></p>

<p><label>Voice:
<input type="text" name="Ecom_ShipTo_Telecom_Phone_Number" />
</label></p>
<p><label>Fax:
<input type="text" name="fax" />
</label></p>

<input type="submit" title="Register" />
</form>
```

Motivation

A browser can autofill much information, even on a form it's never encountered before, if the form uses standard names for input fields. This helps all of us who hate to waste time retyping repetitive content. However, it's especially helpful to physically impaired users (including the very young and very old) who have much greater difficulty typing than average.

You're also more likely to collect accurate and correct information if the browser automatically fills in the values than if the user types them. Not only is the browser less likely to make random typos, but many users actively fake the information they input into many web forms.

Potential Trade-offs

You'll probably have to rewrite some back-end code to support this.

You may also need to introduce an additional level of indirection if the database or program that receives data from the form uses the field names in its own code. This is probably a net positive, though, because it will increase the flexibility of the back-end code.

Mechanics

Search your forms for common input. In particular, look for the following:

- Personal names
- Contact information: snail mail addresses, telephone numbers, e-mail addresses
- Credit card details: number, name, expiration date, billing address, and so on
- Usernames and passwords

All of these can use standard field names that browsers can recognize and that are defined in RFC 3106. For example, the first line of the street address should be named `Ecom_ShipTo_Postal_Street_Line1`. The city for the billing address should be named `Ecom_BillTo_Postal_City`. These field names are defined by RFC 3106 and are summarized in Table 6.1. Yes, the names are a little unwieldy, but users won't see them. It's worth imposing a small extra burden on the site's developers to assist users in this way.

Most of these fields have a certain minimum length that's allowed. Some have other constraints. For example, the currency field should be ready to accept an ISO currency code such as USD or GBP.

Not all fields fit into this scheme. For instance, there's no standard name for a fax number. That's fine. Most forms collect some unique and original information. Not everything needs to have a standard name. However, you should enable the browser to autofill as much as possible.

You'll need to make any changes to field names in at least two places: the form itself and the server-side program that receives input from the form. If the form is a heavy user of JavaScript, as many forms are, you'll need to update the scripts as well to use the new names.

Many autofill tools can also recognize standard labels, as well as field names. In many cases, the name and the label will be the same, perhaps modulo a small case change. However, because the label is user-visible, you'll often want to customize or translate it, rather than using the standard field names. By contrast, the field name is invisible and irrelevant to the end-user.

If these names are too much to stomach, most autofill tools will recognize reasonable variations of them. For instance, you may be able to use `PostalCode` instead of `Ecom_ReceiptTo_Postal_PostalCode`.

TABLE 6.1   Standard Field Names

Name	Meaning	Minimum Length
Ecom_ShipTo_Postal_Name_Prefix	Ship to title	4
Ecom_ShipTo_Postal_Name_First	Ship to first name	15
Ecom_ShipTo_Postal_Name_Middle	Ship to middle name	15
Ecom_ShipTo_Postal_Name_Last	Ship to last name	15
Ecom_ShipTo_Postal_Name_Suffix	Ship to name suffix	4
Ecom_ShipTo_Postal_Company	Ship to company name	20
Ecom_ShipTo_Postal_Street_Line1	Ship to street line1	20
Ecom_ShipTo_Postal_Street_Line2	Ship to street line2	20
Ecom_ShipTo_Postal_Street_Line3	Ship to street line3	20
Ecom_ShipTo_Postal_City	Ship to city	22
Ecom_ShipTo_Postal_StateProv	Ship to state/province	2
Ecom_ShipTo_Postal_PostalCode	Ship to ZIP/postal code	14
Ecom_ShipTo_Postal_CountryCode	Ship to country	2
Ecom_ShipTo_Telecom_Phone_Number	Ship to phone	10
Ecom_ShipTo_Online_Email	Ship to e-mail	40
Ecom_BillTo_Postal_Name_Prefix	Bill to title	4
Ecom_BillTo_Postal_Name_First	Bill to first name	15
Ecom_BillTo_Postal_Name_Middle	Bill to middle name	15
Ecom_BillTo_Postal_Name_Last	Bill to last name	15
Ecom_BillTo_Postal_Name_Suffix	Bill to name suffix	4
Ecom_BillTo_Postal_Company	Bill to company name	20
Ecom_BillTo_Postal_Street_Line1	Bill to street line1	20
Ecom_BillTo_Postal_Street_Line2	Bill to street line2	20
Ecom_BillTo_Postal_Street_Line3	Bill to street line3	20
Ecom_BillTo_Postal_City	Bill to city	22
Ecom_BillTo_Postal_StateProv	Bill to state/province	2
Ecom_BillTo_Postal_PostalCode	Bill to ZIP/postal code	14
Ecom_BillTo_Postal_CountryCode	Bill to country	2
Ecom_BillTo_Telecom_Phone_Number	Bill to phone	10
Ecom_BillTo_Online_Email	Bill to e-mail	40

TABLE 6.1   Standard Field Names *(Continued)*

Name	Meaning	Minimum Length
Ecom_ReceiptTo_Postal_Name_Prefix	Receipt to title	4
Ecom_ReceiptTo_Postal_Name_First	Receipt to first name	15
Ecom_ReceiptTo_Postal_Name_Middle	Receipt to middle name	15
Ecom_ReceiptTo_Postal_Name_Last	Receipt to last name	15
Ecom_ReceiptTo_Postal_Name_Suffix	Receipt to name suffix	4
Ecom_ReceiptTo_Postal_Company	Receipt to company name	20
Ecom_ReceiptTo_Postal_Street_Line1	Receipt to street line1	20
Ecom_ReceiptTo_Postal_Street_Line2	Receipt to street line2	20
Ecom_ReceiptTo_Postal_Street_Line3	Receipt to street line3	20
Ecom_ReceiptTo_Postal_City	Receipt to city	22
Ecom_ReceiptTo_Postal_StateProv	Receipt to state/province	2
Ecom_ReceiptTo_Postal_PostalCode	Receipt to ZIP/postal code	14
Ecom_ReceiptTo_Postal_CountryCode	Receipt to country	2
Ecom_ReceiptTo_Telecom_Phone_Number	Receipt to phone	10
Ecom_ReceiptTo_Online_Email	Receipt to e-mail	40
Ecom_Payment_Card_Name	Name on card	30
Ecom_Payment_Card_Type	Card type	4
Ecom_Payment_Card_Number	Card number	19
Ecom_Payment_Card_Verification	Card verification value	4
Ecom_Payment_Card_ExpDate_Day	Card expire date day	2
Ecom_Payment_Card_ExpDate_Month	Card expire date month	2
Ecom_Payment_Card_ExpDate_Year	Card expire date year	4
Ecom_Payment_Card_Protocol	Card protocols	20
Ecom_ConsumerOrderID	Consumer order ID	20
Ecom_User_ID	User ID	40
Ecom_User_Password	User password	20
Ecom_SchemaVersion	Schema version	30
Ecom_WalletID	Wallet ID	40
Ecom_TransactionComplete	End transaction flag	
Ecom_Merchant	Merchant home domain	128

TABLE 6.1   Standard Field Names *(Continued)*

Name	Meaning	Minimum Length
Ecom_Processor	Processor home domain	128
Ecom_Transaction_ID	Transaction identifier	128
Ecom_Transaction_Inquiry	Transaction URL inquiry	500
Ecom_Transaction_Amount	Transaction amount	128
Ecom_Transaction_CurrencyCode	Transaction currency	3
Ecom_Transaction_Date	Transaction date	80
Ecom_Transaction_Type	Transaction type	40
Ecom_Transaction_Signature	Transaction signature	160
Ecom_TransactionComplete	End transaction flag	

You might even discover that `zip` or `zip_code` works for some users. However, support will vary among autofill tools and even among users, depending on which other forms they've already filled in. It's best to use the names in Table 6.1 if at all possible. Even if it's not, stay away from meaningless names such as `field4` and `q17a`.

Turn on Autocomplete

Remove `autocomplete="off"` attributes where appropriate.

```
<form action="/login" method="post" autocomplete="off">

<p><label>E-Mail Address:
<input type="text" name="e1" autocomplete="off"/>
</label></p>

<p><label>Password:
<input type="password" name="p1"  />
</label></p>
```

```
<input type="submit" title="Login" autocomplete="off"/>

</form>
```

```
<form action="/login" method="post" autocomplete="off">

<p><label>E-Mail Address:
<input type="text" name="e1" />
</label></p>

<p><label>Password:
<input type="password" name="p1"  />
</label></p>

<input type="submit" title="Register" />

</form>
```

Motivation

Autocompletion helps users avoid wasting time retyping repetitive content. It's especially helpful to physically impaired users (including the very young and very old) who have much greater difficulty typing than average.

Autocompletion also improves security in login forms by avoiding the need for users to write down passwords or to reuse the same password from site to site. Login forms that prevent users from using autocomplete are far more likely to be compromised by out-of-band mechanisms such as shoulder surfing.

Potential Trade-offs

Many webmasters believe that autocompleting logins is a security risk. Indeed, it may be so on a shared computer, such as one in a public library. However, only the end-user can determine whether their computer is shared. Users are always free not to remember a username or password or to tell the browser to forget stored information, if they use a shared computer. That being said, I do recommend that lab managers configure their computers to forget all stored information (not just forms, but also cookies, bookmarks, history, and other potentially private data) between browser restarts.

Mechanics

Search your HTML pages for `autocomplete="off"`. This can appear on the `form` element or on individual `input` elements. When you find it, consider whether this is really appropriate.

Some forms really do expect different input each time. For instance, the main query field in a search engine likely doesn't see a lot of repeated content from the same user, or at least not enough to make autocomplete helpful. Most users search for something different every time they visit. These forms may legitimately use `autocomplete="off"`. Therefore, you should not perform a blanket search and replace that removes all `autocomplete="off"` attributes.

However, in the vast majority of cases, `autocomplete="off"` merely inconveniences users for little or no good reason. If you're in doubt, remove it. The user never has to use autocompletion, but should not be prevented from doing so by the server's whim.

Add Tab Indexes to Forms

Add a `tabindex` attribute to every editable, nonhidden form control.

```
<form action="login.php" method="post">
<p><label>Username:
  <input type="text" name="log" size="18" />
</label></p>
<p><label>Password:
  <input type="password" name="pwd" size="8" />
</label></p>
<p><label>
  <input name="stayloggedin" type="checkbox"
         id="stayloggedin" value="remember" />
Remember me on this computer</label>
```

```
</p>
<p class="submit">
  <input type="submit" value="Login" />
</p>
</form>
```

```
<form action="login.php" method="post">
<p><label>Username:
  <input tabindex="1" type="text" name="log" size="18" />
</label></p>
<p><label>Password:
  <input tabindex="2" type="password" name="pwd" size="8"/>
</label></p>
<p><label>
  <input tabindex="3" name="stayloggedin" type="checkbox"
      value="remember" />
  Remember me on this computer</label>
</p>
<p class="submit">
  <input tabindex="4" type="submit" value="Login" />
</p>
</form>
```

Motivation

Keyboard navigation is greatly simplified if the user can tab from one control to the next. This is especially important on forms that will be used frequently—for example, by a data entry clerk. It is also important for users with lesser manual dexterity who aren't able to reliably or easily target fields with a mouse. However, even dexterous, one-time users expect to be able to tab between fields and will attempt to do so. Make sure that when they press the Tab key, the focus advances to the next logical field.

Potential Trade-offs

The proper tab order is not always obvious, and it may vary from one user to the next, especially in forms where input fields advance both horizontally across the screen and vertically down the screen. Nonetheless, any carefully considered and assigned tab order is likely to be better than the default order the browser guesses when no tab order is specified by a form.

Mechanics

Seven elements support the `tabindex` attribute:

- a
- area
- button
- input
- object
- select
- textarea

Unifying these is the fact that they are all some form of user input. Thus, each can have an explicit `tabindex` attribute.

The value of the `tabindex` attribute is an integer between 0 and 32,767. (If you have more than 32,768 of these elements, split the page. It's too large.) Tabbing begins with 1 (or the lowest positive value) and continues in order to the highest value.

On a page whose main purpose for existing is to get the user to fill out a form, it's reasonable to guess that the tabs should hit the form fields first. Give each form input element a `tabindex` attribute, ordered from start to finish, and make the submit button the last `tabindex`. I either don't assign tabindexes to links on such a page or I assign higher tabindexes to them than to the form fields so that they'll be tabbed through after the form.

In many forms, you need to consider not only the logical order of the fields, but also which fields are likely to be filled out. This is sometimes a hard call to make, but if a field is used only infrequently and is positioned off to the side, I sometimes leave it out of the tab order to enable the user to more quickly advance through the common fields.

The `tabindex` attribute has page scope. Consequently, you need to consider the logical order of the forms, links, and other controls on the page, not merely the order of controls within any one form. It may seem as though 32,767 is more indexes than you'll need, but it does allow you to do things such as assign numbers from 1 to 500 to the first form; 501 to 1,000 to the second; and so forth.

If your site does not currently use `tabindex` attributes, you can simply search for all input fields to find the fields you need to augment. If `tabindex` attributes are already in use on your site, you can use this regular expression pattern to find nonhidden input fields that don't yet have a `tabindex`:

```
<input/s+((id|class|title|style|dir|lang|value|type|src|size
|name|maxlength|checked|alt|align|accept|accesskey|onfocus
|onblur|onselect|onchange|onclick|ondblclick|onmousedown
|onmouseup|onmouseover|onmousemove|onmouseout|onkeypress
|onkeydown|onkeyup)\s*=\s*("[^"]+"|'[^']+')\s*)*>
```

You will need to consider each page individually to determine an appropriate tab order. There are no automated tools to help.

Several other elements also support the `tabindex` attribute, most notably `object` and `a`. I don't usually place `tabindex` attributes on a elements because the default beginning-to-end order is normally sufficient for links, especially on simple, linear pages. However, if you're faced with a page where less important links precede more important ones—for instance, links in a left sidebar precede links in the main content—you can add `tabindex` attributes to a elements as well.

It is especially important to assign explicit tabindexes on pages that mix links with form fields. Often, links are used to provide help or explanatory text about the form or its fields, and that's good. However, the tab order should always jump from one field to the next and should never hit any link in between them. If you use the default tab order, the user can easily tab into what they expect the next field to be, but will end up on a link instead. At best, this will be annoying when they begin to type and realize their text isn't showing up. At worst, a user will fail to submit crucial data because they typed it into a link instead of a field.

For example, consider the Brooklyn Public Library login form in Figure 6.4. A user will typically click the mouse in the Name field,

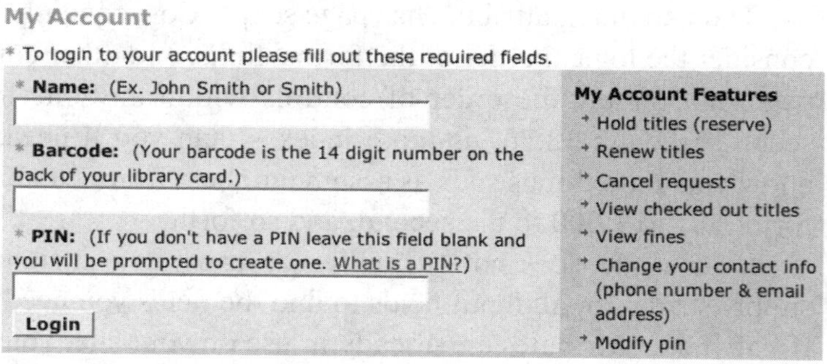

My Account

* To login to your account please fill out these required fields.

* **Name:** (Ex. John Smith or Smith)

* **Barcode:** (Your barcode is the 14 digit number on the back of your library card.)

* **PIN:** (If you don't have a PIN leave this field blank and you will be prompted to create one. <u>What is a PIN?</u>)

Login

My Account Features

* Hold titles (reserve)
* Renew titles
* Cancel requests
* View checked out titles
* View fines
* Change your contact info (phone number & email address)
* Modify pin

FIGURE 6.4   A form that mixes input fields and links

press Tab, fill out the barcode from a library card, press Tab, and then type in the PIN. Only the last tab doesn't actually place the cursor in the PIN field. Instead, the focus is on the "What is a PIN?" link, so the text is lost. The tab order should be explicitly specified so that the user advances directly from the Barcode field to the PIN field.

Introduce Skip Navigation

Place an "invisible" link at the beginning of each page that jumps straight to the main content on the page.

```
<body>
<div id="header">Blah blah blah</div>
<div id="leftnav">Blah blah blah</div>
<div id="main">Blah blah blah</div>
<div id="footer">Blah blah blah</div>
</body>
```

⬇

```
<body>
<div id="header">
<a href="#main"><img src="blank.png"
                alt="Jump to Main Content"
                width="1" height="1" tabindex="1"/></a>
```

```
Blah blah blah
</div>
<div id="leftnav">Blah blah blah</div>
<div id="main">Blah blah blah</div>
<div id="footer">Blah blah blah</div>
</body>
```

Motivation

Reading a site with a screen reader is hard enough without being forced to slog through a long sidebar or header on every page. Blind users really appreciate being able to jump straight to the unique content of each page.

Potential Trade-offs

None.

Mechanics

The first step is to identify the pages where skip links are likely to be helpful. On some sites with common sidebars and headers, this is pretty much every page. On other sites, it is only certain pages. The usual pattern is that a header or left sidebar, or both, precede the actual content of the page when viewed in HTML:

```
<div id="header">Blah blah blah</div>
<div id="leftnav">Blah blah blah</div>
<div id="main">Blah blah blah</div>
```

The visual layout of what comes first does not matter as much, though how much it matters can vary from one screen-reading program to another. (Some screen readers just follow the raw HTML. Others try to scrape the text off the screen after the browser has laid it out and rendered it.)

Regardless, a skip link right at the beginning is helpful. You can place this just inside or immediately preceding the first `div` on the page:

```
<div id="header">
  <a href="#main">Skip to main content</a> Blah blah blah
</div>

<a href="#main">Skip to main content</a>
<div id="header">Blah blah blah</div>
```

Whichever approach is more convenient for you is fine.

Some sites aren't bothered by the extra link at the top and just choose to show it to everyone. However, it's not hard to hide if you don't like it. The simplest approach is to set the CSS `display` property to `none`:

```
<a href="#main" style="display: none">Skip to content</a>
```

Like most things CSS, this is inconsistently supported across browsers, but it's not a big deal if a browser shows it anyway. More seriously, some screen readers may omit it, too.

The second approach is the perennial white-on-white trick (or whatever your background color happens to be). This trick is normally used for black-hat search engine optimization, but here we use it for a good cause. For example:

```
<a href="#main" style="color: white">Skip to content</a>
```

Again, this is not a perfect solution, but it's good enough most of the time.

My favorite variation is to make the link content a small image that matches the background color. Then place the text, such as "Skip to main content," in the `alt` attribute. This way, only screen readers will see it.

```
<a href="#main"><img src="blank.png"
                 alt="Skip to main content"
                 width="1" height="1"/></a>
```

Whether you display the link or not, the key is to make sure the page has one so that blind readers can skip to the main content. It's hard enough to listen to a page without being forced to listen to three minutes of navigation links from a sidebar.

Add Internal Headings

Place h1–h6 elements at reasonable breaks throughout long pages.

```
<div class="title">The Ungrammatical Times</div>
<div class="headline">Mill Employees Refuse to Work After
Death</div>
<div class="headline">First time offenders cut in
half</div>
```

```
<h1>The Ungrammatical Times</h1>
<h2>Mill Employees Refuse to Work After Death</h2>
<h2>First time offenders cut in half</h2>
```

Motivation

Assistive software enables both visually and physically impaired readers to jump to the next headline on a page with a single keystroke. However, this works only when those headings are identified with proper HTML markup.

Potential Trade-offs

You may need to rewrite the stylesheets for the page to restore the original look and feel. However, this shouldn't be hard.

Mechanics

There's no easy way to find mislabeled headings. They can be p elements, div elements, even span or dt elements. On most sites, though, the problems tend to be consistent from page to page. Once you've identified how a site is formatting headings, you can devise a search and replace to find and fix them. For instance, if a site has identified each heading as a `headline` class, it's simple to search for `class="headline"`.

One thing you may wish to consider is adding subheads to medium-to-long pages that don't already have them. Users of all abilities tend to scan pages rather than reading them from beginning to end. They zero in on only the sections they're most interested in. Descriptive subheads on the page make the scanning process easier.

Move Unique Content to the Front of Links and Headlines

Place the most important, most distinct content first in each heading and link.

```
<h1>Cheney Alleges Canada has Weapons of Mass
Destruction</h1>
<ul>
<li>Dick Cheney says Tuva Has Weapons of Mass
Destruction</li>
<li>Dick Cheney says Mexico Has Weapons of Mass
Destruction</li>
</ul>
<a href="finance.html">SuperPortal: Finance</a>
<a href="sports.html">SuperPortal: Sports</a>
<a href="news.html">SuperPortal: News</a>
```

```
<h1>Canada has Weapons of Mass Destruction, alleges
Cheney</h1>
<ul>
<li>Tuva Has Weapons of Mass Destruction,
    says Cheney</li>
<li>Mexico Has Weapons of Mass Destruction,
    says Cheney</li>
</ul>
<a href="finance.html">Finance SuperPortal</a>
<a href="sports.html">Sports: SuperPortal</a>
<a href="news.html">News: SuperPortal</a>
```

Motivation

Readers listening to a page with a screen reader scan by jumping from link, list item, or heading to the next item without listening to the entire item. Do not make readers listen to more than they have to in order to determine whether the link or headline is relevant to them.

Potential Trade-offs

On occasion, the language can become a little stilted, especially when complete sentences are involved.

Mechanics

Visually impaired users often scan pages by listening to the first two or three words of each successive link or heading. Those words have to count.

You can inspect easy link, heading, and table title to see whether it needs to be reordered. It's easy enough to write an XPath expression that will find all of these in any given document. For example:

```
//html:a | //html:h1 | // html:h2 | //html:h3 | //html:h4
| //html:h5 | //html:h6
```

A regular expression is not much harder:

```
<a\s+.*>.*</a> | <h([1-6])\s+.*>.*</h\1>
```

Fixing them, however, requires real human intelligence. Given the state of the art, this cannot be automated.

For each item, ask yourself whether the most important content comes first. For example, the heading "Johns Hopkins scientists find cure for cancer" should be rewritten as "Cancer cure found by Johns Hopkins scientists." The most important information is that a cure for cancer was found, not who found it. A sighted user may in fact pick up on that in the first form because the word *cancer* is likely to jump out at him even before he has read the sentence (especially if it's been emphasized with em or strong tags). However, a blind reader may hear the words "Johns Hopkins scientists" and jump to the next heading on the page because she's not all that interested in scientists or Johns Hopkins.

This inverted style of writing can, of course, be more than a little stilted and distracting when it occurs in the middle of body text. I don't customarily use it in links inside paragraphs and narrative text. However, it's very important for lists of links, such as tables of contents and the like. In these, the auditory user is going to scan down the page very, very quickly, listening to just two or three words of each item.

Consequently, one thing you should avoid at all costs is lists in which each item starts with the same two or three words. For example:

```
<ul>
  <li>Clothing: Shoes</li>
  <li>Clothing: Shirts</li>
  <li>Clothing: Pants</li>
  <li>Clothing: Belts</li>
  <li>Clothing: Accessories</li>
</ul>
```

The more words of text in common at the start of each link, heading, or list item, the more annoying this is. Rewrite all such lists as soon as possible, and then improve other links and headings as time permits.

Make the Input Field Bigger

Make sure all your forms have enough space for the user to comfortably type in the requested values.

```
<label>Subject:
  <input name="subject" id="subject" size="25"
       maxlength="240" type="text" /></label>
<label>Describe the problem:
  <textarea name="message" id="message" cols="40" rows="8">
  </textarea></label>
```

↓

```
<label>Subject:
  <input name="subject" id="subject" size="80"
       maxlength="240" type="text" /></label>
<label>Describe the problem:
  <textarea name="message" id="message"
          cols="80" rows="32">
  </textarea></label>
```

Motivation

There's nothing quite as frustrating as trying to write an essay in a 40-column by 20-row box. Make sure all text areas have enough space to allow the users to enter what they need to enter. It's better to have too large a box than too small.

Potential Trade-offs

Expanding a form's width may require some adjustment of the surrounding layout to provide more space for the form, especially on three-column pages, or pages with a sidebar on the right. However, it should have no effect on the back-end processing. Small text areas do not prevent users from entering large quantities of text. They just make it inconvenient for them to do so.

Mechanics

You can find many pages you need to check just by searching for `<textarea`. More often than not, the cols and rows fields that determine the size of the box are on the same line, and you can do quick visual inspection for the smallest ones. These are the ones you'll probably want to fix first.

The proper width and height may vary, depending on what you're asking the user to enter. A customer filling in a mailing address may only need six rows or fewer. A journalist filing an article may need hundreds. For width, I'm suspicious of anything less than 60 columns wide; 80 is probably a better choice. For text areas, the width is typically set by the `cols` attribute. The height is set by the `rows` attribute. For single-line input fields, the width is set by the `size` attribute. For text and password input, this size is measured in characters. For other types of input, the size is measured in pixels.

If an input field or a text area is by itself on a line (very common for text areas, not uncommon for input fields) or at least has no content to the right of it, it's often appropriate to allow it to expand horizontally. You can do this with CSS by specifying a percentage width that will override the default width. Usually somewhere between 80% and 100% is reasonable; 90% is often a good median value. This gives the user as much space as the browser has to give, and the browser window can be maximized if more space is required.

```
textarea { width: 90%; }
```

Height depends heavily on what information the form is requesting. However, 6 lines is usually the minimum I'd allow, and 12 are probably better for small amounts of text such as mailing addresses and brief messages. For serious writing, such as for web mail and blog comments, go taller: 20, 24, 36, or even 40 rows high. I don't suggest going so tall that the text area fills the page. It will scroll if it has to, and there's likely to be other content on the page that the user will want to see at the same time. However, it's simply easier to write when you have a larger window on your text rather than squinting at it through a four-line peephole. For example:

```
<textarea name="problems" id="problems"
        cols="80" rows="36" ></textarea>
```

If in doubt, err on the side of too much room rather than too little. It's no big deal if the user has some blank space in the form, but it's much more troublesome if they can't fit the text. Always allow for extra room. Many users will have different, larger fonts than you do, whether because of different platforms, different preferences, worse eyesight, or other reasons.

Introduce Table Descriptions

Add a caption element and/or a summary attribute to each table. Add a th element for each row or column label.

```
<table>
  <tr>
    <td>Species</td>
    <td>Spring</td>
    <td>Summer</td>
    <td>Fall</td>
    <td>Winter</td>
  </tr>
  <tr>
```

```
<td>Pied-Billed Grebe</td>
  <td>Uncommon</td>
  <td>Very rare</td>
  <td>Uncommon</td>
  <td>Fairly Common</td>
 </tr>
 <tr>
  <td>Mourning Dove</td>
  <td>Common</td>
  <td>Common</td>
  <td>Common</td>
  <td>Common</td>
 </tr>
 <tr>
  <td>Worm-eating Warbler</td>
  <td>Uncommon</td>
  <td>Rare</td>
  <td>Very rare</td>
  <td>Not Present</td>
 </tr>
</table>
```

```
<table summary="The Pied-billed grebe spends the winter.
 The Worm-eating Warbler passes through on migration,
 while the Mourning Dove is a year-round resident.">
 <caption>Species Frequency in Prospect Park</caption>
 <tr>
  <th scope="col">Species</th>
  <th scope="col">Spring</th>
  <th scope="col">Summer</th>
  <th scope="col">Fall</th>
  <th scope="col">Winter</th>
 </tr>
 <tr>
  <th abbr="pied-billed" scope="row">
     Pied-billed Grebe
  </th>
  <td>Uncommon</td>
  <td>Very rare</td>
  <td>Uncommon</td>
  <td>Fairly Common</td>
 </tr>
 <tr>
  <th abbr="mourning" scope="row">Mourning Dove</th>
  <td>Common</td>
  <td>Common</td>
<td>Common</td>
```

(continued)

```
    <td>Common</td>
  </tr>
  <tr>
    <th abbr="worm eating" scope="row">
      Worm-eating Warbler
    </th>
    <td>Uncommon</td>
    <td>Rare</td>
    <td>Very rare</td>
    <td>Not Present</td>
  </tr>
</table>
```

Motivation

Although tables are an excellent means of presenting certain kinds of data to sighted readers, they challenge blind readers who must access a page linearly. Consider the code immediately preceding this paragraph. Presented linearly in HTML, does it really make a lot of sense? This is how a blind user is likely to see it. Presented two-dimensionally as in Table 6.2, it's a lot easier to read.

Many sight-impaired users prefer to just get a quick summary of a table rather than trying to read the entire thing. When they do need to drill down into a table, it's very helpful to have marked-up headers for rows and columns that help them determine where they are.

Potential Trade-offs

Captions are shown to sighted users as well as users with screen readers. If you really don't want a caption, this can be a problem. In this case, you might choose to provide a `title` attribute instead.

TABLE 6.2   Species Occurrence

Species	Spring	Summer	Fall	Winter
Pied-billed Grebe	Uncommon	Very rare	Uncommon	Fairly common
Mourning Dove	Common	Common	Common	Common
Worm-eating Warbler	Uncommon	Rare	Very rare	Not present

However, even fully sighted users often prefer to be told what a table means rather than carefully inspecting the data for themselves. Indeed, often the table is really a reference for readers who want to know more, rather than something intended for everybody to read. A caption is usually a good addition for everyone, not just users listening to the page with a screen reader.

Mechanics

Neither the `caption` element nor the `summary` attribute is required by the XHTML strict DTD. You can search for `<table` to find all `table` elements and then quickly inspect them manually to see whether they need captions or summaries or both.

Some accessibility tools do notice if these are missing. Tidy will warn you about missing summaries and headers with this message:

> The table summary attribute should be used to describe the table structure. It is very helpful for people using nonvisual browsers. The scope and headers attributes for table cells are useful for specifying which headers apply to each table cell, enabling nonvisual browsers to provide a meaningful context for each cell.

However, human intelligence and effort are required to fill in the values for each additional summary and caption. There's no easy way around that.

The `caption` element contains marked-up text more fully describing the table. It can contain inline elements such as `strong` or `a`, but not block elements such as `p` or `div`.

The `summary` attribute contains plain text describing the table. However, the real difference between the two is that everyone sees the caption text, whereas usually only screen readers will notice the `summary` attribute. Because only users with screen readers are likely to read the `summary` attribute, it's usually the best place to put the most detailed prose description of the table's contents. The caption typically includes a less descriptive (though more marked-up) title that describes what's in the table without attempting to repeat the actual data.

If you don't include a caption in the table, you should add a `title` attribute to the table that serves as a caption for nonsighted readers. This is in addition to the summary. For example:

```
<table title="Species Frequency in Prospect Park"
  summary="The Pied-billed grebe spends the winter.
  The Worm-eating Warbler passes through on migration,
  while the Mourning Dove is a year-round resident.">
```

Of course, some sighted and nonsighted users alike are going to want to drill down into the table, at least some of the time. To assist with this, you should mark up each header in a `th` element rather than in a `td` element. This element can be used for both row and column headers and may appear anywhere a `td` element can appear. Browsers often style the header differently than a regular cell, and if they don't, CSS can. Furthermore, screen readers can repeat table headers as necessary to keep a listening user from getting lost in the table.

The `th` element is used for both row and column headers. To indicate which it is, each such element should have a `scope="row"` or `scope="col"` attribute. You can also set scope to `rowgroup` or `colgroup` to cover the group to which the header belongs. Visual browsers don't make much use of the `scope` attribute, but screen readers do.

In more complicated tables, it may not be possible to cleanly associate each `th` header with exactly one row or column. In this case, individual table cells (`td` elements) may each have a `headers` attribute that contains a whitespace-separated list of the IDs of the headers (`th` elements) that apply to that cell. A screen reader can read the names of the headers before reading the content of each cell.

Because screen readers do repeat table headers from time to time, each multiword header should have a shorter `abbr` attribute (not the same thing as an `abbr` element) that screen readers can use in preference to the full heading. The longer the heading is, the more important this becomes.

Finally, simplify your tables to the extent possible. Do not nest tables, and try to avoid columns and rows that span more than one cell. Even when a table is truly a data table and not a layout table, it still poses a challenge for screen readers and sight-impaired users. Complicated nested table markup can move difficult but possible-to-read content over the line into unintelligible.

Introduce Acronym Elements

Wrap abbr and acronym tags around abbreviations and acronyms.

```
<label>Subject:
Gleaning Resource Descriptions from Dialects of Languages
(GRRDL) defines Extensible Stylesheet Language
Transformations (XSLT) stylesheets that can transform
Hypertext Markup Language (HTML) documents into Resource
Description Framework (RDF) triples.
```

```
<acronym title="Gleaning Resource Descriptions from
Dialects of Languages">GRRDL</a> defines <abbr
title="Extensible Stylesheet Language
Transformations">XSLT</abbr>
stylesheets that can transform <acronym title="Hypertext
Markup Language">HTML</a> documents into <acronym
title="Resource Description Framework">RDF</acronym> triples.
```

Motivation

Screen readers need to know when they should try to pronounce an entire word and when they should just spell it out.

Not all your readers necessarily know all the acronyms that you use. Many browsers will show a tool tip to tell the reader what the acronym means if you mark it up appropriately in the source document. This avoids the need to explain everything for the larger portion of your audience who does know what the acronym means.

Potential Trade-offs

Some browsers put some really ugly dotted lines under marked-up acronyms and abbreviations. This also throws off the line spacing. However, you can counter this with CSS.

Mechanics

For purposes of HTML, an abbreviation is made up of the first letters of the words in a phrase. It is pronounced by spelling out the words. For example:

```
<abbr>BBC</abbr>
<abbr>GNP</abbr>
<abbr>IBM</abbr>
```

By contrast, an acronym is normally pronounced like a word, rather than by spelling it out. Examples include:

```
<acronym>NAFTA</acronym>
<acronym>GATT</acronym>
<acronym>Inc.</acronym>
```

These aren't quite the dictionary definitions of *abbreviation* and *acronym*—in fact, an acronym is really a type of abbreviation—but they do reflect how speech synthesizers decide to pronounce each unfamiliar abbreviation.

Each abbr or acronym element should have a `title` attribute that expands the abbreviation. For example:

```
<abbr title="British Broadcasting Corporation">BBC</abbr>
<abbr title="Gross National Product">GNP</abbr>
<abbr title="International Business Machines">IBM</abbr>
<acronym title
  ="North American Free Trade Agreement">NAFTA</acronym>
<acronym title="General Agreement on Tariffs and Trade">GATT</acronym>
<acronym title="Incorporated">Inc.</acronym>
```

Some browsers will show a small tool tip with the title if the user mouses over the element. One big benefit is that this avoids the need to explicitly define an acronym or abbreviation that 99% of people understand the first time you use it.

Introduce lang Attributes

Add `lang` and `xml:lang` attributes to each root element identifying the primary language of the document. Add superseding `lang` and `xml:lang` attributes to any element in that document that is written in a different language.

```
<html xmlns="http://www.w3.org/1999/xhtml">
<body>

<p>Pierre shouted, "Vive la France!"</p>

</body>
</html>
```

```
<html xmlns="http://www.w3.org/1999/xhtml"
      lang="en-US" xml:lang="en-US">
<body>

<p>Pierre shouted,
  "<span lang="fr" xml:lang="en-US">Vive la France!</span>"
</p>

</body>
</html>
```

Motivation

Proper language identification is important for pronunciation by screen readers.

Language identification also assists search engines. Your French pages are more likely to be picked up by google.fr and your German pages by google.de if the content is properly tagged.

Finally, language identification assists you when authoring pages, especially when working in something other than a system's primary language. It enables editors to choose the proper dictionary for spell checking.

Potential Trade-offs

None. This is only for the good.

Mechanics

If you know none of your documents already contains a `lang` or `xml:lang` attribute, and that they're all written in the same language, it's easy to search for `<html` and replace it with `<html lang='en' xml:lang='en'`.

If you aren't certain whether there are any such attributes already, try searching for `lang\s*=\s*['"a-zA-z]`. If nothing turns up, it's highly likely that there aren't any.

If you do find that some of your documents have such attributes already and some don't, the following regular expression should find most documents that do not have a `lang` or `xml:lang` attribute on their root `html` element:

```
<html\s+((id|class|dir|xmlns)\s*=\s*("[^"]+"|'[^']+')\s*)*>
```

This will find most cases you need to deal with.

The language codes themselves are standardized in the IANA Language Subtag Registry. Where possible, you should use the standard two-letter codes as shown in Table 6.3. This is an abbreviated list. You can find the full list at www.iana.org/assignments/language-subtag-registry.

Although there are many more codes than I've shown in Table 6.3, there are even more languages on the planet (about 6,000) than there are two-letter codes. Less common languages now use three-letter codes. For instance, Coptic has the code cop. There are also dialect subcodes you can use. For example, en-US is English as spoken in the United States, whereas en-GB is English as spoken in Great Britain. This might matter a little to search engines or spell checkers. However, getting this right is not nearly as important as identifying the primary language.

Although they are redundant, you should include both `lang` and `xml:lang` attributes, at least for now. Older browsers only recognize `lang`, and some generic XML tools only recognize `xml:lang`. Going forward, `lang` will be eliminated in XHTML 1.1 and `xml:lang` will be the only option. However, that is still a few years in the future, at least.

TABLE 6.3 Common Language Codes

Language	Code
Amharic	am
Arabic	ar
Czech	cs
German	de
Greek	el
English	en
Esperanto	eo
Spanish	es
French	fr
Hindi	hi
Indonesian	id
Italian	it
Japanese	ja
Korean	ko
Dutch	nl
Portuguese	pt
Russian	ru
Vietnamese	vi
Chinese	zh

Chapter 7
Web Applications

In Web 2.0, many sites aren't just static pages anymore, or even static pages plus a few forms to fill out. They're full-blown applications for data entry, word processing, calendar management, human resources, games, and anything else you can imagine. In this chapter, we focus on issues that specifically arise in improving such web applications.

Replace Unsafe GET with POST

Redesign unsafe operations so that they are accessed via POST rather than GET.

```
<a class="delete"
href="article.php?action=delete&amp;id=1000517&amp;nonce=76a62"
onclick="return deleteSomething('post', 1000517,
'You are about to delete this post &quot;POST vs.
GET&quot;.\n&quot;OK&quot; to delete,
&quot;Cancel&quot; to stop.'
);">Delete</a>
```

```
<form method="post" action="articles.php">
  <input name="action" value="delete" type="hidden" />
  <input name="id" value="1000517" type="hidden" />
  <input name="nonce" value="76a62" type="hidden" />
  <input type="submit" value="Delete" />
</form>
```

Motivation

URLs accessed via GET can be and are spidered, prefetched, cached, repeated, and otherwise accessed automatically. Unsafe operations such as confirming a subscription, placing an order, agreeing to a contract, and deleting a page should be performed only via POST to avoid accidentally taking such actions without explicit user request and consent.

Potential Trade-offs

Browser users can only access POST functionality through HTML forms. They cannot simply follow a link. To be honest, this is a feature, not a bug. However, it does tend to restrict the formatting you can apply to an operation.

You may also discover that some firewalls and proxy servers are configured to allow GET requests through but block POST requests. Thus, switching from GET to POST may prevent some people in high-security installations from accessing your site. Again, this is a feature, not a bug. HTTP is designed to enable network administrators to control their network traffic and separate safe requests from potentially unsafe ones. If the network administrator has chosen to block POST, that is their decision and right, not yours. Do not attempt to subvert other sites' security policies by tunneling POST through GET.

Mechanics

Consider each action on your site that is serviced by a script or program rather than a static file. In particular, look at URLs that include query strings. Ask yourself, "Would it bother me if Googlebot followed this URL?" For the moment, ignore the temptation to say, "Google could never find this" or "Google would not have the right user authentication cookies to be allowed in" or anything like that. Simply consider whether it would be a problem if Googlebot did somehow get in. Would it do anything you wouldn't want it to do?

Next, ask yourself what would happen if a real user got a timeout on a page and resubmitted the form. Would a credit card be charged twice? Would they have printed two copies of a book instead of one?

Would anything have happened that they did not want to happen and had not asked for?

If the answer to any of these questions is yes, the form should be using POST rather than GET. POST is intended for potentially unsafe operations. POST operations are not cached, bookmarked, prefetched, or even resent from the back button without an explicit user request. POST operations are at least sometimes dangerous and irrevocable. Consequently, user agents such as browsers take special care to make sure the user does not accidentally POST data without really meaning to. By contrast, URLs accessed via GET are commonly downloaded without any human intervention or consent whatsoever. They are for browsing, not buying. They should be safe and free of side effects.

The following operations should be done with POST:

- Purchasing an item
- Agreeing to a legal document
- Posting a comment on a blog
- Deleting a page from a content management system (CMS)
- Signing a petition
- Sending e-mail
- Inserting new content into a database
- Printing a map
- Controlling a machine

This is just a sample. There are many more.

By contrast, the following operations should be done with GET, because they are safe and do not obligate the reader:

- Reading a legal document
- Downloading an editable copy of a document from a CMS
- Reading e-mail
- Viewing a map
- Inspecting the current state of a machine

Again, this is just a sample. There are many more.

A few operations straddle the line. For example:

- Adding an item to a shopping cart (but not immediately purchasing it)
- Previewing a comment on a blog

I'd probably use POST for adding an item to a shopping cart simply because I don't want a browser to do this automatically. This may not commit the user to buy the item, but it still changes the state of the shopping cart. If an item were added automatically, the user would then have to remove the item from the cart.

Whether I implemented previewing as GET or POST might depend on implementation details and convenience. It would not be a problem for a browser to prefetch a preview or for someone to link to it. However, if the preview in some sense actually creates the comment resource but just doesn't allow it to be shown to the other users yet, POST is more appropriate.

Using GET where POST is called for can have potentially disastrous consequences. In the worst case I know of, Google deleted an entire government web site that had used GET for all operations.

Do not rely on cookies, nonces, hidden form fields, nonhidden form fields, JavaScript, HTTP authentication, referrer checking, or other tricks to hide the GET links from spiders. The Google web accelerator caused massive problems for many diverse web sites that weren't expecting users' browsers to begin following every link on the page. In this case, users were already logged in and had all necessary credentials to perform dangerous operations.

These are only the most famous examples. There have been many others over the years. The bottom line is this: HTTP is designed to clearly separate what you do with POST from what you do with GET. When you design web applications to use POST for what POST was designed for and GET for what GET was designed for, everything works and works well. When you mix them up and try to tunnel GET through POST or POST through GET, trouble ensues. You can spackle over the problems and spend your life putting out fires as one problem after another crops up, or you can use HTTP the way it was meant to be used.

If you do uncover any forms or links that are using GET where they should be using POST, fix them. The only client-side change that's usually needed is changing `method="get"` to `method="post"` on the `form` element.

If the unsafe operation is being triggered by a link, replace it with a form. You can use hidden fields to fill in the values of the query string variables. For example, suppose you have this link:

```
<a href="/admin.php?action=approve&amp;id=1798">Approve</a>
```

It has two fields: `action` with the value `approve`, and `id` with the value 1798. Each field in the query string becomes a hidden field in an equivalent form shown in Listing 7.1. The text of the link becomes the text on the submit button.

LISTING 7.1   Link Converted to a Form

```
<form method="post" action="/admin.php">
  <input type="hidden" name="action" value="approve" />
  <input type="hidden" name="id" value="1798" />
  <input type="submit" value="Approve" id="approve" />
</form>
```

Browsers will show a single button for this action. Some more modern browsers, including Firefox, let you style the button so that it looks more like a link with a CSS rule such as this one:

```
input#approve {
  border: none;
  background: white;
  color: blue;
  text-decoration: underline;
}
```

However, other browsers, including Safari, always show a button no matter what styles you apply. I think using a button instead of a link is no big deal. It's probably friendlier to users who associate buttons with taking an action and following links with simple surfing. However, if you really, really hate buttons, there's something else you can do. You can retain the original link but have it point to a page containing a confirmation form. No action is actually taken until the confirmation form is submitted, so the link can still use GET. The confirmation form uses

POST. This seems a little involved to me, but it does allow you to keep buttons off the main page and retain the overall look, feel, and layout of that page while still using the proper HTTP verbs.

On the server side, a little more work is usually required to switch from GET to POST, but not an excessive amount. The details of how you switch from GET to POST on the server side will vary depending on the environment in which your server-side programs are written. In most cases, though, it's straightforward. For instance, if you're using Java servlets, you can handle many cases merely by renaming the doPost() method to doGet(). The arguments and the logic are the same. If you're using PHP, you may well be able to just change $_GET['name'] to $_POST['name'].

The ease with which such frameworks enable one to switch between methods, combined with some bad early tutorials that were widely disseminated, has created a common antipattern in which scripts are written that accept requests via both GET and POST, and do the same thing in each case. This is dangerous and almost always a mistake. Most server-side programs should accept arguments via one or the other, not both.

It is possible to design a system in which a script takes different actions when you access it via GET or POST. For example, http://www.example.com/cars/comments might return a page with all the comments when you access it with GET and add a new comment to the page when you access it with POST. However, this pattern is uncommon in practice. Usually separate pages are set up to receive GET and POST requests.

Replace Safe POST with GET

Redesign safe operations so that they are accessed via GET rather than POST.

```
<form method="post" action="listarticles.php">
  <p><label>Display
    <input name="number" value="10" type="text" />
    articles </label></p>
```

```
<p><label>Sort by: <select name="sort">
  <option value="Reverse">Most recent first</option>
  <option value="Forward">Publication order</option>
  <option value="Author">By author</option>
  <option value="Title">By title</option>
</select></label></p>
<p><input type="submit" value="List articles" /></p>
</form>
```

```
<form method="get" action="listarticles.php">
  <p><label>Display
    <input name="number" value="10" type="text" />
    articles</label></p>
  <p><label>Sort by: <select name="sort">
    <option value="Reverse">Most recent first</option>
    <option value="Forward">Publication order</option>
    <option value="Author">By author</option>
    <option value="Title">By title</option>
  </select></label></p>
  <p><input type="submit" value="List articles" /></p>
</form>
```

Motivation

URLs that can be accessed with GET can be linked to, spidered, book-marked, prefetched, cached, printed in books, painted on the sides of buildings, and more. GET URLs enable the use of the back button. A GET operation is just overall friendlier to the user than a POST operation.

GET URLs are also friendlier to search engines, and they improve your site's search engine ranking. POST-only URLs are effectively invisible to spiders and search engines. Other sites and people can link to your GET URLs, which improves your traffic directly when people follow the links and indirectly when search engines notice the links and boost your page rank accordingly.

Finally, representations of GET URLs can be cached, which dramatically improves both client and server performance.

Potential Trade-offs

Done right, none. However, you do need to be careful that your operations are really free of side effects. Using GET where it's inappropriate can cause massive damage, up to and including the complete deletion of an entire site. However, it's not hard to understand when GET is and is not appropriate.

Due to caching, GET URLs may measure fewer hits than a page accessed via POST. This might mean less advertising revenue or budget. However, because GET URLs are so much more search-engine- and user-friendly, you'll more than make up for any reduced hits due to caches with increased hits due to actual visitors. Furthermore, some simple modifications of cache-control headers can eliminate this issue entirely, without using POST.

Mechanics

You should use GET for all operations that do not cause side effects. If following a URL simply results in the server transferring some data to the client and nothing else, GET is appropriate. Anything that can be thought of as simple browsing should be handled with GET, whether it's implemented with static files or with a server-side script. The distinction should be irrelevant to the browser. Ideally, users shouldn't be able to tell whether they're being served static files, live database queries, or cached database queries.

However, if a connection has major side effects, it should not be accessed with GET. For example, if the user is charged a penny for each page loaded or each image viewed, those pages should only be loaded with POST. Similarly, a user should read a contract with GET but only agree to it with POST.

Trivial side effects such as hit counters and log file entries don't need to be considered here. The real concern is that users not be obligated in any way by following a link and GETting a URL. They don't buy anything. They don't promise anything. They don't make anything happen. They're simply browsing through the store.

Query String Limits

There's a common myth that GET can be used only in cases where the data embedded in the query string will be less than 256 characters long. This was true a long time ago, but hasn't been true for at least ten years. All browsers from this millennium can easily handle URLs that are up to 2,000 characters long, and more modern ones go well past that limit.

The big problem is Internet Explorer, which as of Version 7 still cannot handle URLs longer than 2,083 characters. This should be long enough for most forms that do not collect free-form input from the user. Forms that do ask the user for unlimited amounts of text (comments on blogs, contact forms, etc.) can usually legitimately use POST anyway.

I have encountered a few cases where *very* long query strings broke a server-side framework (PHP 4 in particular). If this happens, you might temporarily use POST where GET is more appropriate. In the longer run, though, you should upgrade to a server framework that does not impose such arbitrary limits.

On the client side, changing a form to use GET instead of POST is easy. Simply change method="post" to method="get" on the form element. On the server side, details vary with framework, but the change is usually easier than it should be. (Most frameworks really don't care whether any given form is submitted via GET or POST, which has contributed to the myth that the difference doesn't matter. Indeed, some poorly written frameworks accept all forms with both methods by default.)

If you're using Java servlets, renaming the doPost() method to doGet() is often all you need to do. In PHP, you may have to do little more than replace $_POST['name'] with $_GET['name'] and carry on as though nothing else had changed. Scripts that pay attention to the URL by which they were invoked—for instance, by echoing the URL back to the user—may also wish to make a point of stripping off the old query string.

Replacing Forms with Links

The really big advantage of switching from POST to GET is that you no longer need to use forms at all. You can still use forms if you like, but you can also create static links that make particular queries. For example, consider the article list form from the beginning of this section. You can now make a link that finds the ten most recent articles:

```
<a href="article.php?sort=Reverse&amp;number=10">
  10 Most Recent Articles
</a>
```

Or you can make a link to the very first article:

```
<a href="article.php?sort=Forward&amp;number=1">
  The one that started it all
</a>
```

Furthermore, not only can you make links such as these, but other people who want to link to your site can mint these URLs, too. They can bookmark your pages and use these URLs in several other ways to drive traffic to you. None of that is possible with POST.

Of course, any such links you write must be properly encoded both according to XHTML's rules and according to URL rules. For XHTML, this means you must encode each & as `amp;`. Thus, a URL such as /article.php?sort=Reverse&number=10 is typed in the XHTML document as /article.php?sort=Reverse&number=10.

URLs further require that all non-ASCII characters as well as the space, the forward slash, the colon, the equals sign, and other nonalphanumeric characters that have special meaning in URLs be percent-encoded. For ASCII characters, this just means replacing the character with a percent sign followed by the hexadecimal value of the character. For example, the space is ASCII 32 in decimal and 20 in hex. Therefore, spaces encoded in your URLs are encoded as %20. The colon is ASCII character 58 in decimal and 3E in hex. Therefore, colons included in your query strings are encoded as %3E. Non-ASCII characters are first converted to individual UTF-8 bytes. Then each byte is percent-encoded.

This is the same encoding used by a browser before it submits a form to the server. One way to figure out the strings you need is simply to create a form that builds them, submit it, and copy the resulting URL out of the browser's location bar.

Redirect POST to GET

Redesign scripts that respond to POST requests to redirect browsers rather than serving the results directly.

```
HTTP/1.1 200 OK
Date: Tue, 08 Apr 2008 20:58:58 GMT
Server: Apache/2
X-Powered-By: PHP/5.2.0
Content-Length: 325
Content-Type: text/html; charset=UTF-8

<html>
<head><title>Order Accepted</title></head>
<body>
<h1>Invoice for your Records: Order #9878932479</h1>

…

<p>Please print a copy if you want to save it.</p>

</body>
</html>
```

```
HTTP/1.1 301 Moved Permanently
Date: Tue, 01 Jan 2008 22:39:42 GMT
Server: Apache/2
Location: http://www.example.com/order/9878932479
Connection: close
Content-Type: text/html; charset=UTF-8
```

Motivation

It's convenient to be able to bookmark, link to, and return to orders, invoices, quiz results, and the like. However, you can't do this with POST because the operation is unsafe. For example, bookmarking a

POST request to check out of a store might order the same items again when the bookmark was activated.

Instead, the server can respond to the initial POST by creating a new static resource for the order status. Instead of returning the status directly, the server redirects the client to this new static resource. Then the client can bookmark and return to that static resource whenever they like.

Potential Trade-offs

The server will need to save the results of POST requests for a reasonable period of time. They don't need to be saved forever if they're not relevant indefinitely. (How many people check on an order six years after it's been delivered anyway?)

Many of these results are at least somewhat private. You'll need to use the same level of authentication for retrieving the results as you do for submitting the form in the first place.

Mechanics

Implementing this requires an additional level of indirection for both client and server. When the client submits the form, do not immediately calculate the result and feed it back to them. Instead,

1. Process the user input.

2. Generate a response for the user and store it.

3. Assign a roughly random URL for the response.

4. Redirect the client to the response.

Of course, the details will depend on exactly how the form is normally processed. Processing the data submitted from the form is usually the same as when responding directly. If you store the data in a database, it's still stored in the database. If the input is e-mailed to someone, it's still e-mailed to someone. If it starts up a robot on the factory floor, it still starts the same robot on the factory floor.

The trick is the next step. We do not form the response HTML document in memory and send it directly to the client in the body of the

HTTP response. Instead, we form the HTML and save it somewhere: in a database, on the filesystem, on another server, or wherever is most convenient. Sometimes you'll save an actual complete HTML document. Other times you'll just save data that can be filled into a template later. If your server is mostly serving static HTML in the first place, static files are likely the simplest. If the server is database-backed and template-driven, storing the data for later insertion in a template is probably easier. The client won't know or care which approach you take.

Either way, you need to associate a URL with the data that can be used to find it later. If everything's in static files, the actual URL of the file is likely enough. Just pick a random name for that file. If the data is stored in the database, you'll probably need to add another table to map randomly chosen URLs to particular records. Either way, when the request comes in, the server will match the URL to what is stored and send out the appropriate document.

Finally, you send the client a 300-level HTTP response redirecting them to this new data. In this case, 301 Moved Permanently is usually what you want. This server will also have a Location header that points to the result document. For example, using Java servlets, some code along these lines would do the trick:

```
response.setStatus(HttpServletrequest.SC_MOVED_PERMANENTLY);
response.setContentType("text/html; charset=UTF-8");
response.addHeader("Location",
  "http://www.example.com/order/9878932479");
OutputStream out = response.getOutputStream();
Writer w = new OutputStreamWriter(out, "UTF-8");
w.write(
  "some HTML in case the browser doesn't follow the redirect");
w.flush();
w.close();
```

PHP, RAILS, and other frameworks have similar abilities.

When the browser receives the 301 response, it will GET the URL specified by the Location header. This page can then be bookmarked, linked to, and so forth. If this page contains private data, the server can require authentication just as it can with any other page. If it's very private, the Location header can redirect the browser to an https URL instead of an http URL. Because this is just a regular GET, it fits well into existing HTTP frameworks and tools on both the client and server sides.

Enable Caching

Apply cache control headers so that dynamically generated pages can also be cached when appropriate.

```
HTTP/1.1 200 OK
Date: Sun, 08 Apr 2007 20:58:58 GMT
Server: Apache/2
X-Powered-By: PHP/5.2.0
Content-Length: 325
Content-Type: text/html; charset=UTF-8
```

```
HTTP/1.1 200 OK
Date: Sun, 08 Apr 2007 20:58:58 GMT
Server: Apache/2
X-Powered-By: PHP/5.2.0
Cache-control: public
Last-Modified: Fri, 03 Dec 2004 11:53:03 GMT
ETag: "6548d4-30a9e-c7f4e5c0"
Content-Length: 325
Content-Type: text/html; charset=UTF-8
```

Motivation

Caching is a crucial part of web performance and scalability. Caching can take place at many levels: on the server with gateway proxies, between the client and the server in proxy servers, and in the browser itself through local history. The fewer connections the client makes and the more it can act on information it already has, the faster both the client and server can run.

Web servers' default configurations are fairly good at managing caches for static files, and you don't need to worry a lot about that. However, web applications that manage their own HTTP headers require more thought and care. Most especially, web applications accessed via POST and ones that make use of URL query strings must be especially considerate of cache control headers because much software does not cache the result of GET requests that use query strings or any POST request. However, by manipulating the HTTP header you can indicate to the client that it is acceptable to cache some of these.

Potential Trade-offs

Not everything should be cached. You do want to be careful before blindly allowing caching. Done wrong, caching can deliver stale information or expose users' private data.

Cacheable pages will measure fewer hits than unncacheable pages. If that's a major problem for you, the next section explains how to prevent caching, rather than enabling more of it. However, most sites benefit heavily enough from caching that they'd like more of it, not less.

You can also use the techniques in this section to enable caching of some resources but not others. For example, you might allow the main HTML pages to be cached but disallow caching of ads. That would enable more precise measurement of just how many people are seeing your ads.

Mechanics

Proxy servers such as AOL's use caches to improve local performance on their network. If 10,000 people request the *New York Times* home page between 6:00 a.m. and 7:00 a.m. every day, AOL has to load it from the *New York Times* only once. Then it can serve its local copy to all of its users. Individually, users often return to the same pages more than once. A browser that has gone to a page before can save time by reloading it from a local cache rather than downloading it from the network again. This saves everyone's bandwidth, reduces latency, and is an all around good thing. It is one reason the Web scales as well as it does.

Usually browsers, proxy servers, and other software cache documents only if the server indicates that's OK. The server does that by setting one or more of the following HTTP headers:

- Last-modified
- Expires
- ETag
- Cache-control

They do not cache documents if

- The document was loaded via https.
- The document required HTTP authentication.
- The document was received in response to a POST.

However, you can modify all of this using the Cache-control header.

If a browser or proxy has stored a document in its cache, it will serve it to a client if the document is not too old. If it is too old, it will first check with the server to see whether the document has changed. It does this using an HTTP HEAD request that does not require the server to send the entire document all over again. If the document has changed, the browser will download a fresh copy of the document. Otherwise, it will serve the document out of its cache.

Usually for static files you don't have to worry about this, as long as you aren't too picky about how long browsers cache documents. If you have frequently updated data, or high-performance requirements, you may want to play with the defaults; but more often than not the defaults are fine. However, content generated dynamically from PHP, JSP, ASP, CGI, and similar technologies requires you to provide the necessary headers to enable caching. Otherwise, the page won't be cached.

The easiest tag to send is `Last-modified`. When a client sees a Last-modified header a reasonable distance into the past, it assumes the page isn't updated every minute or two and makes a reasonable guess as to how long it can cache the page. In PHP, you can send this and all other headers with the `header` function like so:

```
header('Last-Modified: Thu, 05 Apr 2007 09:41:05 GMT');
```

You must call the `header` function *before* writing any other output to the client.

If you want to precisely specify when the cached copy should expire, you can send an Expires header instead of or in addition to the Last-modified header. The value of the Expires header is a date in the future after which the cache should be flushed and a new copy loaded.

For example, this header sets the expiry time for Wednesday, August 8, 2012:

```
Expires: Wed, 08 Aug 2012 09:41:05 GMT
```

This is much longer than most browsers will hold on to a document by default. You might choose such a long time for static images that are very unlikely to change. You can also try setting an Expires header in the relatively distant future for each separate embedded component on a page: scripts, stylesheets, Flash animations, and the like. In Apache, you can do this by setting the `ExpiresDefault` property in your .htconfig file like so:

```
ExpiresDefault "access plus 2 weeks"
```

The downside of this is that many surfers will continue to use the cached components until the time period expires. To get around this, when you change one of them, also change its name. Sometimes it's helpful to just add a version number to each such resource: stylesheet_111.css, stylesheet_112.css, and so forth.

You can use the `ExpiresByType` directive to override the expiry time for particular types of documents. For instance, if the HTML files change frequently, you may want them to expire very quickly. This sets them to expire after 3,600 seconds:

```
ExpiresByType text/html M3600 # HTML expires after one hour
```

You can use the Cache-control header to specify a relative expiry time. For example, this header sets the expiry time one hour (3,600 seconds) after the client has first retrieved the page:

```
Cache-Control: max-age=3600
```

Prevent Caching

Apply cache control headers so that rapidly changing pages are always loaded fresh from the server.

```
HTTP/1.1 200 OK
Date: Sun, 08 Apr 2007 20:58:58 GMT
Server: Apache/2
X-Powered-By: PHP/5.2.0
Cache-control: public
Last-Modified: Fri, 03 Dec 2004 11:53:03 GMT
ETag: "6548d4-30a9e-c7f4e5c0"
Content-Length: 325
Content-Type: text/html; charset=UTF-8
```

```
HTTP/1.1 200 OK
Date: Sun, 08 Apr 2007 20:58:58 GMT
Server: Apache/2
X-Powered-By: PHP/5.2.0
Cache-control: no-cache
Last-Modified: Fri, 03 Dec 2004 11:53:03 GMT
ETag: "6548d4-30a9e-c7f4e5c0"
Content-Length: 325
Content-Type: text/html; charset=UTF-8
```

Motivation

Not everything should be cached. You do want to be careful before blindly allowing caching. Done wrong, caching can deliver stale information or expose users' private data. Stock prices need to be updated from second to second. So do sensor readings from laboratory equipment.

Or perhaps you simply want better user statistics. You want to know how many users are seeing your ads without having to guess how many users equate to each AOL proxy server. Cacheable pages will measure fewer hits than uncacheable pages. Marking pages as uncacheable inflates, and usually more accurately reports, site traffic.

Potential Trade-offs

Uncacheable pages place much higher loads on a server. Worse yet, the effect is multiplied at times of high traffic, such as an online store the weekend before Christmas or any site that gets dugg. If you're turning caching off purely to improve hit counts and user tracking, be ready to turn it back on again if traffic spikes. Ideally, you should build in automatic governors that notice the traffic is spiking and reenable caching without manual intervention.

Mechanics

One way to prevent caching is to make all requests go through POST, because POST requests are never cached (at least not by decent clients and proxies). However, that's the wrong solution. Using POST to prevent caching is like using SAP to run a mom-and-pop candy store. It's much too big a solution for too small a problem, and consequently it will cause more problems than it solves.

The right solution is to send HTTP cache control headers with the pages that should not be cached. For example, if you simply wanted to prevent all caching of a page, you'd tell the HTTP server to set `Cache-Control` to `no-cache`. Then it would send an HTTP header such as this one before the page:

```
HTTP/1.0 200 OK
Cache-Control: no-cache
Date: Sat, 05 Apr 2008 15:52:40 GMT
Server: Apache/2
Last-Modified: Thu, 05 Apr 2008 09:41:05 GMT
ETag: "8aeb10-b6e7-5ea4ae40"
Content-Length: 46823
Content-Type: text/html; charset=iso-8859-1
Connection: close
```

Or perhaps the data is tied to a single user. It's OK for that user's browser to store the data in its local cache, but you don't want shared proxy servers to send the same page to a different user. Then you'd set `Cache-Control` to `private`:

```
Cache-Control: private
```

You can set an explicit amount of time for which the cache is valid using max-age. For instance, if you want caches to hold on to a page for no more than an hour, set max-age to 3600 (seconds):

```
Cache-Control: max-age=3600
```

You can specify multiple values for Cache-Control separated by commas. For example, this header requests only private caching for no more than an hour:

```
Cache-Control: private, max-age=3600
```

Table 7.1 lists the values you can use to control caching for GET requests.

Dynamically generated pages written in PHP and the like can use the customary mechanisms to set Cache-Control headers. For static pages, details vary from server to server. In Apache, you can use the mod_headers module to specify per-file and per-directory Cache-

TABLE 7.1   Cache-Control Header Values

Value	Meaning
public	Completely cacheable
private	Can be cached only by single-user caches, such as in a browser; must not be cached by multiuser caches in proxy servers
no-cache	Do not cache under any circumstances.
no-store	Like no-cache but stronger. Do not even write the data to disk, not even temporarily. In practice, this is not very reliable.
no-transform	Cache only as served—do not convert image formats, for example.
must-revalidate	Do not allow the client to use a stale response, even if the user has asked it to.
proxy-revalidate	Do not allow a proxy to use a stale response, even if it has been configured to do so.
max-age = *seconds*	Serve from the cache only until the specified number of seconds since the original request has elapsed

Controls. This module is not typically compiled in by default, and it may require a custom compilation to use. Assuming it is turned on, you can place a `Header` directive in any Files, Directory, or Location section in your .htconfig file, or you can place it in an .htaccess file to make it apply to every file in the same directory. For example, this line requests that only private caching be performed:

```
Header append Cache-Control "private"
```

This line requests that the pages be cached but revalidated:

```
Header set Cache-Control "public, must-revalidate"
```

The use of the `set` keyword instead of `append` means that this header will replace any other Cache-Control headers that might be set by other modules, rather than being merged with them.

Introduce ETag

Provide ETags for semistatic pages generated by web applications.

```
Date: Mon, 09 Apr 2007 13:41:12 GMT
Server: Apache/2
X-Powered-By: PHP/5.2.0
Expires: Wed, 11 Jan 1984 05:00:00 GMT
Last-Modified: Mon, 09 Apr 2008 13:41:13 GMT
Cache-Control: no-cache, must-revalidate, max-age=0
Content-Style-Type: text/css
Keep-Alive: timeout=15, max=98
Connection: Keep-Alive
Transfer-Encoding: chunked
```

```
ETag: "6548d4-30a9e-c7f4e5c0"
Date: Mon, 09 Apr 2008 13:41:12 GMT
Server: Apache/2
X-Powered-By: PHP/5.2.0
```

(continued)

```
Expires: Wed, 11 Jan 1984 05:00:00 GMT
Last-Modified: Mon, 09 Apr 2007 13:41:13 GMT
Cache-Control: no-cache, must-revalidate, max-age=0
Content-Style-Type: text/css
Keep-Alive: timeout=15, max=98
Connection: Keep-Alive
Transfer-Encoding: chunked
```

Motivation

ETags enable a client to quickly check that a page has not changed without downloading the entire page again. This saves server and client bandwidth and speeds up page load times.

Potential Trade-offs

You shouldn't provide ETags for pages that update very frequently, in particular more frequently than a client will access them.

ETags can also take non-negligible CPU time to calculate. This usually isn't a big deal, but on a server that is CPU-limited (as opposed to bandwidth-limited), this might be a concern.

Mechanics

ETag stands for "entity tag." It's a server-scoped identifier for the data sent by a server to a client in response to a request for a particular URL. It's supposed to change when the entity changes and stay the same otherwise. The first time a browser or other client requests a page from a server, it notes the entity tag of that page. The next time it needs to request that page, it can include the ETag in an If-None-Match header, like so:

```
GET /foo.html HTTP/1.1
If-None-Match: "6548d4-30a9e-c7f4e5c0"
Host: www.elharo.com
User-Agent: Mozilla/5.0 (Macintosh; U; PPC Mac OS X Mach-O;
en-US;rv:1.8.1.3) Gecko/20070309 Firefox/2.0.0.3
Accept: application/xhtml+xml,text/html,text/*;q=0.8,*/*;q=0.5
Accept-Language: en-us,en;q=0.5
Accept-Encoding: gzip,deflate
```

```
Keep-Alive: 300
Connection: keep-alive
```

If the server recognizes that the ETag matches the current ETag of the requested resource, it responds with a 304 Not Modified response, like this:

```
HTTP/1.1 304 Not Modified
Mon, 09 Apr 2007 15:21:10 GMT
```

It really doesn't have to say anything else. In particular, the server does not send the body of the resource as it would if there were no ETag. Instead, the client loads its old copy of the resource from its cache. It can do this even if the expiration date of the resource in the cache has passed because it has checked with the server that the old representation is still fresh. For large documents, this can save significant bandwidth.

Web servers today send ETags for static files, and you don't have to do anything extra for those. However, dynamic pages generated by PHP and similar frameworks are trickier. Sometimes every request to the server creates a different byte stream. If this is the case, don't bother sending an ETag. It will never help. However, many scripts sit somewhere in the middle. For example, suppose a script responds to a request for http://www.example.com/isbn/0691049548/ by making several SQL queries against a database and then formatting the results as HTML. If nothing in the database has changed, there's no need for clients to keep requesting that data. However, clients won't know that unless the server gives them an ETag.

ETags versus Caching

ETags have a complex but partially orthogonal relationship to caching. Caches and cache control headers determine when a browser does or does not check back with a server before showing an old copy to a client. ETag headers come into play after a browser has decided to check back with a server.

There are no special rules for how one constructs an ETag. Conceptually you can think of it like an MD5 or SHA-1 hash code for a document. However, because ETags do not need to be secure, and because these algorithms are computationally expensive, they are not the best choice for this purpose. Instead, consider what actually distinguishes one request from the next, and see if you can devise a simple hash code algorithm from that. For example, if the only difference between pages is in the SQL queries used to access a database, and if no new data is inserted into the database, you could form a hash code based on the SQL queries themselves. If the database is updated, but only occasionally, you might devise a scheme in which ETags are generated from SQL queries plus a random identifier that is changed every time the database is modified. However, if the database is written as frequently as it is read, you have to base the hash code on the data the queries return. Possibly, though, you could make it depend on just some of the fields in the response rather than all of them.

For example, I have published a simple PHP program that generates a plain text file containing Fibonacci numbers. The only relevant input is the number requested. Thus, I can make that the ETag, like so:

```
$generations = $_GET['generations'];
header('Etag: "' . $generations . '"');
```

If I ever change the format this script generates, I'll need to adjust the ETags as well. Alternatively, I could use weak entity tags. By default, entity tags are assumed to be strong, which means that two representations have the same entity tag if and only if they are byte-per-byte identical. However, if you put W/ in front of the quoted string, it becomes a weak entity tag. Documents that share a weak entity tag mean the same thing, but may not be byte-per-byte identical. For instance, if I converted a JPEG to a GIF, I could keep a weak entity tag the same, but not a strong one. A weak entity tag looks like this:

```
ETag: W/"6548d4-30a9e-c7f4e5c0"
```

There are few limits on what you can put in an ETag. It must be ASCII text. It cannot contain any control characters, including carriage returns, line feeds, and tabs. It must be double-quoted. Otherwise, use any format that works for you.

The second step for the web application to support ETags is to recognize when someone sends it an ETag and sending a 204 response instead. Clients can send multiple entity tags in a header separated by commas to indicate that they have multiple representations prestored. For example:

```
If-None-Match: "6548d4-30a9e-c7f4e5c0", "756ed4-44a5e-1cf56c09"
```

In this case, the server should send a 304 Not Modified response if any of the supplied entity tags match the current state of the resource along with the ETag that matches.

Replace Flash with HTML

Convert Flash sites to HTML. Provide pure-HTML alternatives for all Flash content.

```
<html xmlns="http://www.w3.org/1999/xhtml"
      xml:lang="en" lang="en">
<head>
 <title>Salkind Agency</title>
</head>
<body>
<object classid="clsid:d27cdb6e-ae6d-11cf-96b8-444553540000"
codebase="http://fpdownload.macromedia.com/pub/shockwave/cabs/
flash/swflash.cab#version=6,0,0,0" width="766" height="670"
id="salkindfinal1" align="middle">
  <param name="allowScriptAccess" value="sameDomain" />
  <param name="movie" value="salkindfinal1.swf" />
  <param name="quality" value="high" />
  <param name="bgcolor" value="#ffffff" />
  <embed src="salkindfinal1.swf" quality="high"
   bgcolor="#ffffff" width="766" height="670"
   name="salkindfinal1" align="middle"
  allowScriptAccess="sameDomain"
  type="application/x-shockwave-flash"
  pluginspage="http://www.macromedia.com/go/getflashplayer" />
</object>

</body>
</html>
```

```
<html xmlns="http://www.w3.org/1999/xhtml"
  xml:lang="en" lang="en">
<head>
```

(continued)

```
  <title>Salkind Agency</title>
</head>
<body>
<div id="Content">
<h1>Salkind Literary Agency</h1>
<p>We've sold over 4,500 books since 1995.</p>
<p>Our largest deal to date: $6,000,000.</p>
</div>
<div id="Nav">
<ul>
<li><a href="about/">About Us</a></li>
<li><a href="books/">Books</a></li>
<li><a href="articles/">Articles</a></li>
<li><a href="contact/">Contact Us</a></li>
</ul>
</div>
</body>
</html>
```

Motivation

Flash is extremely inaccessible. In most cases, a Flash site might as well be a black box to blind users, and it is often hostile to color-blind, deaf, and motion-impaired users as well. Although accessibility has been improved somewhat in the latest versions of Flash, most Flash applications are still vastly less accessible than plain old HTML.

It's not just handicapped users who have problems with Flash either. Even people with no handicaps do not have Flash-enabled browsers or browsers with the latest version of Flash installed. The lowest estimates I've seen are that 1 person out of 20 does not have Flash installed. Based on my experience, I expect that number is severely biased by self-selection effects and that likely a much higher percentage of users do not have Flash at all. Regardless of the exact numbers, though, there's no question that Flash is a crippling inconvenience to many users.

Finally, Flash is almost completely inaccessible to Google and other search engines. Even if users can view a Flash site, if it's all Flash, they'll never find it. My book agent (who's also an author and professor) recently converted to an all-Flash site. If you search for his name on Google, you'll find his faculty page, his Amazon page, his Barnes & Noble page, some listings at other bookstores, some eBay listings for his books, and more detritus no user would ever wade through. It isn't until the fourth page of Google results, near the bottom, that his literary agency that shares his name shows up.

Potential Trade-offs

There are some things you can't do in plain old HTML. If you really want a bouncing, singing greeting card or another Tetris knockoff, go ahead and use Flash.

There are even some more serious uses to which Flash can reasonably be put. For example, a Flash animation can show how to disassemble a complicated piece of equipment or demonstrate the flow of money in an economy. Done well, such animations will assist sighted users. However, you should also have a complete plain HTML version of all such content, for both unsighted users and Google.

Flash is sometimes used to attempt to lock in content. Flash content cannot be copied as easily as HTML and JavaScript. YouTube and Google use Flash video to try to force people to link to them and watch their ads rather than downloading their own copies of videos. However, there's a world of difference between "cannot be copied as easily" and "cannot be copied." Numerous tools are available today that enable users to download Flash videos, decompile Flash files, and extract text, images, and movies from them. Encoding content in Flash merely impedes legitimate users while not seriously hindering pirates.

Mechanics

Chances are you probably know where the Flash files are on your site. If for some reason you don't, just search for `d27cdb6e-ae6d-11cf-96b8-444553540000` and `application/x-shockwave-flash`. Unless you're publishing Flash tutorials, these strings only appear in documents that embed Flash.

Once you've found a Flash file, you'll need to play it to see what it's doing. If it's doing something that really can't be done with HTML, such as a twitch game, you may be OK leaving it. However, you should still add some HTML content to the page to at least describe the game for Google and other viewers who may not be able to play it. Please don't just leave them with a message saying, "This site requires that you have the latest version of the Flash player" or, worse yet, a completely blank page. At the very least, tell them why they might want to download Flash to view your site.

However, what really needs a rethink are sites such as my agent's that use Flash for tasks that HTML can do perfectly well. In particular, the following common things should never be written as Flash applications:

- Navigation
- Text content
- Noninteractive images
- Slide shows
- Data entry forms
- Invoices

All of these and many, many more can and should be handled by pure XHTML+CSS. On occasion, you might even throw in a little JavaScript, though I mostly try to avoid that too. There is no excuse for using Flash for any of these things.

There are a couple of cases where I can see the use of Flash, but it's not strictly necessary. These are sound and video. For pure sound, you're better off doing a podcast as an MP3 file. Users are unlikely to sit in front of their computers in their cubicles and listen to a 30-minute show, but they may download it to their iPod and listen to it on their commute home. However, for background sound on web pages (the Web's equivalent of elevator music), you may as well use Flash as anything else. Please, please give users a way to turn the sound off if you do so, though. Nothing makes a user close a window and leave your site faster than hearing the Black Eyed Peas unexpectedly start blasting "My Humps" in the middle of a crowded office.

For video, Flash actually does seem to be the most reliably cross-platform format. QuickTime doesn't run on Linux. Most Windows Media files don't play on the Mac without a variety of hard-to-find plug-ins most users haven't installed. MPEG is covered by a variety of patents, and nobody's sure exactly which ones or how many. And even if you can sort out the confusing mess that is video codecs, you are then faced with the problem that the means of embedding videos in a page vary from one browser and platform to the next. It's invalid and nonstandard.

For the moment, Flash really may be the best choice here, as hard as that is to believe. For the longer term, though, help is on the way. Several patent-free, open video standards, such as Ogg Theora, are under development. (They're already supported on Linux, but not yet widely available on more mainstream platforms.) HTML 5 seems likely to add a video element and maybe even an audio element to go with the existing img element. However, for the time being, using Flash for video and audio is not out of the question.

Finally, there are what I consider to be the truly evil uses to which unscrupulous webmasters have put Flash. In particular:

- Animated ads
- User tracking

If someone asks you to do these things, just say no. Users hate animated ads, and these days more users block them than don't. Indeed, some users block all Flash content by default just to avoid these ads (and other equally annoying animated content that is not technically ads). If you really want to waste your time and your client's/company's money on animated ads, be my guest, but I guarantee you that your effort and intelligence would be better spent on improving your site's usability and customer conversion than on making the ads blink.

As to using Flash data storage to replace cookies, if a user is smart enough to block your cookies, chances are they are smart enough to set Flash's persistent storage to zero, too. If your client insists on such scummy tactics, fire the client. If your boss orders you to do this, find a better job. (Don't worry too hard about this. Most such bosses/clients have their hair cut too pointy to know about this in the first place. If you don't tell them it's possible, they'll never know to ask for it.)

Add Web Forms 2.0 Types

Identify the type of expected data by adding a `type="email | url | date | time | datetime | localdatetime | month | week | number"` attribute to input text fields in forms.

```
<form action="http://www.example.com/formhandler" method="post">
<p><label>E-mail: <input name="email" /></label></p>
<p><label>Date: <input name="date" /></label></p>
<p><label>Time: <input name="time" /></label></p>
<p><label>Date and time:
        <input name="datetime" type="text" /></label></p>
<p><label>Local date and time:
        <input name="localdatetime" type="text" /></label></p>
<p><label>Month: <input name="month" /></label></p>
<p><label>Week: <input name="week" /></label></p>
<p><label>Number: <input name="number" /></label></p>
<p><label>URL: <input name="url" /></label></p>
<p><label><input type="submit" value="Send data" /></label>
</form>
```

```
<form action="http://www.example.com/formhandler" method="post">
<p><label>E-mail: <input type="email" name="email" /></label>
</p>
<p><label>Date: <input type="date" name="date" /></label></p>
<p><label>Time: <input type="time" name="time" /></label></p>
<p><label>Date and time:
        <input type="datetime" name="datetime" /></label></p>
<p><label>Local date and time: <input type="datetime-local"
                          name="localdatetime" /></label></p>
<p><label>Month: <input type="month" name="month" /></label></p>
<p><label>Week: <input type="week" name="week" /></label></p>
<p><label>Number: <input type="number" name="number" /></label>
</p>
<p><label>URL: <input type="url" name="url" /></label></p>
<p><label><input type="submit" value="Send data" /></label>
</form>
```

Motivation

These new types enable browsers to provide more appropriate GUI widgets to input data. For example, a browser can show a calendar control to allow the user to select a date, as shown in Figure 7.1.

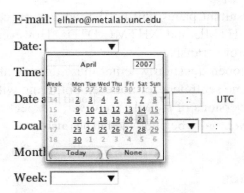

FIGURE 7.1 Opera 9's calendar control

Browsers can also check the input data on the client side and refuse to accept it or submit the form if it's incomplete or incorrect. Figure 7.2 shows Opera refusing to accept a value that's outside the specified range.

Potential Trade-offs

Not all browsers support these types yet. In fact, so far only Opera 9 does. More support is coming soon, but in the meantime, these forms still work perfectly well in today's legacy browsers. Users just don't get all the neat new features to help them with data entry.

Input validation helps users be sure they don't make a mistake. However, it does not substitute for server-side validation. Not all clients check these inputs, and hackers can trivially submit values outside the expected ranges.

Pick a number between 1 and 12: ☐ 15

15 is too high. The highest value you can use is 12.

Time: ☐ :

FIGURE 7.2 Opera 9 won't allow the user to submit a value outside a specified range for a numeric typed field.

The resultant pages will not be valid when compared against the traditional HTML and XHTML DTDs. However, this will have no effect on browser display.

It's an open question whether these documents will ever be valid. There's some sentiment for not even bothering with schemas or DTDs for future versions of HTML. However, I expect that DTDs and schemas will eventually be published.

Mechanics

You can easily do a multifile search for `<form` just to find the pages that would benefit from closer inspection. Once you've found a form, consider it field by field to figure out what types are likely to be a good fit. There's not a lot you can do to automate this process.

Once you've found the forms, check each input field to see whether it matches any of the expected types. There are ten new types you can use:

- `email`
- `date`
- `time`
- `datetime`
- `datetime-local`
- `month`
- `week`
- `number`
- `url`
- `range`

Adding one of these types only affects the client and has no effect on the server. However, you need to make sure that the format the server is accepting is indeed the format the client is sending. For example, dates are sent in the ISO standard form YYYY-MM-DD (e.g., 2008-06-23). If you expect dates in a different form, such as MM/DD/YYYY, you'll need to change the form processor on the server to accept the new format before deploying this on the client.

email

The `email` data type is used for e-mail addresses of the usual syntax: elharo@metalab.unc.edu, for example. When you tag an input field as type `email`, the browser can inspect the user's address book to offer options for autocompletion, as shown in Figure 7.3.

date

The `date` type is used for specific days in history, such as January 23, 1987, or September 18, 2012. The attributes `min` and `max` can be applied to limit the range of values the user can choose. For example, this input field asks the user for a date in 2008:

```
<input type="date" name="date"
       min="2008-01-01" max="2008-12-31"/>
```

The form for date data entry is the ISO standard form YYYY-MM-DD (e.g., 2008-06-23). If you expect dates in a different form, such as MM/DD/YYYY, you'll need to change the form processor on the server to accept the new format before deploying this on the client.

When you tag an input field as type `date`, the browser can offer a calendar control so that the user can pick a date.

time

The `time` type is used for times of day, such as 12:31 a.m. or 3:17:05 p.m. The default precision is 60 seconds (i.e., one minute), though you can adjust this with the `step` attribute. You can also specify minimum and maximum times with the `min` and `max` attributes. For example, this

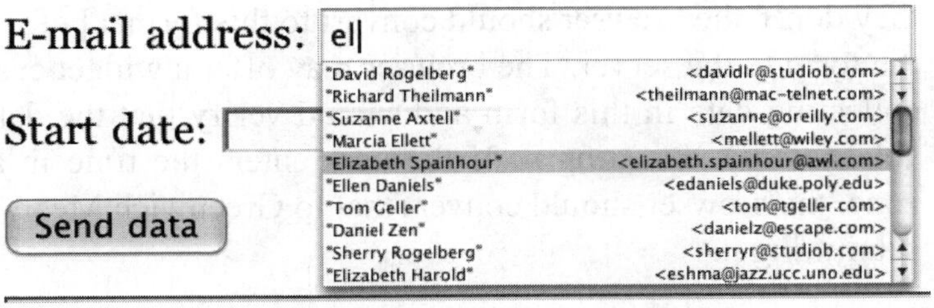

FIGURE 7.3 Autocompleting e-mail addresses

field requests a time between 9:00 a.m. and 5:00 p.m. on the hour or half hour:

```
<label>Start time:
  <input type="time" min="09:00" max="17:00"
        step="30" name="st" />
</label>
```

The form for time data entry is the ISO 8601 standard form HH:MM:SS.xxx (e.g., 03:45:13.23 for 3:45 a.m. and 13.23 seconds). Seconds are optional. Times after noon use a 24-hour clock—for example, 14:37, not 2:37 p.m. Time zones are not used.

When you tag an input field as type `time`, the browser can offer a more specific time control, as well as check that the user indeed entered a valid time.

datetime

The `datetime` type is used when you want the user to enter a specific moment in history—for example, not just 3:45 p.m. or December 12, 1982, but 3:45 p.m. on December 12, 1982. Data will be submitted in the form YYYY-MM-DDTHH:MM:SS.fffZ. Seconds and fractions thereof are optional. For example, 3:45 p.m. on December 12, 1982, would be sent as 1982-12-12T03:45Z or 1982-12-12T03:45:00.0000Z. Here the Z stands for Greenwich Mean Time (a.k.a. Coordinated Universal Time, UTC, or Zulu time). The data can be provided in a different time zone by using a plus sign (+) and an offset from Greenwich Mean Time. For example, Eastern Standard Time is five hours earlier than Greenwich Mean Time, so the same time is 10:45 a.m. EST.

The user does not necessarily have to type in this format, but if they don't, the browser should convert to this format before submitting the form to the server. The browser may offer a widget customized for collecting data in this form and should verify that the data is reasonable before submitting it. If the user enters the time in a local time zone, the browser should convert that to Greenwich Mean Time before submitting it.

datetime-local

The datetime-local type is the same as datetime, except there's no trailing *Z*. Furthermore, the time is assumed to be given in the user's local time zone rather than in UTC. For example, 3:45 p.m. on December 12, 1982, would be sent as 1982-12-12T03:45 or 1982-12-12T03:45:00.0000.

month

The month type represents a specific month in a specific year, such as December 1952 or July 2028. Data is submitted in the form YYYY-MM. For instance, December 1952 is 1952-12 and July 2028 is 2028-07. The user can enter months in any form the browser accepts as long as the browser converts it to this form before submission.

week

The week type represents a specific week in a specific year, such as the first week of 1952 or the thirty-second week of 2009. Data is submitted in the form YYYY-Www. For instance, the first week of January 1952 is 1952-W01. The thirty-second week of 2009 is 2009-W32. All weeks begin on a Monday. The first and fifty-second weeks may extend across year boundaries.

number

The number type requests that the user enter a number. The default precision is 1, so by default the user can only enter an integer. However, you can adjust this downward with the step attribute to allow the user to enter a decimal number. For example, this input field requests a number between 1 and 12, including fractional numbers such as 2.72 but not 2.71828:

```
<label>Pick a  number between 1 and 12:
<input type="number" name="guess"
       min='1' max='12' step='0.01'/>
</label>
```

range

A range control is similar to a numeric control. The crucial difference is that the exact value is not considered important in the range, just that it's somewhere in the vicinity. An example would be a thermostat. You want the temperature around 22° Celsius, but you don't really care whether it's 22.5 or 21.6, as long as it's in the ballpark. For example:

```
<label>Temperature:
<input type="range" name="temp"
       min='-20' max='90' step='0.5'/>
</label>
```

The browser may present this as a slider, scroll bar, or some other kind of input control that does not provide precise control rather than making the user type a value in a text field.

url

The url type requests an absolute IRI (like a URL, except that it can contain non-ASCII letters such as é) from the user, such as http://www.elharo.com/blog/ or ftp://ftp.ibiblio.org/.

Browser Support

Not all browsers support these types. In fact, currently only Opera 9 does. However, Firefox and Safari are likely to in the future and others may follow. However, if they don't, much of this can be supplied with JavaScript and AJAX. Google has released a JavaScript library to add support for these types (and other Web Forms 2.0 features) and functions to your web pages in legacy browsers such as Firefox 2 and Internet Explorer 5. Simply copy the JavaScript library from http://code.google.com/p/webforms2/ to your site and add this script element to the head of your document:

```
<script type='text/javascript' src='webforms2.js'></script>
```

Even if that's not an option, Web Forms 2.0 has been carefully designed to degrade gracefully in legacy browsers. Visitors with older browsers will simply see normal input fields when they reach a page using these new types. They'll have to wait for the server to tell them if they've input a bad value, rather than being told before they submit. It's no worse than the status quo.

Data Validation

It's important to remember that client-side validation in no way guarantees anything about the data the server receives. Always validate any input received from a client. Some browsers do not support these types at all and will allow users to submit any data they choose. Crackers can and do submit deliberately invalid data to attempt to penetrate systems, deface web pages, steal passwords, and otherwise do naughty things. Always verify the input you receive from the client on the server, regardless of these types or any other client-side validation logic.

Replace Contact Forms with mailto Links

Turn contact forms into real mailto links.

```
<form action="http://www.example.com/email" method="post">
  <input type="hidden" value="support@ticcorp.com"/>
  <p><label>Subject:
    <input type="text" name="subject" /></label></p>
  <p><label>Message:
    <input type="text" name="message" /></label></p>
  <p><input type="submit" value="Send e-mail"/></p>
</form>
```

```
<a href="mailto:support@ticcorp.com?Subject=Support%20request">
  Send E-mail to TIC support
</a>
```

Motivation

E-mail programs give users much more powerful and comfortable editing and archiving facilities. You will receive better communications when users can use their e-mail program of choice to compose their messages to you.

Furthermore, users will be able to maintain a record of their correspondence for easier reference in the future. This will make the communication more effective.

Potential Trade-offs

Users working from public terminals may not have an e-mail program installed or properly configured. You may wish to provide contact forms *and* mailto links. That way, users can choose what works best for them. However, do make sure the e-mail address is prominently displayed and visible on your site. Don't make users hunt for it.

Users who rely on web mail providers such as Yahoo! Mail and Gmail will need third-party extensions and various hacks to make mailto links work for them. Many have already installed such extensions.

E-mail may not tie into back-end bug tracking and customer management systems as easily as a web form. When shopping around for such systems, you should insist on e-mail management as a core feature. Even if your system does accept e-mail input, you may not be able to organize the requests into such neatly fielded responses. You'll need to be ready to parse information such as order dates, problem categories, and more out of the plain text of the e-mail. This usually requires human intelligence. That is, a person has to sit down and read the e-mail to figure out what it means. You do more work so that your customer does less. However, if this is too onerous, there are some tricks you can play to still use fielded forms while enabling your customers to use their real e-mail programs.

Publishing e-mail addresses on web sites opens them up to spam. In fact, even without that, they're probably getting a lot of spam already. I'll address techniques for minimizing this in the next chapter.

Mechanics

A mailto link is straightforward. In fact, it's much easier to create than a contact form and associated back-end machinery for processing the form. It just requires a standard a element and a mailto URL. The URL is just mailto: followed by the address. For example, here's a mailto link you can use to reach me:

```
<a href="mailto:elharo@metalab.unc.edu">
  E-mail Elliotte Rusty Harold
</a>
```

You can encode additional headers in the URL's query string. For example, here's an e-mail link that sets the Subject line to "Refactoring":

```
<a href="mailto:elharo@metalab.unc.edu?Subject=Refactoring">
  E-mail Elliotte Rusty Harold
</a>
```

You can encode non-ASCII characters and non-URL legal characters by first converting them to UTF-8 and then encoding each UTF-8 byte as a percent sign followed by two hexadecimal digits. For example, a space is %20, so this link sends e-mail to me with the subject "Refactoring HTML":

```
<a href=
  "mailto:elharo@metalab.unc.edu?Subject=Refactoring%20HTML">
  E-mail Elliotte Rusty Harold
</a>
```

You can separate additional headers from each other with ampersands (which must themselves be encoded as & in the XHTML). For example, this link CCs the message to another address of mine:

```
<a href=
 "mailto:elharo@metalab.unc.edu?Subject=Refactoring%20HTML&amp;
CC=elharo%40macfaq.com">
  E-mail Elliotte Rusty Harold
</a>
```

You can even set a default body for the e-mail using the query string variable Body. Here's one example:

```
<a href=
"mailto:elharo@metalab.unc.edu?Subject=Refactoring%20HTML&amp;
Body=I%20love%20Refactoring%20HTML.">
  E-mail Elliotte Rusty Harold
</a>
```

These techniques should suffice to reproduce most contact forms in regular e-mail. I really believe that all e-mail should be read and responded to by a human being. However, if you need some greater level of automation, you can achieve it with a two-step process. First, set up a classic contact form that collects a series of fielded data from the user. The first submission sends it into your CMS and assigns it a unique ID by which it can be tracked. However, the response, rather than a simple thank you, is actually a confirmation screen that invites the user to e-mail the response to you. You can provide both a form and a mailto link for doing this. The mailto link is configured by the server-side script to already contain the right tracking ID, as well as all the detailed information the user filled out. The user can then mail that in.

One final note: Please don't respond to forms or any e-mail from a "Do not reply to this address" address. Every e-mail you send out should come from an actual person who can carry on a conversation (possibly by delegation) if necessary. Yes, spam is a problem. Install a good spam filter, but don't use spam as an excuse for hiding from your customers.

Practicing What I Preach

You find my real, unobscured e-mail address prominently displayed in multiple locations in my books and on most of my web pages. I read all mail sent to me.

Block Robots

Add robots.txt files in directories you wish to block. Install a honey pot to detect and block impolite robots and venomous spiders.

```
User-agent: *
Disallow: /scripts/
Disallow: /styles/
Disallow: /management/
Disallow: /support/
Disallow: /DTD/
```

Motivation

Robots waste your bandwidth. Robots can discover and expose private pages.

Potential Trade-offs

Blocking robots prevents search engines from indexing your site and keeps people from finding your pages. Be careful to only block sub-trees you really don't want to be public.

Mechanics

First identify and catalog those parts of your URL hierarchy that should be invisible to search engines and other spiders. Remember to look at this from the perspective of an outside user looking in. This is based on the apparent URL hierarchy, not the actual layout of files on a disk. For example, here's a typical list of URLs you might want to exclude:

- /cgi-bin
- /store/checkout
- /personaldata/
- /experimental
- /staging

Of course, the details will vary depending on your site layout. I suggest blocking even those directories a robot "can't" get into. Defense in depth is a good thing.

Place each of these in a file called robots.txt, preceded by `Disallow:` like so:

```
User-agent: *
Disallow: /cgi-bin
Disallow: /store/checkout
Disallow: /personaldata/
Disallow: /experimental
Disallow: /staging
```

Place this file at the root level of your web server. That is, it should be able to be retrieved from http://www.example.com/robots.txt. Remember that URLs are case-sensitive, so ROBOTS.TXT or robots.TXT and similar variations will not work.

You can also block robots by User-agent. For example, if you have a grudge against Google and want to keep it out of your pages, the following robots.txt will do that while allowing other search engines in:

```
User-agent: Googlebot
Disallow: /
```

Note that this works only on robots. This would not allow you to exclude real browsers such as Mozilla and Internet Explorer, no matter what you put in the User-agent string. The goal here is precisely to block robots while allowing real people in.

You can even specify different rules for different robots. For example, this blocks all robots from /cgi-bin, blocks Googlebot from /staging and /experimental, and blocks Turnitin from the entire site:

```
User-agent: *
Disallow: /cgi-bin

User-agent: Googlebot
Disallow: /staging
Disallow: /experimental

User-agent: TurnitinBot
Disallow: /
```

The syntax here is quite minimal. In particular, there's no "Allow" command. You cannot block all user agents from a directory and then allow one in particular. Similarly, you cannot block a root directory but allow access to one or more of its file or subdirectories. Robots.txt is a pretty blunt instrument.

You can also specify a `robots` meta tag in the head of HTML documents. However, few robots recognize or respect this. You really should use a robots.txt file to prevent robotic visits.

The especially dangerous robots are those that don't follow the rules and spider your site whether you permit them to or not. To prevent these you have to detect them and then block them by IP address.

Detecting them isn't hard. You just set up a few links in your pages that only robots are likely to find. For example, you can have a link with no content, like this:

```
<a href="hidden/dontgohere.html"></a>
```

Block the hidden directory in robots.txt so that well-behaved robots will ignore it:

```
User-agent: *
Disallow: /hidden
```

Then check your server logs to see which IPs have actually loaded that file. Also check to see what other files those IPs have loaded. If it's just a few files, widely separated in time, I'd ignore it. But if I see that IP address has been hitting every other page on my site, I'll block it in my Apache .htconfig file, like so:

```
<Directory "/www/xom">
    Order allow,deny
    Allow from all
    Deny from 212.0.138.30
    Deny from 83.149.74.179
    Deny from 66.186.173.166
</Directory>
```

This prevents it from hitting any page on my site, not just the protected ones. However, chances are that spider is up to no good, so I don't mind doing this.

You can also use `mod_rewrite` to block robots by User-agent. However, it's so easy to change the User-agent string that I rarely bother with this. I find it hard to believe that a spider that's ignoring robots.txt is not going to fake its User-agent string to look exactly like a perfectly legitimate copy of Firefox or Internet Explorer.

Some people have automated this procedure or used other means of detection. In particular, if anyone is hitting your site more than 12 times per minute, he may well be up to no good. However, this requires quite a bit more server intelligence than simple IP blocking.

Escape User Input

Escape all user-supplied data.

```
$query = "SELECT price FROM products WHERE sku='"
         . $GET_['sku'] . "';";
```

↓

```
$escaped_sku = mysql_real_escape_string($GET_['sku']);
$query = "SELECT price FROM products WHERE sku='"
         . $escaped_sku] . "';";
```

Motivation

SQL injection is the single most common source of security breaches on the Web today. It's probably easier to find a database-backed site with a SQL injection vulnerability than a site without one. SQL injection has led to theft of confidential customer data, web-site defacement, credit card fraud, privacy breaches, denial of service, spam, phishing, virus propagation, and almost every other computer-assisted crime you can imagine.

Potential Trade-offs

None.

Mechanics

Never treat user-supplied data as code, be it SQL, JavaScript, XSLT, or anything else. Only treat it as data. In particular, do not build executable statements by simple string concatenation of user-supplied values with code. This is begging for trouble.

To demonstrate the problem, consider a simple search form such as this one:

```
<form name="search" action="/search.php" method="get">
 <input size="12" name="terms">
 <input type="submit":" value="Search"/>
</form>
```

It looks innocuous enough, but it can easily hide some serious security holes. For example, suppose it's handled by a very basic PHP script such as this one:

```
$keywords = $_GET['terms'];
$query = "SELECT url, title FROM pages WHERE content LIKE '%"
        . $keywords . "%';";
$result = mysql_query($query);
```

You may very well have given hackers the ability to delete every row in your database. For example, imagine they search for this:

```
foo%'; DELETE * FROM pages; SELECT * FROM pages
  WHERE content LIKE '%
```

This closes the initial search early, adds a second SQL command that deletes all data from the pages table, and then performs the first part of the next query to make sure the complete set of statements is syntactically correct.

Don't fool yourself into thinking that nobody could possibly figure out how to do this. These attacks happen all the time, and hackers have gotten very good at working their way into databases in this fashion. Although the details depend on the database structure and the back-end code, this is not a theoretical attack.

Start with libraries such as Hibernate's Criteria API that clearly separate the data from the code. Use parameterized queries and stored procedures where possible. When that's not possible, make sure you escape all significant characters such as ' and " before forming the string.

Many APIs have built-in functions to perform this escaping. For example, PHP provides the `mysql_real_escape_string` function for escaping strings in a form suitable for use in MySQL. You could safely write the preceding code as follows:

```
$keywords = $_GET['terms'];\
$query = "SELECT url, title FROM pages WHERE content LIKE
'%"$safe_keywords = mysql_real_escape_string($keywords);
        . $safe_keywords . "%'";
$result = mysql_query($query);
```

Many other environments have something similar.

You can limit the possible damage by restricting the access your web server has to the database. Most databases have functions for assigning different users different levels of privilege. Many queries can be run as a user who has only SELECT access to the database but not INSERT, UPDATE, or DELETE. This will limit the damage an attacker can do. However, attackers may still be able to trick the database into revealing information that was supposed to be secret, even if they can't modify it.

A number of automated security testing tools such as Sprajax and PHP Security Scanner look for such problems. By all means use them. However, the nature of code means these tools are not perfectly adequate. They can miss some problems while reporting many false positives. The best solution is to carefully review all code that accepts input from the user with an eye toward these sorts of security problems. Make sure every point where input is accepted from outside the program is properly escaped as appropriate for your environment.

Variations

I've focused on SQL injection here because it's by far the most common instance of this pattern. However, other non-SQL systems may be vulnerable as well. Anytime you take data from a user and execute it as code, you're at risk. This can crop up in XPath, XQuery, XSLT, LDAP, and other systems as well.

Though details vary, the defenses follow the same basic pattern. Carefully inspect all user-supplied data for reserved characters (whatever those may be in the language of concern) and escape them. If possible, use vendor-supplied escaping functions instead of hand-rolled ones. Never treat client-supplied data as code.

Chapter 8
Content

So far, we've focused almost exclusively on the markup of the page and relatively little on the content. Markup may be where the code is, but content is why readers come to a site in the first place. Chances are there are some significant improvements you can make in your content too that will pay immediate dividends.

Correct Spelling

Check all text with a spell checker.

> In the new milennium, the inteligent playright endeavers to avoid the embarassment that arises from superceding good judgement with exceedingly dificult to spell words of foriegn derivasion at every occurence.

> In the new millennium, the intelligent playwright endeavors to avoid the embarrassment that arises from superseding good judgment with exceedingly difficult to spell words of foreign derivation at every occurrence.

Motivation

Proper spelling makes a site appear more professional. It enhances the trust readers have in your site. Sites that can't spell look bad and drive away readers. This is especially critical for any site attempting to close a sale with a visitor. Web surfers have learned to associate poor spelling (and grammar) with hackers and impostors. They are far less likely to hand over a credit card number to a site that's full of spelling errors.

Proper spelling also improves search engine placement. You get no Google juice for a term you've misspelled (unless everyone else is misspelling it, too).

Potential Trade-offs

None.

Mechanics

Most decent HTML editors, such as BBEdit and Dreamweaver, have built-in spell checkers. By all means, use them. Unlike the spell checkers built into products such as Microsoft Word, they're smart enough to realize that kbd is misspelled but <kbd> isn't. Make sure all people editing any page on your site have their spell checker turned on and running so that it draws a little squiggly red line under every misspelled word as soon as it's typed. Do not give writers the opportunity to forget to spell-check their content before submitting it.

Of course, for the content that already exists on your site, you'll need something a little more automated. It's well worth spending a day or two on a complete and thorough proofread of a site. If you don't have a solid day, work on one page at a time, but by all means, devote some effort and energy to this.

The trick is to generate a good custom dictionary that matches your site and all its unique terms, brand names, proper names, and other words the default dictionary does not contain. Although you can certainly check each page individually and build the dictionary as you go, I find it more efficient to work in larger batches. The basic procedure is as follows.

1. Generate a list of all possibly misspelled words in all documents.
2. Delete all actually misspelled words from the list. This requires the services of a native speaker who is an excellent speller. What remains is a custom dictionary for your site.
3. Rerun the spell checker on one file at a time using the custom dictionary. This time, any words it flags should be genuine spelling errors, so you should fix them.

Be sure to store the dictionary you create for later use. You will occasionally need to add new words to it as the site grows and changes.

At least for English, the gold standard is the GNU Project's Aspell. This is really a library more than an end-user program, but you can make it work by stringing together a few UNIX commands. Here's how I use it.

First I check an entire directory of files with this command:

```
$ cat *.html | aspell --mode=html list | sort | uniq
```

This types all HTML files in the directory, passes the output into the spell checker, sorts the results, and *uniquifies* them (deletes duplicates). The result is a list of all the misspelled words in the directory, such as this:

```
AAAS
AAC
AAL
ABA
ABCDEFG
ABCNEWS
ACGNJ
...
ystart
yt
yvalue
zephyrfalcon
zigbert
ziplib
zlib
zparser
```

Of course, looking at a list such as this, it will immediately strike you that most of these words are not in fact misspelled. They are proper

names, technical terms, foreign words, coinages, and other things the
spell checker doesn't recognize. Thus, next you inspect the output and
use it to build a custom dictionary.

Pipe or copy the output into a text editor and delete all clearly misspelled words. (I am assuming here that you're a solid speller. If not,
hire someone who is. This is especially important if you're not a native
speaker of the language you're checking.) If you're in doubt about a
word, delete it. You'll want to look at it in context before deciding.

Save the remaining correctly spelled words in a file called custom-
dict.txt. If the file is too large to inspect manually, you may want to
start with a smaller sample. Then compile this text file into a custom
dictionary, like so:

```
$ aspell --lang=en create master ./webdict < customdict.txt
```

This creates the file webdict in the current working directory.

Now run the command again with the --add-extra-dicts=./
webdict option, like so:

```
$ cat *.html | aspell --mode=sgml --add-extra-dicts=./webdict
  list | sort | uniq
```

This time, Aspell will generate a list of words that are much more
likely to be actually misspelled. When I recently checked my site, my
initial list comprised more than 11,000 misspelled words. After scanning them and creating a custom dictionary, the potential spelling
errors were reduced to 1,138, a much more manageable number.

At this point, I would take each word in this new shorter list and
search for it using this regular expression:

```
\bmisspelling\b
```

The \b on both ends limits the search to word boundaries so that I
don't accidentally find it in the middle of other words. For example, if
I'm correcting *adn* to *and*, I don't want to also change *sadness* to
sandess.

If I'm uncertain about whether a word is correctly spelled, I may
open the file and fix it manually. If I know it's obviously wrong, I'll
just replace it.

The alternative to this approach, and one that may be more accessible to some people, is to use a traditional GUI spell checker, such as those built into BBEdit and Dreamweaver, and check files one at a time. That's certainly possible, but in my experience it takes quite a bit longer, and the larger the site, the longer it takes. Spelling errors are not independent. The same ones tend to crop up again and again.

A nice compromise position is to use Aspell to build up a custom dictionary and then use that custom dictionary as you check individual files, whether with Aspell or with some other GUI tools. Most decent tools should be able to import a custom dictionary saved as a plain text file.

For many sites, that may be enough. Anything this process catches is certainly something you'll want to fix. However, professional sites that convey your image to the world are worth a little more effort. Some things a machine can't catch. For instance, I know of one site where a spell checker did not notice an omitted *l* in the word *public* with consequently embarrassing results. If at all possible, I recommend hiring a professional proofreader to catch these and similar mistakes, as well as errors of grammar, meaning, and style that a computer program just won't recognize.

Although I usually say that hiring a professional proofreader is optional, there is one exception. If you are publishing a site in anything other than your primary native language, professional native assistance is mandatory. Even well-educated, truly bilingual people rarely have formal education in more than one tongue. Any commercial site publishing in a non-native language should insist on a native proofreader.

However you go about this, correcting spelling errors can take awhile. The effort involved is roughly linear in the size of the site after you get your initial custom dictionary set up. As usual, you may not have to do it all at once. Start with your home page and other frequently accessed pages, as indicated by your server logs. Then work your way forward from there. Don't feel like you have to do it all at once. Every error you correct is one less error for site visitors to notice and to think less of you for.

Repair Broken Links

Repair broken links if possible. Delete them if not.

```
<a href="http://deadsite.example.com/">Dotcom, Inc.</a>
<a href="http://www.example.com/reorganized/site">Learn More</a>
```

```
Dotcom, Inc.
<a href="http://www.example.com/new/location">Learn More</a>
```

Motivation

Dead links annoy users and waste their time. In the worst case, they can be offensive. Many disgusting spammers make a habit of buying up abandoned domain names of failed companies and replacing them with pages of ads for subprime mortgages, get-rich-quick schemes, and outright pornography. Many web sites are pointing to porn and don't even know it.

Dead links also reduce search engine placement for both your site and the sites linked to it.

Potential Trade-offs

None.

Mechanics

Checking links is fairly easy to automate. As a result, many tools will do this for you. Some are built into authoring tools, and they usually work on a single page. Others are stand-alone programs that run on your computer. Still others are web-based services. For a quick check on one page, I'll either use what's built into my editor or hop over to the web-based checker at http://validator.w3.org/checklink. Googling for "online link checker" will find many similar tools.

For more automated testing of an entire site, on Windows I use Xenu Link Sleuth, http://home.snafu.de/tilman/xenulink.html; and on UNIX I use Linklint, www.linklint.org/. Once again, these are just two choices. There are many others. Each can scan a site remotely or locally and attempt to follow each link it finds. If a link can't be followed, or if it is redirected, an error message is logged. For example, here's some output from checking one of my sites with Linklint:

```
$ ./linklint -http -host www.cafeaulait.org -doc results /@

Checking links via http://www.cafeaulait.org
that match: /@
1 seed: /

Seed:     /
    checking robots.txt for www.cafeaulait.org
Checking /
Checking /oldnews/news2007March26.html
Checking /mailinglists.html
Checking /javafaq.html
...
-----     /oldnews/news2007March30.html
-----     /oldnews/news2007March23.html

Processing ...

writing files to results
wrote 21 txt files
wrote 19 html files
wrote index file index.html

found  64 default indexes
found 112 cgi files
found 923 html files
found   2 java archive files
found 130 image files
found  86 applet files
found 593 other files
found 1076 http links
found  26 ftp links
found 249 mailto links
found  13 news links
found 542 named anchors
-----      3 actions skipped
----- 100 files skipped
ERROR   1 missing directory
ERROR   4 missing cgi files
ERROR  28 missing html files
ERROR   1 missing java archive file
ERROR  12 missing image files
ERROR   6 missing applet files
```

```
ERROR  19 missing other files
ERROR 104 missing named anchors

Linklint found 1910 files and checked 1000 html files.
There were 71 missing files. 160 files had broken links.
175 errors, no warnings.
```

This tool writes its results into a directory specified on the command line (here, the results directory) in both plain text and HTML format. The most useful results file is errorF.html, which contains a list of the file containing the broken links, as well as the links that were broken. Typical output looks like this:

```
file: errorF.txt
host: www.cafeaulait.org
date: Sun, 01 Apr 2007 14:55:15 (local)
Linklint version: 2.3.5

#---------------------------------------------------------------
# ERROR 160 files had broken links
#---------------------------------------------------------------
/
    had 1 broken link
    /&

/books.html
    had 3 broken links
    /&
    /books/beans/a
    /javafaq/

/books/
    had 1 broken link
    /books/&

/books/beans/
    had 2 broken links
    /books/javasecrets.html
    /index.html
```

Most such tools are highly configurable and have numerous options for specifying exactly what to check and not to check. Usually the defaults are fine. One option you may want to consider is differentiating between checking for broken internal links and broken external links. Broken external links are bad, but broken internal links are ten times worse (and are usually easier to fix). In the case of Linklint, the default is to check only for internal links. To check external links as well, add the -net option:

```
$ linklint -http -host www.cafeaulait.org -net /2000march.html

Checking links via http://www.cafeaulait.org
that match: /2000march.html
1 seed: /2000march.html

Seed:     /2000march.html
    checking robots.txt for www.cafeaulait.org
Checking /2000march.html
-----     /1999november.html
-----     /1999may.html
-----     /1999september.html
-----     /1999december.html
-----     /1999october.html
-----     /2000february.html
-----     /1999july.html
-----     /1999august.html
-----     /2000january.html
-----     /1999june.html

Processing ...

found  11 html files
found   2 image files
found  61 http links
-----  10 files skipped
ERROR   1 missing other file
ERROR   1 missing named anchor

Linklint found 13 files and checked 1 html file.
There was 1 missing file. 1 file had broken links.
2 errors, no warnings.

checking 61 urls ...

bluej.monash.edu/
  could not find ip address
conferences.oreilly.com/java/
  moved
  conferences.oreillynet.com/java/
  not found (404)
crushftp.bizland.com/
  access forbidden (403)
developer.apple.com/java/text/download.html
  moved
  developer.apple.com/java/download.html
  ok
developer.apple.com/mkt/swl/
  moved
  developer.apple.com/softwarelicensing/index.html
  ok
fourier.dur.ac.uk/%7Edma3mjh/jsci/index.html
  timed out connecting to host
fred.lavigne.com/
  ok
```

```
homepage.mac.com/mheun/jEditForMac.html
  moved
  www.mac.com/account_error.html
  ok
java.sun.com/aboutJava/communityprocess/maintenance/JLS/index.html
  moved
  jcp.org/aboutJava/communityprocess/maintenance/JLS/index.html
  ok
java.sun.com/products/personaljava/index.html
  not an http link
java.sun.com/products/personaljava/pj-cc.html
  ok
java.sun.com/products/personaljava/pj-emulation.html
...
found   39 urls: ok
-----   12 urls: moved permanently (301)
-----   14 urls: moved temporarily (302)
ERROR    2 urls: access forbidden (403)
ERROR    1 url: could not find ip address
ERROR    9 urls: not found (404)
ERROR    2 urls: timed out connecting to host
warn     8 urls: not an http link

Linklink checked 61 urls:
    39 were ok, 14 failed. 26 urls moved.
    3 hosts failed: 3 urls could be retried.
1 file had failed urls.
There were 2 files with broken links.
```

Of course, Linklint does not spider the remote pages. It merely checks that they're where they're expected to be. As you can see, a link can be broken for several reasons. These include:

- could not find ip address

  The entire host has been removed from the Net and has not been replaced. In some cases, you can find the replacement host with a little Google work. Otherwise, you should delete the link.

- moved

  The page has moved to a new location, but the host is still there. If the ultimate response is OK, you can update the link, but it's not essential and not an immediate problem. If the location is not found, though, you need to fix the link.

- access forbidden

  Usually this means the directory has been deleted. You'll need to fix or delete the link.

- `timed out`

  The host is still there, but it doesn't seem to be responding at the moment. It may be a temporary glitch, or the site may be gone for good. Try again tomorrow.

The exact terms vary from one tool to the next, but the reasons and responses are the same.

Note that this process does not just find broken links. It also finds redirected links—that is, links where the server sends the browser to a new page. These are worth a second look, especially if the server the user is being redirected to is not the original server. Too often, the browser is being redirected to a spam page that's been set up at a dead domain. Other times it's the home page of the correct site, but the page you were actually linking to is missing. You may need to verify these manually.

In many ways, checking for broken links—especially external links—is one of the most annoying refactorings. Most of the refactorings described in this book have the advantage of being stable. That is, once you fix a page, it stays fixed, at least until someone edits it. Not so with link checking. A page can be perfectly fine one minute and have two dozen broken links the next, and there's not a lot you can do about it. The best you can hope for is to notice and quickly fix any problems that do arise. For example, set up a cron job that runs Linklint periodically and e-mails you the results. You can't stop other sites from breaking your links to them, but you can at least repair the problems as time permits.

Repairing Links

Sometimes you can fix links automatically with search and replace. For example, when Sun's Java site changed its URL from java.sun.com to www.javasoft.com, it was easy for me to replace all the old links with new ones just by searching for java.sun.com and changing it to www.javasoft.com. Then when Sun changed the host name back to java.sun.com a few years later, I just did the search and replace in reverse.

Most changes aren't this easy. You'll often need to spend some time surfing the targeted site and Googling for new page locations. Sometimes you'll find them. Sometimes you won't. If you do find them, updating the old link to point to the new location is easy. If you don't find it, delete the link. Depending on context, you can delete the entire a element, the `<a>` and `</a>` start tag and end tag, or just the `href` attribute. If you delete only the `href` attribute, you can move the old URL into the `title` attribute for archival purposes, so you'll still have it somewhere if the site comes back:

```
<a title="http://www.example.com/foo/">Foo Corp.</a>
```

There's one important exception. If the link points into your own site, rather than to an external site, you should either delete the entire element or fix it to point to the new page. However, there's something else you have to do to. You'll want to set up a redirect so that other sites and bookmarks linking to this page will be redirected to the new location as well. I'll take this up in the next section.

Move a Page

Reorganize your URL structure to be more transparent to developers, visitors, and search engines, but always make sure the old URLs for those pages still work.

```
http://www.example.com/framework/wo/9t5oReW4DX1d7/0.0.1.172.1.1
http://www.example.com/boredofdirectors/bios/
http://www.example.com/2007/05/23/1756?id=p12893
```

```
http://www.example.com/products/carburetors/
http://www.example.com/boardofdirectors/bios/
http://www.example.com/pr/TIC-patents-new-fuel-efficient-engine
```

Motivation

In the words of the W3C, "Cool URIs don't change." Once you publish a URI, you should endeavor to make sure that content remains at that URI forever. Other sites link to the page. Users bookmark it. Every time you reorganize your URL structure you are throwing away traffic.

However, you do need to move pages. Sometimes it's a matter of search engine optimization. Sometimes it's mandated by a change to a new content management system (CMS) or server-side framework. Sometimes it's necessary just to keep the development process sane by keeping related static files close together.

Thus, the compromise: Move pages as necessary, but leave redirects behind at the old URLs to point users to the new URLs. Done right, users will mostly never notice that this has happened.

Potential Trade-offs

As long as you don't actively break links, most external sites that point to you won't bother to update their links. Then again, most of them won't update their links no matter what you do. That's why you need to keep the old links working.

Mechanics

Every time you move a page, set up a redirect from the old page to the new page. In other words, configure your web server so that rather than sending a 404 Not Found error when a visitor arrives at the old location, it sends a 301 Moved Permanently or 302 Found response.

For example, when I published my first book, I put the examples at www.cafeaulait.org/examples/. When I published my second book, I needed to split that up by book, so I moved those files to www.cafeaulait .org/books/jdr/examples/. However, if you go to www.cafeaulait.org/ examples/, the server sends this response:

```
HTTP/1.1 302 Found
Date: Fri, 06 Apr 2007 17:34:27 GMT
Server: Apache/2
Location: http://www.cafeaulait.org/books/jdr/examples
Content-Length: 298
Content-Type: text/html; charset=iso-8859-1

<!DOCTYPE HTML PUBLIC "-//IETF//DTD HTML 2.0//EN">
<html><head>
<title>302 Found</title>
</head><body>
<h1>Found</h1>
<p>The document has moved
```

```
<a href="http://www.cafeaulait.org/books/jdr/examples">here</a>
</p>
<hr>
<address>Apache/2 Server at www.cafeaulait.org Port 80</address>
</body></html>
```

Most users never see this. Instead, their browser silently and immediately redirects them to www.cafeaulait.org/books/jdr/examples/. I was able to move the page but keep the old links working.

Consult your server documentation to determine exactly how this is accomplished with different servers. In the most popular server, Apache, this is achieved with mod_rewrite rules placed in the httpd.conf or .htaccess files. For example, the preceding redirect is accomplished with this rule:

```
RewriteEngine On
RewriteOptions MaxRedirects=10 inherit
RewriteBase    /
RewriteRule    ^examples(.*) books/jdr/examples$1 [R]
```

Regular expressions indicate exactly what is rewritten and how. In this case, after turning on the engine and setting a couple of options to prevent infinite redirect loops, the base for the rewrites is set to /, the root of the URL hierarchy. This is where all further matches begin.

The actual rule looks for all URLs whose path component begins with /examples, followed by any number of characters. The ^ character anchors this expression to the rewrite base of / set in the previous line. The .* matches everything that comes after /examples, and the parentheses around .* enable us to refer back to those matched characters in the next part of the expression as $1.

The third string on the last line, books/jdr/examples$1, is the replacement rule. It replaces the matched string from the first line with books/jdr/examples/ and the piece that was matched by (.*) in the search string.

Finally, [R] means that the client should be told about the redirect by sending a 302 response. If we left it out, the new data would still be sent to the client, but it would appear as though it had come from the old URL. That's usually not what you want, because keeping the same page at several URLs reduces your search engine impact. (However, such silent redirects are very useful if you're trying to put a sensible URL structure on top of a messy internal database-backed system. WordPress uses this technique extensively, for example.) If you'd rather send a 301 Moved Permanently response, change [R] to [R=301].

This one rule creates many redirects. For instance:

- /examples/chapters/01 is redirected to /books/jdr/examples/chapters/01.
- /examples is redirected to /books/jdr/examples.
- /examples/chapters/01/HelloWorld.java is redirected to /books/jdr/examples/chapters/01/HelloWorld.java.

By adjusting the regular expression and the base, you can create other redirects. For example, we could redirect requests for .html files but not .java files:

```
RewriteRule   ^examples(.*)\.html books/jdr/examples$1.html [R]
```

Or suppose you've changed all your HTML files to end with .xhtml instead of .html. This rule redirects all requests for .html to new names with .xhtml instead:

```
RewriteRule   ^(.*)\.html $1.xhtml [R]
```

Rules aren't always so generic. Sometimes you just want to redirect a single file. For example, suppose you discover you've published a document at /vacation/picures.html and it should really be /vacation/pictures.html. You can rename the file easily enough and then insert this rule in your .htaccess file so that requests for /picures.html are now redirected to /vacation/pictures.html:

```
RewriteRule   /vacation/picures.html /vacation/pictures.html [R]
```

Another common case is when the site name changes. For example, suppose your company changes its name from Foo Corp to Bar Corp. Of course, you'll continue to hold on to the www.foo.com domain, but you do want to send users to the new www.bar.com domain. This rule does that:

```
RewriteCond %{HTTP_HOST}   !^www\.bar\.com [NC]
RedirectMatch ^/(.*) http://www.foo.com/$1 [L,R=301]
```

This says the host is exactly www.bar.com (except for case) and the request should be redirected to www.foo.com, from which the same path and query string will be requested.

Remove the Entry Page

Put the content on the front page.

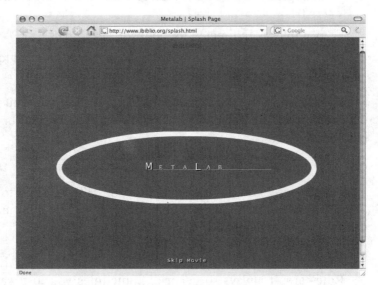

FIGURE 8.1   Flash intro page for IBiblio

FIGURE 8.2   The real IBiblio home page

Motivation

Don't waste visitors' time. Every extra click you put in their way is one more opportunity for them to leave your site and go elsewhere. Put everything people need to start using your site on the front page. If it's too complicated to put everything on the front page, put the first step on the front page.

This will also make the site simpler for users to navigate because they'll have a clear root.

Potential Trade-offs

None.

Mechanics

Many sites make you click through some sort of entry page before they let you do what you came to do. At best, these pages are a minor annoyance. At worst, they make you sit through an all-singing, all-dancing Flash extravaganza before you can actually get any work done. These pages are occasionally impressive (though usually the main people they impress are the site's own designers), but more commonly they're just annoying.

Remember, for most sites repeat visitors are far more important than first-time customers. Someone who has already bought your product or viewed your site and then comes back a second time is far more likely to do it again. I don't care how brilliantly designed your front page is or how clever a Flash animation you've put there. Users will be bored with even the best after the first time. (For all but the best, many users will get bored and leave the first time.)

Ask yourself why people come to your site, and make sure they can do it on page one. If they come to read news, make sure the first page is where they'll find it. If they need to log in, put the login box on the front page, not hiding behind a link. If they want to shop, make sure they can begin browsing and adding to their shopping cart right away. And because search is one of the preeminent ways users navigate a site, make sure the search box is prominently displayed on the front page.

Amazon and Google are two examples of sites that get this right. You go to Google to search and that's what you do on Google's very first page. Amazon's is a more complex site, but it lets you start shopping right away without even logging in. Sites that get this wrong are a lot less common than they used to be, though I do notice that musician and artist sites are disproportionately fond of entry pages. I suspect they view it as art in itself. Maybe that makes some sense for them. For the rest of the world, though, move the content upfront. Visitors arrive for the content, not to admire a beautifully orchestrated entry page.

In the short term, the simplest way to support this is to set up a `mod_rewrite` rule that automatically transfers visitors from the entry page to the real front page—that is, the page users used to go to after clicking on the entry page. For example, this rule in .htaccess redirects from the root to realcontent.html:

```
RewriteRule ^/$ /realcontent.html
```

It does not use an [R], so the change is transparent to the end-user. The redirect happens exclusively on the server.

It doesn't take that much longer to go in the other direction. Move the real home page from its old location to the root of the filesystem. Then set up a redirect so that anyone going to the old home page is redirected to the root of the site:

```
RewriteRule ^realcontent\.html$ / [R=301]
```

This example specifies a permanent redirect code so that bookmarks can be updated.

Finally, search for all links that pointed to the old location and update them with links to the root.

Hide E-mail Addresses

E-mail addresses published on web pages should be encoded to prevent spambots from harvesting them.

```
<a href="elharo@metalab.unc.edu">E-mail Elliotte Harold<a/>
elharo@macfaq.com
```

```
<a href="&#109;&#97;&#105;&#108;&#116;&#111;&#58;
elharo%40metalab%2Eunc%2Eedu">E-mail Elliotte Harold</a>
elharo&#x40;macfaq&#x2E;&#x43;om
```

Motivation

Spammers run spiders that screen-scrape HTML pages for e-mail addresses to spam. However, the spiders aren't especially smart, don't follow the relevant specifications, and thus can usually be fooled fairly easily.

Potential Trade-offs

Taken to extremes, hiding e-mail addresses from spambots hides them from your legitimate customers and readers, too. You don't want to do this. Don't go overboard. Make sure your applications allow people to find you. No solution will be perfect. You cannot block all spammers and let in all humans, but it is far more important not to block any humans than it is to keep out the last 1% of spam robots.

Mechanics

Finding e-mail addresses is fairly straightforward. This regular expression will pick up most of them:

```
[\w\-\.\+]+@([\w\-]+\.)+[a-zA-Z]{2,7}
```

You can also search for `mailto:` to find mailto links. Indeed, it is the ease of mechanically extracting e-mail addresses from text that makes spambots so effective. Most spambots don't do anything more sensitive than this very search. That's what makes it possible to fool them.

The first and most obvious technique is to break the address in a way that's easy for a human to repair but hard for a robot. For example:

```
elharo /at/ metalab.unc.edu
```

or:

```
elharo@delete.this.part.metalab.unc.edu
```

The problem is that this keeps the addresses from being copied and pasted without manual editing. Thus, I prefer not to do this.

Some people embed the e-mail address in an image instead:

```
<img src="elharoemail.png" width="167" height="28" />
```

Of course, this is now completely opaque to a blind user. You can add an `alt` attribute to rectify that:

```
<img src="elharoemail.png" width="167" height="28"
    alt="elharo@metalab.unc.edu"/>
```

However, spambots that are just matching a regular expression will find this, and this still has several disadvantages for legitimate visitors. First, it prevents the address from being copied and pasted. Second, it doesn't work in a mailto link. Finally, it has the additional disadvantage of being relatively difficult to implement on a site-wide basis because you need to create a new picture for each address you publish.

The approach I recommend, at least until spammers start to recognize it, is to use some HTML and XML encoding tricks that the browser will slip right through but the regular expression engine used by various spambots will ignore. In particular, I make use of numeric character references, either decimal and hexadecimal or both, like so:

```
&#x65;&#x6c;&#x68;&#x61;&#x72;&#x6f;&#x40;
&#x6d;&#x65;&#x74;&#x61;
&#x6c;&#x61;&#x62;&#x2e;&#x75;&#x6e;&#x63;
&#x2e;&#x65;&#x64;&#x75;
&#101;&#108;&#104;&#97;&#114;&#111;&#64;
&#109;&#101;&#116;&#97;&#108;
&#97;&#98;&#46;&#117;&#110;&#99;&#46;&#101;&#100;&#117;
```

Very few regular expressions will recognize those as e-mail addresses, but browsers will.

When the e-mail address is a URL, a third level of escaping is possible. We can replace some of the characters with percent escapes. For example, here I escape the @ sign and the periods:

```
<a href="mailto:elharo%40metalab%2Eunc%2Eedu">E-mail Me</a>
```

Of course, you can combine these techniques. This link hides the mailto scheme in decimal character references while encoding the e-mail part of the URL with percent escaping:

```
<a href="&#109;&#97;&#105;&#108;&#116;&#111;
&#58;elharo%40metalab%2Eunc%2Eedu">E-mail Me</a>
```

This isn't impenetrable by any means, but it's enough to fool most spambots.

If you like, you can generate the e-mail addresses out of JavaScript instead of including them directly in the page. Few if any spambots will run the scripts. For example:

```
<script type="text/javascript">
<!--
address=('elharo@' + 'metalab.unc.edu')
document.write(
  '<a href="mailto:' + address + '">' + address + '</a>')
 //-->
</script>
```

The disadvantage to this approach is that many users disable JavaScript for a variety of reasons. This technique hides the e-mail address from those users as well. One of those JavaScript-disabled users is Googlebot, so users won't be able to search for the e-mail addresses. I tend to think this is a bad thing because I often search for e-mail addresses, but you may feel differently.

Appendix A
Regular Expressions

Regular expressions enable one to search for common patterns in text files. Many tools support regular-expression-based search and replace. Although there are small differences in syntax from one tool to the next, most of the syntax and the basic ideas are much the same.

Characters That Match Themselves

The first rule of regular expressions is that most normal characters match themselves. A "normal" character is a letter, a digit, or a space. Thus, the regular expression "Al Gore was elected president in the year 2000" matches exactly the string "Al Gore was elected president in the year 2000" and no others. Searching for that string will find all occurrences of that exact string in the searched document or documents. However, it will not find even slight variations, such an extra space between the words *Al* and *Gore*. Table A.1 shows some more examples.

To be specific, the following characters match themselves:

- All ASCII letters A–Z and a–z
- The ASCII digits 0–9
- The space character
- All non-ASCII characters: é, ç, . . . and so on

- The following ASCII punctuation characters:

!
"
#
%
'

,
/
:
;
<
=
>
@

‑
`

~

Parentheses vary according to dialect. In some regular-expression dialects, parentheses match themselves, and in some they don't. In jEdit, parentheses are metacharacters that do not match themselves.

TABLE A.1   Characters That Match Themselves

Pattern	Matches	Example
Foo	The string Foo	Foo
foo	The string foo	Foo
foo bar	The string foo bar	foo bar
2000	The string 2000	2000
ανερ	The string ανερ	ανερ
<!DOCTYPE	The string <!DOCTYPE	<!DOCTYPE
<p>	The string <p>	<p>
</p>	The string </p>	</p>

Metacharacters

Other ASCII characters are reserved and must be escaped if you wish to match them. For noncontrol characters, you do this with a backslash. For example, to match a period, you use \.. (This is also called a *character representation.*) To match a question mark, you use \?. To match a left parenthesis, you use \(. To match a right parenthesis, you use \). To match a backslash, you type \\, and so forth. Table A.2 shows some more examples.

There are also character representations for many control characters, such as these seven:

- \r for carriage return
- \n for line feed
- \t for tab
- \f for form feed
- \a for alarm
- \b for backspace
- \e for escape

However, we don't use these a lot when refactoring HTML because these characters aren't very important in HTML. Usually what you care about is whether there's some whitespace, not exactly which character

TABLE A.2 Metacharacters

Pattern	Matches	Example
<!\[CDATA\[	The string <![CDATA[	<![CDATA[
<\?xml-stylesheet	The string <?xml-stylesheet	<?xml-stylesheet
\(\)	The string ()	()
2**3	The string 2**3	2**3
2 \+ 2 = 4	The string 2 + 2 = 4	2 + 2 = 4
\$19\.95	The string $19.95	$19.95

it is. The last four characters are not even legal in XML documents, including XHTML documents. The form feed, \f, is the only one of these that's even remotely common. It would not be a bad idea to do a quick search for \f. If you find any, inspect the document where it appears to find out what purpose it serves. You can likely replace it with a br element, a p element, or a single space.

Wildcards

So far, we haven't described anything you couldn't find with a simple literal search. The power of regular expressions is that you can write strings that match several similar strings. For instance, you can write an expression that matches any start-tag, not just a particular start-tag. To do this, you need wildcards that can stand in for more than one character.

The first such wildcard is the period. It matches any single character except a line break. For example, the regular expression 200. matches 2000, 2001, 200Z, 200!, and many more strings. The regular expression a....b matches any six-character string that begins with *a* and ends with *b,* such as abbbbb, aaabbb, aDCEFb, ab bc b, and many more. Table A.3 shows more examples.

The only characters the period doesn't match are the carriage return and the line feed. Because HTML does not usually consider line breaks to be significant and tags can extend across multiple lines, this is problematic. Some regular-expression dialects, including Perl's, allow you to modify this behavior so that the period does not match a line break. However, jEdit's does not.

To match any character, including a line break, you can use the character class [.\s]. More on this shortly.

Of course, sometimes a period is just a period. If you want to match a literal period, escape it with a backslash. For example, the regular expression other\. would find sentences that end in the word *other.*

TABLE A.3 The Period Wildcard

Pattern	Matches	Example
Foo.Bar	Any string beginning with Foo, followed by a single character, followed by Bar, not containing any line breaks	FooZBar FoozBar Foo Bar Foo9Bar
.Foo	Any four-character string whose last three letters are Foo	AFoo fFoo 9Foo -Foo Foo
....	Any four-character string not containing any line breaks	<em> This that I am Cat. 2008
..c..	Any five-character string not containing any line breaks whose middle character is the letter *c*	Faced a cat abcde

Quantifiers

A period or a literal character by itself always matches exactly one character. However, you can append a quantifier to it to indicate that the character may appear a variable number of times.

Zero or One: ?

A normal character suffixed with a question mark indicates that the character appears only optionally (zero times or once). For example, the regular expression a?b matches ab and b. The a is optional. The regular expression a?b?c? matches abc, ab, bc, ac, bc, a, b, and c, as well as the empty string.

You can suffix a period with a question mark to indicate that any character may or may not appear. For example, the regular expression 200.? matches 200 as well as 2000, 2001, 200Z, and 200!.

Zero or More: *

An asterisk (*) suffix indicates that the preceding character appears zero or more times. For example, a*b matches ab, aaab, aaaaab, and b. However, it does not match abb or acb.

You can put an asterisk after a period to indicate that any number of any characters may appear. For example, a.*b matches ab, aaab, aaaaab, abb, acb, a123b, and "a quick brown fox jumped into the tub".

Unlike UNIX shell globs, the asterisk alone does not match anything. It must be suffixed to something else. For example, to list all the HTML files in the current working directory, you'd usually type something such as this:

```
$ ls *html
```

However, in most regular-expression dialects, the regular expression that matches all strings ending in *html* is .*html. *html without the initial period is a syntax error.

One or More: +

A plus sign (+) suffix indicates that a character appears one or more times. For example, a+b matches ab, aaab, and aaaaab. However, it does not match a single b, abb, or acb.

Of course, a plus sign after a period indicates that one or more of any character is required. The regular expression a.+b requires at least one character between the a and the b, so it matches aaab, aaaaab, abb, acb, and a123b but not a simple ab.

A Specific Number of Times: {}

You can specify that a character must appear a specified number of times using curly braces. For example, a{3} is the same as the pattern aaa. It stands for exactly three *a*'s in a row.

TABLE A.4 Quantifiers

Pattern	Matches	Example
\</?p>	A p start tag or end tag	\<p> \</p>
\<br */>	A br start tag containing any number of spaces before the closing />	\ \ \
\<p.*>	A complete p start tag, followed by all other text through the last > on the same line	\<p> \<p id='c4'> \<p id='c4'>This is text\</p>
\<a+>	Any number of *a*'s, but no other characters, in angle brackets	\<a> \<aa> \<aaa> \<aaaa>

You can also specify a range of possible occurrences using a comma. A{3,5} allows three to five *A*s in a row. That is, it matches AAA, AAAA, and AAAAA but not AA or AAAAAA.

You can omit the second, maximum value to indicate that at least a certain number of repetitions is required but more are allowed. For example, a{3,} matches aaa, aaaa, aaaaa, aaaaaa, and any larger sequence of *a*'s. Table A.4 shows some more examples.

Class Shorthands

Several backslash sequences match particular types of characters. For example, \d matches any digit: 0, 1, 2, 3, 4, 5, 6, 7, 8, or 9. \D matches any character that is not a digit. (Capitalization often reverses the sense of a pattern.) Other such classes include the following.

- \s

  A whitespace character: space, tab, carriage return, or line feed. This is very important in HTML because usually in HTML these four characters are interchangeable. \s does not match the non-breaking space.

- \S

  Any nonwhitespace character.

- \w

  Any word character—that is, any letter or digit but not punctuation marks or spaces. However, the underscore, _, is considered to be a word character in most regular-expression dialects. Whether non-ASCII characters are considered individually or excluded as a group varies according to dialect.

- \W

  Any nonword character.

- \d

  Any digit from 0 to 9. In some dialects, this also matches non-ASCII digits such as (the Japanese 1) and (the Arabic 1) as well.

- \D

  Any character except 0 to 9; in some dialects, any character that is not a digit.

Character Classes

Bracketed expressions enable you to define your own character classes that match some characters and not others. Just place the characters you want to match inside square brackets.

For example, suppose you want to search for all hexadecimal digits. You can easily enumerate those characters as [0123456789abcdefABCDEF]. This matches any *one* of those characters. Then, to match any potential hexadecimal number, which will include one or more of these characters, you suffix the brackets with a plus sign to form this regular expression:

```
[0123456789abcdefABCDEF]+
```

Of course, this also matches words composed purely of these 22 characters, such as *Decaf* and *fed*.

This is simple enough, but enumerating all the characters can be tedious. Sometimes what you want is a range. Use a hyphen between two characters to indicate all characters from one's ASCII value to the other. For example, [a-z] matches any lowercase letter. [A-Z] matches any uppercase letter.

You can combine ranges. [a-zA-Z] matches any upper- or lowercase letter. For example, we can match hexadecimal numbers a little more simply as:

```
[0-9a-fA-F]+
```

You can negate a character set or range by placing a caret, ^, immediately after the opening bracket. For example, [^a-z] matches any character except a lowercase ASCII letter. [^a-zA-Z] matches any character except a lower- or uppercase ASCII letter.

Warning

Ranges are determined by character value, as measured in ASCII or Unicode. This works pretty much as you expect within any one obvious range. However, beware of ranges that cross script, case, or type boundaries, such as [a-Z], [0-F], or [A-Ω]. These almost certainly don't do what you want or expect.

Table A.5 shows some more examples.

TABLE A.5   Character Classes (a.k.a. bracketed expressions)

Pattern	Matches	Example
</[a-zA-Z1-6]+>	All HTML end-tags	</p> </TABLE> </Span> </foo> </h2>
</[a-z1-6]+>	All XHTML end-tags	</p> </table> </span> </foo>
[a-zA-Z]+\s*=\s*"[^">]*"	Double-quoted attributes	id="c1" id = "c1" id=c1
<p.*>	A complete p start-tag, followed by all other text through the last > on the same line	<p> <p id='c4'> <p id='c4'>This is text</p>
([a-zA-Z0-9]{1-63}\.) [a-zA-Z]+	Domain name	example.com www.example.de server4.nbc.ge.com

Groups and Back References

You can group expressions inside parentheses and then use the repetition operators after the group. For example, suppose you wanted to find all runs of <br> tags. The regular expression (<br>)+ will match <br>,

,

, and so forth.

You can further combine the expressions. For example, (
\s*)+ will match all runs of <br> tags, even if they have whitespace in between them.

Even more powerfully, you can refer back to a group later in the expression. The first parenthesized match is \1. The second is \2, the third \3, and so forth. (If the groups nest, they are counted from the left parenthesis only.) For example, suppose you want to find all simple HTML elements in the form <foo>Blah Blah Blah</foo>. That is, you want to find all the elements without any attributes and that don't contain any child elements. Furthermore, you really want to find all the elements from the beginning of the start-tag to the end of the end-tag.

We can start with the expression <[a-zA-Z]+> to find the start tags. We can use the expression </[a-zA-Z]+> to find the end-tags. However, we want only those pairs that match. So, first we put parentheses around the start-tag, like so:

```
<([a-zA-Z]+)>
```

Then we refer back to that in the end-tag expression as \1—that is, </\1>. If the start-tag was div, the end-tag will be div. If the start-tag was em, the end-tag will be em, and so forth:

```
<([a-zA-Z]+)> </\1
```

Finally, we need to put a character class in the middle that excludes less-than signs but allows line breaks. This will avoid nested child elements and some overly greedy matches:

```
<([a-zA-Z]+)>[^<]*</\1
```

Even more important, you can use the back references \1, \2, and so on in replacement strings. For example, I was recently faced with this list:

```
<ul>
<li>marquee</li>
<li>basefont</li>
<li>bgsound</li>
<li>keygen</li>
<li>bgsound</li>
<li>spacer</li>
<li>wbr</li>
</ul>
```

I wanted to put the contents of each list item in a code element. Therefore, I searched for this:

```
<li>([a-z]+)</li>
```

I replaced it with this:

```
<li><code>\1</code></li>
```

This gave me the following:

```
<ul>
<li><code>marquee</code></li>
<li><code>basefont</code></li>
<li><code>bgsound</code></li>
<li><code>keygen</code></li>
<li><code>bgsound</code></li>
<li><code>spacer</code></li>
<li><code>wbr</code></li>
</ul>
```

As another example, suppose you have a table of species count data organized like this:

```
<tr> <td> Great Egret </td> <td> 7 </td> </tr>
<tr> <td> Redhead </td> <td> 1 </td> </tr>
<tr> <td> Mallard </td> <td> 56 </td> </tr>
<tr> <td> House Finch </td> <td> 3 </td> </tr>
```

Now suppose you decide to swap the columns so that the counts go on the left and the species on the right. You search for this:

```
(<td>.*</td>) (<td>.*</td>)
```

Then you simply replace it with the following:

```
\2\1
```

This very quickly turns the HTML into this:

```
<tr> <td> 7 </td><td> Great Egret </td> </tr>
<tr> <td> 1 </td><td> Redhead </td> </tr>
<tr> <td> 56 </td><td> Mallard </td> </tr>
<tr> <td> 3 </td><td> House Finch </td> </tr>
```

Groups and back references are critical anytime you need to chop data apart and put it back together again in a slightly different order.

Whitespace

Matching whitespace is quite tricky and but still quite important. Precisely because HTML does not consider whitespace to be hugely significant, it's important to pay attention to it. Four whitespace characters are likely to appear in HTML documents:

- The space itself
- The carriage return, \r
- The linefeed, \n
- The tab, \t

The space character has no special representation in regular expressions. To match a space, you simply type a space. Just be careful that you type the right number of spaces, because it won't usually be obvious if you're trying to match two where one is called for or vice versa.

\n is particularly tricky. In some dialects, this represents the literal line feed character, ASCII 10. However, in others, including jEdit's, it means any line break character including carriage return, line feed, and a carriage return-line feed pair. Finally, in still other dialects, it means the platform's native line-terminating character. Thus, it can match a carriage return on the Mac, a line feed on UNIX, and a carriage return line feed pair on Windows.

This is quite troublesome for working with HTML because HTML documents are not platform-bound. You are likely to find all three line-ending conventions in your document collection, sometimes even in the same file. Consequently, we usually do one of several things instead:

- Use [\r\n(\r\n)] to match all line breaks, regardless of type.
- Use \s to match all whitespace, line breaks or otherwise.
- Use ^ and $ to anchor the pattern to the beginning and/or end of a line.

Line breaks are usually not significant in HTML, so more often than not we use the second option.

You may encounter documents that include other characters such as a form feed or a vertical tab. These have no defined meaning in HTML and should usually be replaced with a single space.

Alternation: |

The vertical bar, |, allows you to choose between two possible values. For example, suppose you want to search for all years in the twentieth or twenty-first century; 1904, 1952, 1999, 2001, 2059, and so on. The basic rule is that the first two characters must be either 19 or 20. The second two characters must be digits. 19\d\d matches all years in the twentieth century.[1] 20\dd matches all years in the twenty-first century. (19\d\d)|(20\d\d) matches both sets of years. We could also write this as (19|20)\d\d—that is, either 19 or 20 followed by two digits.

Alternation is also important for matching HTML tags. For example, suppose you want a general expression for matching all start tags. The problem you run into is that there are three ways an attribute can appear, and each has its own regular expression:

- name=value

  [a-zA-Z]+\s*=\s*[^\s'">]+

- name="value"

  [a-zA-Z]+\s*=\s*"[^">]*"

- name='value'

  [a-zA-Z]+\s*=\s*'[^'>]*'

---

1. Pedants beware: Because there was no year 0, 1900 is really in the nineteenth century and 2000 is the twentieth, but I'm going to ignore that.

We can combine these regular expressions with an alternation, like so:

```
<[a-zA-Z]+\s*([a-zA-Z]+\s*=\s*[^\s'">]+
|[a-zA-Z]+\s*=\s*"[^">]*"|[a-zA-Z]+\s*=\s*'[^'>]*')*>
```

This finds all single-quoted, double-quoted, and nonquoted attributes. (It also finds `name=value` parameters in URL query strings, which was not intended.)

Greedy and Nongreedy Matches

By default, all matches are greedy. That is, they match the maximum length of text they can get away with. For example, suppose you have the following paragraph:

```
<p>
<q id='g1'>Take your seats,</q> said the guard.<q id='g2'>Going
by the train, sir?</q>
</p>
```

Now suppose you want to match all the q start tags, and consequently you use the regular expression `<q.*>`. In fact, this will find:

```
<q id='g1'>Take your seats,</q> said the guard. <q id='g2'>
```

The regular expression `<q.*>` matches everything from the first `<q` on the line to the last `>`. The only reason it stops there is that the period does not match line breaks. The match is said to be *greedy*.

You specify a nongreedy match that stops at the first opportunity by putting a question mark after the quantifier. You can also use such a question mark after another question mark or after a plus sign. Thus, if I had written the regular expression as `<q.*?>`, it would have stopped with the start-tag `<q id='g1'>`.

You can also use nongreedy matches with the other quantifiers, such as ? and +. For example, a+? will match at least one *a*, but then it will stop if it can. However, if this is part of a larger pattern, such as a*?b or a+?b, it will match as many *a*'s as it needs to get to the first *b*.

Position

Several metacharacters anchor the regular expression to a particular location in the document without actually matching anything themselves. These include

- ^

    The beginning of a line.

- $

    The end of a line.

- \b

    A word boundary, including a space or line break.

- \B

    Any location that is not a word boundary.

- \A

    The beginning of the document.

- \z

    The end of the document.

- \Z

    The end of the document, unless the document ends with a line break. In this case, it is the position immediately before the final line break.

Because HTML is not very line-oriented, we tend not to use ^ and $ very much. However, \b and \B are quite useful, and \A, \Z, and \z sometimes are, too. For example, \bcat\b matches the word *cat* but does not match inside the words *category, catheter,* or *abdicate.* (Some GUI tools, including BBEdit but not jEdit, give you an option to only match entire words. This is essentially the same as putting \b before and after your expression.) Other possible uses include

- \A\s*(<html|<HTML)

    Find all documents that start with <html or <HTML and thus don't have a DOCTYPE declaration or a byte order mark.

- \A\s*(<body|<BODY)

Find all documents that start with <body or <BODY and thus don't have a proper html root element.

- </[hH][tT][mM][lL]>\s*\Z

Find all documents that end with </html> in various combinations of case, optionally followed by whitespace.

Table A.6 summarizes all of these patterns.

TABLE A.6   Regular-Expression Syntax

Pattern	Matches
.	Any one character
^	Beginning of line
$	End of line
c*	Zero or more c's
c+	One or more c's
c?	Zero or one c
c*?	Zero or more c's, as few as possible
c+?	One or more c's, as few as possible
c??	Zero or one c, as few as possible
c{count}	Exactly count c's
c{count,}	At least count c's
c{min,max}	At least min c's and at most max c's
[a-zA-z]	Any one of the characters from a–z or A–Z
[abc]	Any one of the characters between the brackets
[^abc]	Any one of the characters not between the brackets
[a-z]	Any one of the characters from a–z
[a-zA-z]	Any one of the characters from a–z or A–Z
\A	Beginning of document
\z	End of document

(continues)

TABLE A.6   Regular-Expression Syntax *(Continued)*

Pattern	Matches
\Z	End of document, but before trailing line break, if any
\b	Boundary of a word, that is, the beginning or end of a word
\B	Not the boundary of a word
\s	Any whitespace character (space, tab, carriage return, line feed)
\S	Any nonwhitespace character
\w	Any word character (letters, digits, and the underscore)
\W	Any nonword character
\d	Any digit (0–9)
\D	Any nondigit
(abc)	The characters *a, b,* and *c* in that order
\1, \2, …	First matched pattern, second matched pattern, …

Note

For more information on regular expressions, including lots more examples, some advanced features I haven't gone into here, and details about dialect variations, I recommend *Mastering Regular Expressions,* 3rd Edition, by Jeffrey E. F. Friedl (O'Reilly, 2006).

Index

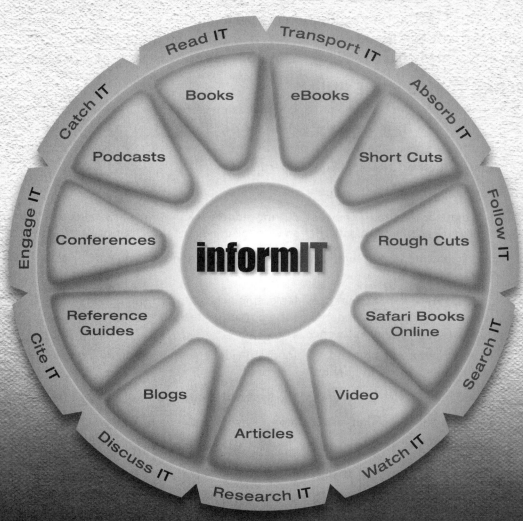

Register
Your Book

at informit.com/register

You may be eligible to receive:
- Advance notice of forthcoming editions of the book
- Related book recommendations
- Chapter excerpts and supplements of forthcoming titles
- Information about special contests and promotions throughout the year
- Notices and reminders about author appearances, tradeshows, and online chats with special guests

Contact us

If you are interested in writing a book or reviewing manuscripts prior to publication, please write to us at:

Editorial Department
Addison-Wesley Professional
75 Arlington Street, Suite 300
Boston, MA 02116 USA
Email: AWPro@aw.com

Addison-Wesley

Visit us on the Web: informit.com/aw